Charlie's Victory

Charlie's Victory

An Autobiography

CHARLIE & LUCY WEDEMEYER

with Gregg Lewis

ZondervanPublishingHouse

Grand Rapids, Michigan

A Division of HarperCollinsPublishers

Charlie's Victory
Copyright © 1993 by Charlie and Lucy Wedemeyer

Requests for information should be addressed to:
Zondervan Publishing House
Grand Rapids, Michigan 49530

Library of Congress Cataloging-in-Publication Data

Wedemeyer, Charlie.
    Charlie's victory : an autobiography / Charlie and Lucy Wedemeyer
with Gregg Lewis.
        p.   cm.
    ISBN 0-310-57710-1
    1. Wedemeyer, Charlie—Health. 2. Amyotrophic lateral sclerosis—
Patients—California—Biography. 3. Football—California—Coaches
—Biography. I. Wedemeyer, Lucy. II. Lewis, Gregg. III. Title.
    RC406.A24W4   1993
    362.1'9683—dc20   93–41753
    [B]   CIP

Edited by John Sloan
Cover design by John Lucas
Photo section by Allie Design

Published in association with Sealy M. Yates, literary agent, Orange,
California.

Printed in the United States of America

93 94 95 96 97 / BP / 9 8 7 6 5 4 3 2 1

This edition is printed on acid-free paper and meets the American
National Standards Institute Z39.48 standard.

The Lord has blessed us with two precious children—Carri Kauihaupuehuehu and Matthew Kaleikapono—to whom we dedicate this book. They have not only lived this story but by God's grace have carried their parents through even the darkest hours with their exceptional faith and love. They continue to light up our lives today with their laughter and contagious joy.

Contents

Prologue   9

Part One: A Change of Game Plan

1. Meet the Coach   15
2. The Diagnosis   23

Part Two: Romance and Dreams

3. Beginnings in Paradise   35
4. Meant for Each Other   43
5. Together in The Big Ten   51

Part Three: Dealing with Disease

6. The Truth Sinks In   59
7. In Search of Cures   67
8. Bumps, Bruises, and Embarrassments   77
9. Independence Lost   85
10. Going Public   95
11. Living with Limits   103

Part Four: Staying Alive

12. In Need of Help   115
13. Accepting Help   125
14. The Battle to Breathe   137
15. It Takes Two to Fight   147

Part Five: Championship Quest

16. Bitter Defeat   161
17. One Quiet Victory   173
18. Unexpected Help   183
19. No Code   193
20. Intensive Care Coaching   203
21. Living on Life Support   213
22. One Last Season   225

Part Six: Living On

23. Sidelined   241
24. A Whole New Challenge   253
25. Offering Hope   261
26. Finding New Strength   269
27. Tomorrow   277
     Appendix one
–To Those Facing Terminal Illness   281
     Appendix two
–The Wedemeyer Story Timeline   287
     Special Thanks   293

Prologue

An attractive blonde waves from the driver's window. A security guard wearing a reflective-orange vest swings the gate wide and motions the mini-bus through. The yellow vehicle pulls across an empty patch of blacktop and coasts to a stop in the deep shadows behind the stands at San Jose State's Spartan Stadium. The engine dies. For a moment all is quiet and dark.

The door of the mini-bus swings open and Charlie Wedemeyer's wheelchair is lowered carefully to the pavement. As a nurse quickly pushes Charlie over alongside a nearby golf cart, the Wedemeyer party climbs out of the bus and scurries after them.

There's a ten-second pause as the group surrounds the golf cart. Then so many people spring into action at once that what happens next might best be described as orchestrated pandemonium. The nurse disconnects the tubing at Charlie's throat. Two other pairs of hands help her transfer a portable respirator and two battery packs from a little shelf under the seat of the wheelchair onto the cart. While this maneuver is being executed, Lucy Wedemeyer "bags" Charlie, manually squeezing breaths of air into his lungs from an ambu-bag, a round, rubberized, balloon-like device that fits over the cuff of Charlie's tracheotomy tube sticking out of his throat. The equipment transferred, a friend bends down beside the wheelchair, hoists Charlie's ninety-five-pound body into his arms and sets him gently into the cart festooned with black and orange balloons and a sign saying "Beat St. Francis."

No sooner is Charlie reconnected to his life support system than a larger throng suddenly surrounds the vehicle. A half-dozen television mini-cams whir, their tungsten spots reflecting off the cart's molded-fiberglass sides and creating a media-made island of light in the chilly early evening darkness of December. Reporters jostle and jockey for position and camera crews elbow back to try to hold their places as the questions begin to fly:

"What does this game mean to you after last year's heartbreaker, Coach?"

"Is your team ready for this one?"

"Have you planned any surprises in your offense for tonight?"

"Any predictions about the outcome?"

"Would you say this is the toughest opponent you've faced?"

"Do you consider this the biggest game of your coaching career?"

Beneath the golf cart canopy, squinting into the glaring lights and struggling to sort out individual voices from the cacophony of questions, Charlie Wedemeyer grins. A few inches below the smile that fills his face, a ribbed-plastic tube protrudes from his throat, snakes over his left shoulder and back to the battery powered machine which every few seconds sends a small puff of air up the tube and into the deflated shell of his body. Charlie's hands lie motionless in his lap; he can't raise them to quiet his questioners. But then even if he could, they wouldn't hear him. His voice is gone, too.

Lucy slides under the cart's steering wheel and next to her husband, raising her hand to speak for him. "Charlie just wants to say that this is what our football team has been working for all year. This is the game he's always wanted to coach. Our opponents have a great team and a great winning tradition. So Charlie expects a tough, competitive game tonight. We'll be glad to talk to each of you and answer all your questions later. But right now, if you'd clear the way, we want to get down to the field and join the team for warm-ups. We have a game to play."

After leaning over to make sure Charlie is belted securely in his seat, Lucy starts the cart, eases it through the reluctantly parting crowd and onto a paved path leading down to field level. At the top of the incline, Lucy stops the cart for a time as both Wedemeyers survey the scene and try to comprehend the significance of this moment, a second chance neither of them had ever imagined possible after last year's shattering defeat.

One reporter, Dave Koga, writing later for The Honolulu Advertiser, *tried to express what is happening on this night with these words:*

> The scoreboard says Charlie Wedemeyer won't win this game. There is no chance for a comeback now. It is only a matter of time.

> There will be no Hail Mary, no Immaculate Reception, no Holy Roller. The gun is cocked, and when it sounds, death will remain undefeated.

> Charlie Wedemeyer has amyotrophic lateral sclerosis. Lou Gehrig's disease. The nerve cells that control the movements of his muscles are dying. His body is wasting away, wilting like an orchid in the noonday sun.

> A respirator breathes for him through a hole in his throat. The days are long and sometimes they are filled with pain.

> All that remains is hope, and right now there isn't much of it left. But for the last 10 years it has been enough.

> The life expectancy of an ALS patient is three years. It has been a decade since doctors told Wedemeyer he had become a statistic.

> He has been hit hard and thrown for huge losses, but somehow he has endured. Somehow, he has managed to juke and sidestep death the way he did tacklers at Punahou School and Michigan State.

> On December 13, 1985, at the age of 40, a rag doll of a man propped up in a golf cart, his wife reading his lips and sending in plays, Wedemeyer coached his team, the Los Gatos (CA) High School Wildcats in the final game of the Central California Coast football championship. . . .

> It's a story that tugs at the heart and touches the soul. There is joy and sadness, hope and despair, victory and defeat. . . .

> And there, too, with Charlie from the beginning, with him all the way is Lucy Wedemeyer, a former Punahou

cheerleader whose unconditional love for her husband now carries them and their children through the hard times.

She is his voice now. Hers are his arms and legs. She is always there—teasing him one minute, suctioning phlegm from his throat the next—and it is clear that she will be there for the duration.

"The day will come, we know that," Lucy says at one point. "We're just not quite ready for it yet. But I think it's made us realize how precious life is. You can't take anything for granted; every second makes a big difference.

"We both feel it's OK if our lives are over at any time," she adds, "because we've had so much."

That is the refrain of this sweet-sad song.

Death is but the conclusion. It doesn't really matter when or how it comes. What counts is the living we squeeze in until then.

Charlie Wedemeyer can't talk, but he is telling us that— loud and clear. When he is sitting in his golf cart, the game unfolding before him, Lucy at his side, his eyes burn with life.

He isn't dying then, he's living. He might be clinging to time—sustained by his undying passion for football and the steadfast love of a remarkable woman—but he's filling every second that's left to him.

And in the end, that's the best that can be said about any of us.

As the golf cart pulls out onto the sidelines someone in the crowd starts a chant that steadily spreads and builds throughout Spartan Stadium, "Char-lie! Char-lie! Char-lie!"

Lucy stops the cart when they reach the fifty-yard marker. Stretching out before them, the carefully-lined expanse of rich green grass sparkles with dew—a football field of dreams. The banks of lights ringing the stadium illumine the shroud of fog that hangs heavy in the air and lends a dreamy aura of fantasy to this unbelievable event—one of many improbable incidents in Charlie and Lucy Wedemeyer's incredible story.

part one

A CHANGE
OF GAME PLAN

chapter one

MEET THE COACH

CHARLIE

If you were meeting me face to face for the first time you would immediately realize some rather obvious things about me. I can't walk; I'm confined to a wheelchair. I can't speak out loud; when I want to communicate my wife has to read my lips. I can't even breathe on my own; my portable life-support system goes wherever I go, twenty-four hours a day.

I've grown used to the reaction my appearance causes any time I venture out in public. Most adults try to stare discreetly when they see an immobile man with tubes connecting his body to a battery powered machine beneath his wheelchair seat. It's usually only young children who are uninhibited enough about their curiosity to walk up to whoever is pushing my chair and ask, "What's wrong with him?"

What's wrong is a progressive disease which eventually destroys the body's ability to control all voluntary muscles. It's terminal. No one knows what causes it or how to cure it. When my doctors discovered I had ALS more than sixteen years ago, they told me I had maybe a year to live. While they were wrong about the timing, they weren't wrong about the diagnosis of the disease that has steadily devastated my body.

I always have mixed feelings about telling people I have ALS because I want others to see beyond my disease. The obvious fact I'm trapped in a body which no longer works like it used to, or that I suffer from an illness which could end my life at any time, doesn't change my basic identity. I'm still Charlie Wedemeyer—a husband, a father, a football coach.

So on one hand I want people to understand ALS has nothing to do with the real person I am, was, and always will be. And yet, on the other hand, I have to admit it has everything to do with who I am because my disease determines how I live. It dictates what I must do, and everything I can't.

It's been more than a dozen years since I could hold my wife Lucy close or even stroke her cheek and run my fingers through her hair. It's been even longer since I could take a Sunday afternoon stroll through a park holding hands with my daughter Carri or go out in the backyard after dinner and play catch with my son Kale. I've proudly watched my children grow up and become adults without ever being able to applaud one of Carri's vocal solos, without ever standing or cheering for one of Kale's dazzling touchdown runs.

I haven't had a swallow of food for more than eight years. I "eat" through a rubber hose that feeds directly into my stomach through a small hole in my abdomen. I've asked my doctors for a wide-mouth model so we could slide in some hamburgers or better yet, a Hawaiian plate lunch of teriyaki chicken, rice and stir-fry. But until they take me seriously I have to make do with a drabber liquid diet of Ensure (a high protein formula used for stomach tube patients), juices, pureed fruit, and a ghastly green mixture of Chinese herbs and vitamins dissolved in water.

I require twenty-four-hour-a-day nursing care and have since I went on a respirator in 1985 (less than four months before that eventful night of the CCS championship playoff game). Because I can no longer swallow, someone must suction out my mouth every few minutes so I don't choke on my own saliva. My trache needs to be suctioned regularly to keep congestion from building up in my chest and lungs and drowning me in my own bodily fluids.

I can't go to the bathroom without assistance. I can't scratch my nose when it itches. I can't even turn to see a hummingbird hovering outside the window of my room without having someone realign my wheelchair, raise my bed, or lift and turn my head.

As someone who always prided himself on his independence, it's been hard to accept being so totally dependent on others. As someone who has always been a perfectionist, it's often frustrating not having things done exactly the way I'd like.

Just getting ready to leave the house requires a two to three hour streamlined routine that took years of practice to perfect. After experimenting with a variety of methods, we've found the best way for me to get a shampoo while lying in bed is to have a large cake pan lined with a garbage bag slid under my head. A pitcher of water is used to wet my hair, after which soap is drizzled in and worked to a lather before a final pitcher of water is poured over my head to rinse. Then the garbage-bag-lined pan is carefully removed and emptied in the sink.

Teeth brushing is only a little simpler. Because I have only limited (and painful) use of my jaw muscles, the nurse pries open my mouth and goes to town brushing, suctioning out the toothpaste when my mouth gets full of foam and then suctioning again to extract the rinse water at the end. Flossing can be a real hassle.

It takes time to teach new nurses how to shave me as close as I like. (I've had some so slow I thought my beard would grow back on one side of my face by the time they finished the other.) Then there's a time-consuming, but never quite zestfully satisfying sponge bath.

Dressing a 155-pound rag doll would be hard enough.

But maneuvering shirts and pants on, over and around trache and stomach tubes without damage adds to the logistical challenge. Because muscle contraction curls my toes downward, a piece of Popsicle stick is taped to the bottom of each toe to keep it straight enough to pull socks on my feet and slide them into my shoes.

Finally, after all this, it's time to get me out of bed.

Transferring me to my wheelchair takes at least two experienced people. They have to lift me into a sitting position, swing my legs around and off the side of the bed, hoist me upright into a standing position (I can still voluntarily stiffen my legs for a few seconds at a time), pivot me on my feet and gently lower me down into the wheelchair. Because my neck muscles no longer support any weight, my head has to be held through the entire procedure to keep it from flopping dangerously and injuring my neck.

This multi-step maneuver must be executed smoothly and quickly because there's no way to do it without temporarily disconnecting the respirator. And as I regularly remind my wife when anything slows the process and I don't get the oxygen I need, "I don't look good in blue."

My wheelchair seat belt must be cinched tightly around my waist so that when I cough or have my trachea suctioned my whole body doesn't slide out of the chair onto the floor. And if I'm pushed over a doorway threshold or a bump in a sidewalk, someone has to hold my head to keep it from falling forward.

Whenever I ride anywhere in my specially equipped van, my chair is strapped tightly to the floor and my head is lashed firmly in place with a padded belt tied around my forehead Rambo-style, making me look like the star of a very strange kung fu movie. Someone has to be right next to me as we drive to help brace me in the turns and to monitor the medical equipment attached to me and my chair.

Flying commercial airlines is an even bigger adventure. Airplane aisles aren't designed for wheelchairs. So I have to be shifted to a narrow dolly-like seat, then tipped and hurriedly wheeled into the cabin like some appliance, lifted into a regular airline seat and reconnected to my power supply. By the time that's done and our entourage has stowed a mountain of life-support and backup medical equipment under seats and in overhead compartments, the other passengers usually have had more entertainment (comedy and drama) than they could get during most in-flight movies. Lucy calls it her "Travels with Charlie" and it's quite a production.

A carefully choreographed production is also required whenever I'm asked to "speak" to civic organizations, conventions, schools or churches. I'm rolled up onto the platform and placed between Lucy and my primary care nurse, Linda Peevyhouse, who alternate between sharing what we decided ahead of time to say and reading my lips to tell the audience my ad-libbed jokes and stories.

When I'm home my routine is constantly changing—TV news, maybe a movie in the VCR, reading, preparation for an upcoming motivational "talk" I've been asked to give, answering correspondence, or entertaining so many friends who drop by for a visit that we've considered installing a revolving door on the front of our house. And, during football season, because I still have a role as an assistant coach for the Los Gatos freshman-sophomore football team, I go to practice every day, spend many hours watching and rewatching game films of upcoming opponents to spot weaknesses, and help plot our offensive game plan.

But even during my most laid-back day, it's the hands of others that punch the controls on the TV remote, turn the pages, open the front door, serve refreshments and take notes. I never have an hour, let alone a day, when I don't have to depend on someone else to do a dozen things I wish I could do myself.

Despite all the nursing help we hire, there are many days when I feel like a terrible burden on my family. Especially on my wife. It's then I have to take comfort in something Lucy said in those first uncertain and frightening days after the diagnosis. She told me, "This isn't your disease, Charlie. It's *our* disease. Whatever happens we'll face it together."

That was a lot easier said than done. But Lucy's lived out that attitude for more than 16 years now. Without that spirit, without her loving commitment and support I wouldn't be alive today. Which is why this book is every bit as much Lucy's story as it is mine.

LUCY

It's true Charlie and I have had to make a lot of adjustments the last fifteen years. But we try to spend more time appreciating the things we have than we do lamenting what we've lost; we try to devote more energy to using the opportunities presented us than we do worrying about those doors that are closed and those things we can't do.

Most days I think we succeed. But I won't try to tell you it's easy.

It hurts to think that it's been more than a dozen years since my strong, handsome husband could wrap his arms around me and pull me close. I still long for his strength, his touch, his physical affection. For more than eight years I've missed hearing the sound of his voice and knowing just by his inflection when he's happy or sad, when he's excited or mad.

We've had to learn new ways of reaching out and touching each other—not only physically but emotionally and spiritually. Yet I think we communicate and understand each other better today than we ever did. While I've learned to read Charlie's lips, I find I often don't have to. His eyes almost always tell me exactly how he feels and his eyebrows punctuate those feelings as they bounce up and down or furrow into a wrinkle. And if you don't think someone in difficult circumstances can find happiness and contentment, if you doubt the contagious quality of joy, well, you've never seen Charlie smile.

Sure, I've cried to see Charlie's frustration at his own growing helplessness. I've cried as I considered the contrast between the man I love who's trapped in a body that betrayed him and the athletically gifted boy I married who used to dodge would-be tacklers and run with the best college athletes in the country.

We've endured a lot of dark storm clouds and passed through many deep valleys in our journey together. There have been numerous times when I felt certain Charlie wouldn't make it, and more than a few when I wasn't sure I could go on myself. When I've cried out to God asking for just one more football season, one more birthday.

I can't count the times I'd have given almost anything for a single day of normalcy in our lives again. Twenty-four hours without the constant sense of urgency and responsibility. A morning when I didn't have to get up and check the nursing schedule to make sure every hour would be covered that day. An afternoon free for an impromptu shopping trip together without a wheelchair, a respirator, freshly charged batteries, a portable suction machine and a large knapsack of medical supplies and backup equipment in case of some emergency. A romantic dinner to share and an evening of privacy alone at home with my husband. Or just one uninterrupted night's sleep.

Instead we do what we have to do. We adjust and accept the facts of life and living with ALS. The steady stream of part-time nurses who pass into and out of our lives as they play such a crucial role in our day-to-day survival. The routine chaos in a household where few things can be done without careful planning, where plans constantly change, everything always takes longer than expected, where even simple activities can suddenly become life-threatening. And those ever-present sounds of Charlie's life—the loud and frequent whine of the suction machine and the quieter, but steady whoosh-whir of the respirator—a rhythmic reminder that death is never more than one breath away, a constant commentary on the preciousness of life.

We've come to accept the fact that our lives are now marked by circumstances very different from what they were in the past, very different from most other people's.

On the surface you might suppose life for Charlie and Lucy Wedemeyer must now be defined by a very different set of principles. And yet those principles aren't so different after all. For we've come to believe the lessons we've learned about life and death, love and marriage aren't unique to us at all.

So we don't tell our story seeking sympathy. We've written this book for a very different reason.

We'd like you to know how we got where we are today. But we have to begin by going back—back to the time years ago when everything *was* different. When life *was* normal.

chapter two

THE DIAGNOSIS

The muscle twitches seemed so insignificant at first that Charlie didn't even think to mention them to Lucy. Not until later, looking back, did he realize the very first signs of a problem probably appeared sometime during the fall of the 1976–77 school year.

CHARLIE

I remember standing at the blackboard in my Los Gatos High School classroom. I picked up a piece of chalk and was writing a problem on the board for my math class when I noticed I had to grip the chalk a little tighter than usual to finish the problem.

Even when this minor weakness recurred in the days and weeks that followed I felt no concern. It wasn't until I began having to grip the chalk with three fingers and my thumb that I sensed any progression or noticeable change.

At that point, when I thought about it at all, I figured it might be the first twinge of arthritis or something of that nature. At age thirty I was probably a little young for arthritis, but my body had taken a beating on the playing field for years—from the time I played Pop Warner, through high school and Big 10 football, until I finally gave up playing competitively after three years of semi-pro ball. I figured any one of a number of old football injuries might have been the cause. And whatever the explanation, the weakness remained only a minor irritation. I compensated for it subconsciously those first few months.

I often played a little basketball in the gym over lunch hour with some of the other assistant coaches and teachers. Early in 1977, as my jump shots consistently fell a little short, I began to sense a loss of strength in my right arm. I quickly made a connection between this new problem and the fact that by this time I had to use all my fingers to hold a piece of chalk. So I mentioned this concern to Lucy for the first time.

LUCY

I remember Charlie sitting on the edge of the bed one night, flexing his wrist and telling me, "I think I may have a little bursitis or arthritis or something in my right arm." He went on to explain about the weakness he'd noticed playing basketball, and about the trouble he had writing on the board. But it was such a casual conversation and Charlie was so matter-of-fact that he made the whole thing seem pretty minor; I wasn't particularly worried.

His theory that it might be somehow connected to an old football injury seemed reasonable to me. I couldn't count the number of concussions, strains, sprains, and fractures Charlie had suffered since we'd begun dating in high school. He'd injured both his neck and back playing high school and college football. And the aftermath of old knee injuries had prompted an orthopedist to tell Charlie he had "the knees of a 70-year-old man." So a little bursitis or even premature arthritis wasn't surprising. But Charlie was, as ever, in great physical shape. He'd always prided himself on his physical and mental toughness; I'd seen him play football games with broken bones. So if he wasn't very concerned about a little unexplained weakness, then neither was I.

We might have given Charlie's physical ailment a little more attention if our already hectic lives hadn't come to a crossroads that spring. In addition to his full-time job teaching high school math, Charlie was an assistant football coach and head frosh-soph basketball coach at Los Gatos High School while also attempting to establish a part-time career as a real estate agent in the summers. I ran my own part-time plant business—taught adult education classes in plant care, helped decorate homes and offices, and consult-ed with clients as a sort of trouble-shooting plant doctor. I'd also recently begun pursuing my own real estate license. And on top of our job-related responsibilities, Charlie and I devoted as much time as possible to our two young children—Carri, nine, and Kale, six.

What complicated our lives even more in that spring of 1977 was a major career decision we had to make. The head football coach at Los Gatos was stepping down. Numerous people connected with the program and the school were encouraging Charlie to apply for the position.

The Wedemeyers talked a lot about the implications and Lucy assured her husband she'd be supportive whatever he wanted to do. At first Charlie hadn't seriously considered the job for fear the added administrative responsibility would take time away from his favorite aspect of coaching—working one-on-one with individual kids. But three major factors began to weigh heavily in his thinking: first, was the sheer number of people (fellow coaches, parents, players, faculty) encouraging him to apply; second, the conviction that it would be best for the program and everyone involved in it for the new coach to come from within the Los Gatos family; and, third, the challenge of heading a football program appealed to him.

Charlie applied for the job. When he got it, he spent every spare minute he could find over the next few months designing the new, complex, multi-set offense he wanted the Los Gatos Wildcats to run the next season.

CHARLIE

I surprised myself by how much I enjoyed my new role.
Like any first year head coach, I had a lot to learn. But after
all my years of playing and my three years as assistant coach
at Los Gatos, there were parts of my personal coaching
philosophy which I determined to implement immediately
and never change.

When I played high school football one of my friends
tried out but was devastated when he didn't make the team.
I made up my mind then that if I ever became a high school
coach, I wouldn't cut anyone who showed me he was
willing to work and learn. And I'd try to help every boy—
whether he was first string or fourth string—to reach his
maximum potential.

The biggest new rule I implemented that first year was,
"No swearing." I had heard so much profanity on football
fields over the years that I decided I wouldn't put up with it
on my team. I wanted the Los Gatos Wildcats to be known
and respected by our opponents and officials for our
sportsmanship. I wanted to instill a lasting sense of discipline and self-respect, so I told the team there would be no
profanity—not in games, practices, in the locker room, on
the bus, or around school. Any player I heard swear would
have to run a mile.

It was amazing how quickly those boys cleaned up their
language.

My complex offensive scheme took longer to implement.
But the players proved so bright and so eager to learn that
they grasped the basics of our sophisticated system much
more quickly than anyone had expected they could.

We needed those brains because we had very little
brawn. We only averaged 168 pounds on our offensive line
that year. Which was why most of my pep talks focused on
the dual theme of "pride and heart." I repeatedly told the
team the only way we could expect to win was if we
believed in ourselves and made up for our lack of size with
big hearts.

And they did it! Everything the coaches asked for—and more. The 1977 Los Gatos Wildcats captured the league championship, winning all our league games and finishing with an impressive 8-2 record overall. I couldn't have been happier for that bunch of boys and my new staff.

LUCY

During his first successful season as head coach, Charlie had many new responsibilities to think about. Yet he remained the exact same person, the same devoted husband, the same attentive father he'd always been. And that impressed me.

Still there was a shadow. It didn't yet seem like a particularly big or dark shadow in the light of such a successful football season. But it was there.

Whatever was wrong with Charlie's hand was clearly getting worse. Sometimes he'd bring his test papers home for me to help grade because he had difficulty gripping a pencil. From time to time I noticed he would drop things he had tried to pick up. While I don't remember feeling very worried about the problem, I was certainly more aware of it. We both were.

One day during the football season, Charlie mentioned the weakness in his hand to our friend Dr. Frank Griffin, a local orthopedist who served as team doctor and whose oldest son played for the Wildcats. Charlie told the doctor his theory about an old football injury, but Dr. Griffin recommended immediate testing to try to get to the bottom of the problem. So Charlie went into a local hospital for a whole battery of tests including a horribly painful myelogram where they inserted a needle into his spine and injected a dye to see if they could spot any abnormalities in the spinal cord.

The only immediate results were a massive migraine for Charlie and an excruciatingly painful trip home from the hospital with Charlie stretched out, face down, moaning like a dying man in the back of our station wagon.

Yet no amount of pain could keep Charlie from thinking

about coaching. Our route home took us right past a rival high school where a football game was in progress. I knew better than to mention the game to Charlie. But my hurting husband heard the sound of a band playing and wanted to know where we were. I told him, "Camden High School."

"What's happening? Can you see the scoreboard?"

"Sorry. It's a little tough to drive and do play-by-play at the same time," I told him.

He said, "Let's stop. I can scout the game."

"I don't think so," I told him. "You're in no condi—"

Looking in the rear-view mirror I saw him lift his head to protest. But before he could utter a word, he slumped back down with an anguished moan. Fortunately he realized he couldn't compile a very helpful scouting report if he was going to pass out with pain every time he raised his head.

A few days later Dr. Griffin told us the tests had been inconclusive. But he did say he'd talked to a friend of his at Stanford University's Medical Center and wanted Charlie to go up there for another series of tests.

Except for the short-term migraines, the medical tests seemed a fairly minor distraction, more of an inconvenience in the middle of a football season than anything we worried or made a big deal about. We didn't deliberately try to keep the tests secret, but very few people knew. Charlie told his assistant coaches, of course, but they didn't have any more reason to be concerned than we did.

I remember one of the assistant coaches, Eric Van Patten, kidding Charlie and saying, "Don't worry. If we have to carry you on a stretcher, you'll be out on the sidelines coaching." Everyone laughed, never imagining how prophetic those words would one day seem.

A week after the Stanford tests Dr. Griffin reported back to the Wedemeyers, saying none of the tests revealed any injuries that would cause Charlie's symptoms. While Charlie and Lucy both felt a little disappointed not to have an explanation, they took the lack of findings as reassurance that they needn't worry. After all, they were caught up in the excitement of Charlie's first football season as head coach.

Not until later, looking back, did they realize there was a lot Dr. Griffin hadn't said. They didn't suspect the tests had ruled out so many things that the doctors could be fairly certain of a diagnosis. They had no idea at the time that their friend Frank Griffin just didn't know how to tell them what he had concluded.

They might have sensed something at Thanksgiving time when Dr. Griffin surprised them with four airplane tickets to Hawaii. He said he wanted Charlie, Lucy and their kids to be able to go back home to visit their families for the Christmas holidays. The Wedemeyers instinctively refused his offer as too generous. But he insisted, pointing out that the modest stipend he received to serve as team doctor more than paid for the tickets.

Charlie and Lucy finally accepted with gratitude and enjoyed a great Christmas celebration with relatives in the islands. But there remained a nagging doubt as to why Dr. Griffin had been so insistent.

CHARLIE

One night, early in February of 1978, Lucy and I had put the children to bed early and were snuggled together on the couch watching a movie on TV about Lou Gehrig the great baseball star. During one restaurant scene, the camera focused on his hand to show his difficulty gripping his fork to eat. Then he reached for some steak sauce, but the bottle slipped out of his grasp and crashed to the table.

At that moment Lucy looked at me. I looked at her. My heart pounded a staccato beat in my chest and a million thoughts raced through my mind at once.

At that instant, I think we both really knew. That scene with the fork and the dropped steak sauce was too real. That could have been me.

LUCY

The next morning after Charlie went to school I headed for the public library to look up amyotrophic lateral sclerosis. I didn't find much about ALS, and what I did find didn't actually describe the disease or even call it a terminal illness.

When I got home from the library I called Dr. Griffin. "You wouldn't believe it, Frank," I told him. "The most amazing thing happened last night. Charlie and I were watching a movie on TV about Lou Gehrig."

"Oh?" the doctor replied.

"Yes, and Lou Gehrig had some of the exact same symptoms Charlie has."

"Is that right?" Dr. Griffin responded. There was a hesitation, an uncertainty in his voice. I wasn't sure if he was brushing aside the idea or if it was something more.

"Well, it's good you called," he continued. "I've been meaning to talk with Charlie."

Maybe there was something. "Frank," I said, "If you have anything serious to tell Charlie, I want to be there."

"Oh, don't worry about that," he told me.

Remembering those words later made me angry. Maybe he just didn't think he could face us both with the news. But it was hard to forgive the doctor for what happened later that afternoon, for the hurt I felt about not being with Charlie when he first heard the diagnosis.

CHARLIE

I didn't know Lucy had already talked to the doctor when I got the message that Frank wanted me to stop by his office on my way home from school that afternoon. I had no way of knowing for sure what he wanted to talk about, but the five minute drive from Los Gatos High to the doctor's office gave me time enough to conclude he must have bad news.

The receptionist sent me right into Frank's office, and he walked in almost immediately. We talked pleasantly for a couple minutes about the great football season we'd had and about the prospects for next year's team. But as we chatted he seemed ill at ease and his discomfort only added to mine. Now I knew the news wasn't good.

He referred to Lucy's call and her mention of the Lou

Gehrig movie. Then he went on to say that because the tests pretty much ruled out any other likely cause for my symptoms, his diagnosis was that I did have ALS, Lou Gehrig's disease.

"Just how serious is it?"

I listened carefully as Dr. Griffin explained briefly that ALS is a degenerative nerve disorder for which there was no known cure.

"That means my condition will continue to get worse?"

The doctor sighed and nodded. He had worked for a time at an ALS clinic and told me, based on his experience with ALS patients, that I probably had only a year or so to live.

I heard his words, but I couldn't believe them because they made no sense. *I don't feel sick. I'm certainly not sick enough to die. It can't be true.*

Frank continued to talk for a short while, but I have no idea what he said. I only remember an overwhelming urge to get out of his office. Not until the drive home did the thought get through to me: *What if he's right?* As I tried to picture the future I realized the doctor had said I didn't have a future. *If that's true, I won't ever be able to see my children grow up!* As I thought about having to leave Carri and Kale and Lucy, tears began to trickle down my face. Suddenly I was overcome with emotion.

I drove right through a red light before I realized I needed to pull over, dry my blurry eyes, and try to regain some control. Somehow I got home. I remember getting out of the car and walking slowly toward the door of the house thinking, *How am I going to tell Lucy?* I still have no idea what I said. I just remember we were in our bedroom, I was holding her, and we both began to cry.

LUCY

Charlie and I are both fuzzy on many of the details of that day. I don't think we realized it then, but we were in conflicting states of shock and denial. While on one level we felt the terrible gravity of what the doctor had said, we couldn't really believe it because Charlie didn't look sick.

I do remember we hugged a lot. But I don't think we said much; words couldn't help. We just held on to each other, seeking some reassuring physical comfort in the face of this sudden emotional cyclone.

I wasn't at all happy with Charlie's decision to keep his plans and leave later that evening for San Francisco with his assistants for a big annual coaches clinic. I certainly didn't want to be 60 miles away from my husband that night. But as upset as I felt, I think part of me realized even then that whether or not this diagnosis was accurate, we couldn't stop living. Charlie needed to keep going. This clinic might help keep his mind off the unthinkable.

But I didn't sleep much that night. The bed seemed so empty. I felt so helpless, so alone.

I must have dozed off toward morning because I remember opening my eyes to daylight. I wanted to tell myself it was all just a bad dream, that Charlie hadn't gone to see Dr. Griffin yesterday, that he couldn't possibly have ALS, and there was no chance he was going to die. But I was already awake enough to realize the horrible truth.

Outside our bedroom window the sun shone on the orange tree in our backyard. The narcissuses were blooming. I could hear warblers singing as they splashed in our birdbath. And I remember a flash of anger as I wondered *How is this possible? How can the rest of the world go on like this when everything has changed?*

Of course, I quickly learned the rest of the universe doesn't come to a stop just because someone says your husband is dying. As disbelieving and unprepared as you might feel, life goes on. Ready or not.

part two

ROMANCE
AND DREAMS

chapter three
BEGINNINGS IN PARADISE

CHARLIE

I'll never forget that first time I set eyes on Lucy.

What a gorgeous Hawaiian day! The tropical sun muted only by a scattering of billowy clouds drifting in from the deep blue expanse of Pacific Ocean stretching to the horizon beyond the hotels marking the skyline of Waikiki. But I wasn't thinking about the view from the hillside campus of Honolulu's Punahou Academy.

I stood with some of my football buddies, talking, laughing and comparing notes on classes, teachers and schedules for our senior year. There she was. I spotted her coming up the stairs beneath the towering poinciana tree which dominated the courtyard in front of the campus cafeteria. *She has to be a new student. I have never seen her before; I would definitely have noticed.*

Suddenly oblivious to the talk around me, I noticed how the rays of sunlight illuminated her blond hair, how her whole face lit up when she smiled, and how easily she laughed at something her friend Jane was saying as they waited in a long line snaking out of the campus bookstore. I thought, *I have to meet that girl.*

Being basically shy, especially around members of the opposite sex, I recruited a couple of my more outgoing buddies as reinforcements. Then we wandered over to the bookstore line where I managed to get introduced (learning she was a new transfer to Punahou and her name was Lucy Dangler) and exchanged brief hellos before letting my more talkative friends carry the conversation.

In the days that followed I couldn't seem to get Lucy Dangler out of my mind. So, after checking around and learning she wasn't going with anyone, I worked up my courage and asked her for a date. I borrowed a car from one of my married sisters and took Lucy out to eat following the first football game of the season.

One date and I knew I was in love.

LUCY

I remember meeting Charlie and thinking he was really cute. While his friends obviously wanted to impress the girls outside the bookstore, he seemed quiet and shy in an appealing sort of way. He didn't have that big-talking personality or the cocky swagger I'd observed in other high school jocks I'd known.

At 5'7" and 160 pounds Charlie didn't look like an imposing athlete. I had no idea he'd already won all-state honors in football (twice), basketball, and baseball (once each), and would again win all-state honors in all three sports his senior year. As a new transfer at Punahou I knew nothing about the already legendary athletic accomplishments that would one day result in his being named Hawaii's Prep Athlete of the Decade for the 1960s. I certainly didn't know when he first asked me out that dating Charlie Wedemeyer would make me the envy of half the high school girls on the island of Oahu.

I probably should have suspected as much when so many girls at school suddenly wanted to be my friend.

But the real tipoff came when Charlie would walk off the field at the end of a football game. Flower leis are a Hawaiian tradition at any and every important event—sporting events are no exception. After ball games mothers, sisters, girlfriends, and other admiring females will converge on their personal "hero" to bestow leis and congratulatory kisses. By the time I could get to Charlie with my lei as he came off the football field after a game, he'd already have a dozen flower strands around his neck.

The night Charlie told me he loved me and asked me to go steady with him, we were sitting in the front seat of his sister's car—the back seat full of leis other adoring girls had given him. I told him "Yes" even as I thought *I must be dreaming!* Not because he was such a popular athlete, but because he was so different from any other boy I'd gone out with.

And I was only beginning to learn who he really was, and what influences had shaped his life.

The foundational force in Charlie Wedemeyer's life, the biggest influence on the person he became was family.

When Charlie was born months after the end of World War II, the Wedemeyers lived in Kalihi Valley, the toughest and probably the poorest area on all of Oahu. On December 7, 1941, the first squadrons of Japanese planes flew out of the rising sun, darted through a mountain pass to the east and roared down through this valley, just hundreds of feet above his family's house en route to bomb the American fleet in Pearl Harbor. So for Charlie, stories of that infamous attack are part of his family's oral history. Time after time he heard his parents and his older brothers and sisters recall that morning, the screaming planes overhead, explosions reverberating in the distance and black smoke filling the sky. Charlie's father, who worked on the docks at Pearl Harbor, often six or seven days a week, didn't go to work on that historic Sunday morning or Charlie might never have been born.

As it was, Charlie came last in a line of nine children born over 18 years to Bill and Ruth Wedemeyer. The oldest was Herman, then Ruth, Jewel, Kenneth, Earl, Winona, Bridget, Penny, and finally Charlie. In his early years Charlie never considered himself "poor"; he thought nothing of the fact his large family lived in a tiny two-bedroom, one-bath house.

Sharing one bedroom with all his siblings (the girls got the bed, the boys slept on the floor) provided a definite sense of family closeness and little if any "personal space." Because the warped bathroom door in that house never closed completely, family members had to hang a towel or a jacket over it if they wanted even a semblance of privacy in the "lua."

Despite their economic hardships, Charlie's family claimed a strong, proud heritage. Like most 20th century Hawaiian families, the Wedemeyers combined a rich mix of cultural heritage—Hawaiian, Irish, English, German, Chinese and French Tahitian. And as Charlie grew up his older siblings added to the mix by marrying spouses with Chinese, Filipino, Japanese, and Hawaiian backgrounds. There was even a mainland "haole" in the family.

CHARLIE

I probably inherited my basically shy personality from my mother. A small, quiet, gentle woman—but a tireless worker—she always seemed more comfortable behind the scenes and out of the limelight. Though reserved, she was also warm and affectionate with our family.

Some of the fondest memories I have of my mother date from early childhood when she'd take me out in the yard with her to "help" garden and care for her flowers—tahitian gardenias, hibiscus, orchids, ti and the fragrant pakalana. I don't remember ever talking much as we weeded and watered, but we were together, just the two of us.

I think another trait I got from my mom was my perfectionism. For despite her economic limitations, she had high expectations and standards for her family. While I never had many, or very fancy clothes, she made sure whenever I left the house for school my clothes were immaculate and impeccably pressed. Mother made ironing an art.

She was just as demanding about our behavior; I knew I

was never supposed to do anything that would bring embarrassment or unfavorable attention to my family. Mother frowned on her children speaking Pidgin, the old colloquial mixture of simple English and other languages that became the standard trading language of the South Pacific and continues as a sort of street slang among many Hawaiians today. We were expected to speak correct English at all times.

My mother might have been poor. But that didn't keep her from being a particular and proper lady.

My father used to tease her by telling people he'd saved her from life as a nun. As a girl she had seriously considered committing her life to service in the church. She remained a very devout Catholic as an adult, making faith and church attendance a crucial part of our family life.

My dad was in many ways her opposite. Outgoing and boisterous, he loved the attention he got spinning yarns and telling jokes. He had a generous streak and a real heart for kids. I can't count the number of times I've seen him at family gatherings surrounded by a flock of youngsters as he teased them, patted their heads, and emptied his pockets of coins he'd hand out one-at-a-time saying, "Here, baby. Here, honey. Here."

I think I inherited a love for children from my dad. But I also inherited some of his temper. He had a short fuse; especially with anyone opposing a member of our family. After one of my Little League baseball games I remember him getting into a scuffle with an umpire he thought had made some lousy calls. Another time when I was older I remember running off the baseball field to help Dad in a fight behind the stands with an opposing fan. He was a loud and loyal personal cheering section who never took his spectator role lightly.

But what I respected him most for was his fundamental attitude toward life. He was a battler who always took life head on and refused to let circumstances limit him. He accepted disadvantages not as barriers but as challenges—a lesson he learned early and modeled the rest of his life.

When Dad was a young teenager, he and some friends decided one day to hop a freight train for a free ride into town. They'd done it often enough to become adept at sprinting along the tracks, reaching out to grab a hold of the ladder on the end of a boxcar and swinging themselves aboard. But on this particular afternoon, as Dad tried to leap aboard the third boxcar from the end of the train, he lost his grip, and sprawled to the ground. Before he had time to recover and roll clear, the next car's wheels rolled over and mangled his left foot.

One of his friends ran for help. And eventually a horse-drawn ambulance carried him to the closest hospital. But there wasn't much in the way of reconstructive surgery at the time; all the doctors could do was clean and sew up the wound, leaving him with a toeless stump.

Amazingly, he didn't let that terrible accident slow him down for long. A great athlete in his day, Dad went on to play semi-pro baseball and even played football in the old Hawaiian Barefoot League. If he ever felt the least bit self-conscious or self-pitying about his handicap, I never saw it. He'd recruit me and some of his grandchildren who were about my age to help wad up newspaper to stuff into his left shoe so it would fit snugly on his stump. All the while he'd regale us with some elaborate and exciting new story he'd made up about how he'd lost all his toes. His favorites involved vicious wild dogs or a giant toe-eating sea turtle that caught him swimming in the ocean. Those exciting adventures always seemed so vivid and real that I don't remember how old I was before I realized the train story was the true one.

With my dad's background as an athlete, it's not surprising that sports played such an important role in our family. My mother too was a life-long fan, her favorite sport being baseball. All my siblings were athletic. One of my sisters became a black-belt in judo. Each of my older brothers played football and other sports. I remember Dad taking me to see Kenneth play football, and I vowed to one day be as quick and tough as Kenneth. But it was my oldest brother Herman who set the Wedemeyer family standard so high, playing college football at little St. Mary's College in California, sharing first-team All America backfield honors his senior year with the legendary Army stars, Glenn Davis and Doc Blanchard. Herman came in fourth in the voting for the Heisman Trophy.

But it was my father's competitive spirit, his never-give-up attitude that inspired my own competitiveness. I never saw him play in his prime. But I served as his bat boy and watched him play in a tough softball league when he was well into his fifties. And when he took up golf he mastered the game so well that when I was a teenager he'd challenge me to a round of golf and beat me using only a driver. While he did it as a competitive challenge, it served the secondary purpose of keeping me humble.

Looking back I believe Hawaii had to be the greatest place in the world for a boy to grow up in the fifties. We had Little League baseball, Pop Warner football, and basketball all year round on the street court in front of the fire station down the block. The fire chief, who was a family friend, would leave on the outside station lights any night we wanted to shoot some hoops under the stars. When my friends and I weren't throwing, hitting, bouncing or shooting some kind of ball there was always the beach. We'd run and explore for miles up and down the beach, swim and dive in the tropical blue waters of the Pacific and body surf Oahu's Makapuu and Sandy Beach.

So the most important factors in establishing the foundation of my self-identity were family and sports. For it was through sports that I lived up to the Hawaiian name my mother gave me—Kalekauwila. "Kale" (pronounced *Kuh-lee*) meant Charlie or Charles, and "kauwila" (pronounced *cow-ee-la*) meant lightning.

Charlie Lightning.

chapter four
MEANT FOR EACH OTHER

LUCY

I reached Hawaii by a different route. Soon after being born in the midwestern U.S., my family moved to the Bay Area of California before my father's sales work with the airlines took us to the islands during my grade school years. I lived with my parents, my younger sister and two younger brothers in an exclusive neighborhood only a block from the beach in Kahala—beyond Diamond Head.

My father, Henry Dangler, had fought as a B-24 pilot in the Army Air Corps during World War II. Shot down over Germany, he bailed out of his flaming aircraft, only to be captured by curious villagers who wrapped his burns in wet newspapers, asked a lot of questions about how a young man with a good German name like Dangler could be an American officer, and finally turned him over to Nazi military authorities. He spent the last months of the war as a POW in the prison camp depicted in Steve McQueen's famous war movie, *The Great Escape*.

His war experience gave him the strength and drive to become a successful sales executive who felt confident and comfortable dealing in the international marketplace. I am told he was a tough, aggressive businessman. While he could be a demanding parent, he was also a devoted and loving father who regularly took the entire family on sailing and tennis outings.

My mother, Marcia Barnum, had a natural air of grace and sophistication—even in the fun-loving side of her character. The *New Yorker* and *Punch* cartoons she regularly clipped out to slip into our school lunch boxes reflected a wry humor. She had a broad streak of perfectionism that sometimes conflicted with my more care-free approach to life. But she was a loving mom, devoted to her family. And she instilled in me, like Charlie's mom did for him, a deep love for gardening, and flowers.

My dad knew and respected Charlie's oldest brother Herman as a business acquaintance and friend, so he approved of Charlie immediately. My brothers, more aware of Charlie's athletic accomplishments than I was to begin with, were impressed to have their sister dating a local sports hero. And Charlie's gentlemanly manners quickly charmed my mother.

In fact, the unquestioned acceptance we received from each others' families is probably the reason I never thought about the significance of Charlie's attendance at the most expensive and exclusive private school in the islands—even though he came from a working class Hawaiian family. I didn't know that his transfer from the all-Hawaiian Kamehameha School in the sixth grade had stirred up controversy and bitterness between the schools. Charlie's brother Herman had encouraged him to accept what amounted to an athletic scholarship at Punahou. But he was charged by many with leaving his heritage at Kamehameha to attend what they considered a *haole* (Hawaiian for "mainlander" or "outsider") school.

Charlie worked in the cafeteria every day at lunchtime, but lots of students took campus jobs to help defer the cost of a Punahou education. Charlie fit in even though he didn't wear the trendy, expensive clothes some of his peers did.

No one looked snappier than he did in his starched and pressed ROTC uniform. He spit-shined his shoes and polished his belt buckle each night. And during the day, when he thought no one was looking, he'd run a comb down the creases in his trousers to keep them crisp and straight.

His family laughingly tells stories of how, when he was younger, he'd slick his hair back along the sides with Brylcreem before bedtime, sleep stiff as a board until morning, and awaken with every hair in place.

At first I thought Charlie's meticulous concern about appearance seemed at odds with his shy, humble nature—until I realized a big part of his motivation was the discomfort he feared should anything about his clothes or his personal grooming call attention to him. He didn't mind being singled out to make a big play in a stadium full of cheering fans, but he hated the thought of standing in the front of a classroom to deliver an oral report, or of walking into a party with a bunch of people he didn't know.

I found this shyness charming and sometimes amusing. I still remember the first time I realized I had publicly embarrassed him. We were on a date, standing in line outside a movie theater when I laughed loudly and he suddenly looked as if he wanted to hide. I didn't understand his reaction until it hit me that my laughter had caused a number of people nearby to turn and look our way.

But I don't think I ever did anything to make him as uncomfortable as his dad did on a regular basis. Charlie's father never missed a chance to tell any listener he could corner about the latest athletic accomplishments of his youngest son. Whenever we came within earshot of his father boasting about "Charlie-boy this" or "Charlie-boy that," Charlie would grab my hand, say "Let's go" and head in the opposite direction.

CHARLIE

Around Lucy I felt an easy self-confidence and acceptance I'd seldom experienced before—except with my family and in my athletics. By the time I became a senior in high school, sports had long been the foundation of my self-esteem.

I'd learned as a shy little kid that my athletic ability was my ticket to respect and acceptance from my peers. I'd felt lost my first day at Punahou, but one week in P.E. class had been enough to prove myself to my peers and bolster my self-confidence. Putting a ball in my hands was a little like pouring spinach into Popeye; the insecurities and self-doubts dropped away and I became a different person— confident, determined, invincible.

Sports also offered me a relational arena in which to establish and build my most meaningful friendships. When I think of my years playing sports at Punahou—all the memories, all the big games, all the honors—what I remember best, what makes me most nostalgic for those bright and glorious days of my youth, is the sense of camaraderie.

Along with my teammates I shared in the pain of some bitter defeats and in the glory of even more sweet victories. The aura of tradition that permeated sports at Punahou bonded us together. Like every Punahou football team for years before us, we spent two weeks before school started in football camp, living together 24-hours a day and enduring grueling two-a-day practice sessions in preparation for the new season. We ended practices with "tiger hunt" drills—a gut-wrenching exercise in which we ran up and down steep grassy slopes to circle the ancient royal poinciana trees standing high on the hillside above our practice field.

Then there was the singing. Music has long been a part of Hawaiian culture; so it held a prominent place in Punahou athletics. We sang traditional Hawaiian songs in the showers after every practice. We sang during bus rides home from games. And the warmest emotional memory I have from my high school sports career, the most moving, spine-tingling sound I remember wasn't the explosion of cheers I heard when I broke through the line of scrimmage and outsprinted my opponents for a touchdown. It was a song.

After every game, win or lose, as the team bus approached the palm-lined entrance gates of the beautiful Punahou campus, everyone on board would fall silent for a moment. Then, as we pulled through the gates, we'd begin singing the team's traditional song, "We are the Sons of Oahu." When the bus braked to a halt beside the field house, the crowd of family and friends waiting to cheer and congratulate us would stand quietly, almost reverently as we finished singing the final chorus.

Perhaps because the islands in the 1960s provided little in the way of college or professional sports, high school athletics were big-time in Hawaii. Every Thanksgiving Day morning, as many as 28,000 fans would fill the old Honolulu Stadium for great rivalries between schools like Punahou and Kamehameha. This so called "Turkey Day Game"—the equivalent of our state championship, was *the* premier sporting event of the football season in Hawaii.

With that kind of attention came a lot of pressure on 16, 17 and 18 year-old kids. Gambling on high school sports was big, but I didn't realize how big at the time. I paid no particular attention to the way so many of my friends' fathers would make a point to ask me how I was feeling, whether the ankle-sprain I got in last week's game was healing well, or how the team looked in practice. I didn't realize they were looking for inside information that might affect the line on the game. Even when I received a threatening phone call before the big Kamehameha game my senior year, I didn't connect the call in my mind to gamblers. But my brother Herman took the threat seriously, insisting I stay at his house near the Punahou campus for the week and go to school with his son Dougie instead of traveling home to the windward side of the island each night.

I enjoyed every sport I played—the thrill of a well-executed fast-break in basketball, the satisfying feel of the bat making solid contact on a wicked curve. But football was always my favorite.

As a quarterback I learned the responsibilities and

assignments of every player, at every position, on every play. The complexities of competing offenses and defenses fascinated me. I also liked the physical aspect of the game— priding yourself in jumping right back to your feet after a hard and clean tackle, the exhilaration of breaking past the line and outsprinting your opponents to the end zone. But what I relished most was the challenge of competing against and beating bigger, stronger opponents. Maybe because I was a little guy, I loved the role of underdog.

LUCY

Charlie and I were soon spending so much time together I think some of our friends resented our closeness. But being so much in love, there never seemed enough time to-gether—what with his practice and game schedule. So not surprisingly, Charlie's sports played a big role in our early relationship.

Watching his football games, it didn't take me long to realize everything people said about him was true. I remember one game when his team was backed up deep in its own territory, Charlie broke through the line and raced eighty-some yards for a touchdown. I can still hear the crowd's cheers turn to groans as we realized a penalty flag had been thrown and Charlie's run was called back. But on the very next play, Charlie took the ball again and ran more than ninety yards for the touchdown as the crowd went absolutely wild. He was a truly gifted athlete who repeat-edly amazed and thrilled his fans.

Sports took up so much of Charlie's time that we had to make the most of every opportunity we had to be together. Charlie would walk me to class whenever he could and then have to sprint across campus to make his next period class. I remember standing with him in the shade of a big tamarind tree before English/Lit until my teacher leaned out of his second story classroom window and good-naturedly called down: "Lucy Dangler, we don't have all day. Say good-bye to Charlie and get up here. We're ready to start class."

We'd steal a few minutes together in the library before school every day. Once I discovered Charlie loved gardenias as much as I did, each morning I'd bring a single blossom from my mother's bushes. Charlie carried the gardenias in his shirt pocket all day and tucked them inside the lining of his football helmet before games. He romantically claimed the gardenia's would inspire him because they'd constantly remind him of me as he played. I never believed the flowers ever had any effect on Charlie's performance, but the thought was sweet, and the pungent fragrance of gardenias certainly had to improve the odor of his sweaty football equipment.

True dates were limited to weekends, and then usually after a ball game—either one Charlie played in or one we attended so he could scout an upcoming opponent. Our favorite place to go for a post-game meal was downtown to Flamingos because Charlie loved their famous banana pie. They'd usually be sold out by the time we could get there after a game, but one of the waitresses always managed to save Charlie a piece or two.

One of our favorite dates was to head down to Waikiki. We sometimes had to laugh at the half-baked tourists (sunburned bright red on one side and pale white on the other) wearing their bright new Hawaiian shirts and mumus. And we'd stroll arm-in-arm along the beach— silhouetted against the moonlit water, warm ocean breezes rustling the majestic palms reaching into the starry night sky overhead. The steady soothing beat of the surf underscored the island music drifting out from the showrooms and lounges of Waikiki's many beach-side hotels. Sometimes we'd slip into one of the shows and catch a number or two; many of the Hawaiian entertainers knew Charlie, his brother Herman, or were somehow related to the Wedemeyer clan, so we seldom had to pay.

But more often than not we just walked along the beach, enjoying each other and the incomparable thrill of young love. Sometimes we'd hold hands and run along the edge of the surf; and I remember Charlie teaching me to juke step as we dodged in and out of the coconut trees in Kapiolani Park at the base of Diamond Head.

Charlie taught me how to pick pineapples and took me horseback riding up into the mountains to pick ginger blossoms. We sometimes went ti leaf sliding down steep hillsides during afternoon rain showers—ending up soaked and covered with mud.

I did manage to get Charlie to go with me, my brother Tim and his future wife, Dian, to an outdoor ballet at the "Shell" in Waikiki. And we often went bird watching on picnics in the mountains with my mother. But Charlie's idea of a fun Wedemeyer family outing was a big volleyball game and potluck picnic on the beach—complete with teriyaki, sushi, manapua, sweet and sour spareribs, Korean barbecue, corned beef and cabbage, and of course the traditional island staple of beans and rice.

Even in those first exciting months together, the high tide of young love seemed more than sufficient to carry us over such dangerous relational reefs as differing backgrounds and personalities. We talked easily and naturally about getting married someday, having a houseful of children and growing old together. We joked about rocking together on a porch in our retirement years, putting in each other's false teeth, and when we got really old maybe even racing each other up and down the beach in our wheelchairs. Toward the end of the school year we talked seriously about going ahead and getting married right after Charlie graduated, but we knew our parents would want us to wait until I could finish high school. And I think we both realized we needed a little more time and maturity. In the meantime, Charlie had another decision to make that would greatly impact our future.

chapter five

TOGETHER
IN THE BIG TEN

CHARLIE

Choosing a college was probably the toughest decision I'd ever made in my life. A number of schools offered me athletic scholarships. I briefly considered staying home and going to the University of Hawaii so I could be near Lucy. But they didn't have a very strong football program at the time.

I also contemplated signing with some West Coast school, but in the end, after a visit to East Lansing, I chose Michigan State in part because MSU had a strong program in hotel and restaurant management; I hoped to one day follow my brother Herman into that field.

Sure, I'd be a long way from home, but I was also swayed by the exciting prospect of Big Ten football. And Coach Duffy Daugherty's island connection had already wooed three Hawaiians I'd played against in high school— Bob Apisa, Dick Kenney, and Roger Lopez—so I figured I wouldn't be alone.

However, I didn't realize just how far Michigan would seem from Hawaii until I climbed on a plane in August knowing I wouldn't see my family or Lucy again at least till Christmas. I'd never known loneliness like I discovered the first two weeks of preseason drills. I spent most of my spare time and almost all my cash for the semester on phone calls before school even started. I think Duffy soon realized how discouraged I was, because he took me aside and kindly told me when I was feeling homesick I could come by the athletic offices and make a long-distance call home.

To me Duffy's offer was a much appreciated act of kindness from a thoughtful man who reached out in compassion to a poor, disheartened and lonely kid half a world away from home.

I still remember the feeling of awe I experienced walking out on the practice field my first day at Michigan State and realizing the incredible talent assembled on one team. Future NFL stars Bubba Smith, Gene Washington and Clint Jones all played for the Spartans in those days. I was one of six freshman quarterbacks who'd been All-American, All-State, all-region or all-something in high school. (I didn't learn until years later that Duffy's philosophy with quarterbacks was to sign every good one he could find so he wouldn't ever have to play *against* them.)

I didn't mind the tough competition. But the recurrence of an old back injury from high school days limited my playing time on the freshman squad and kept me near the bottom of the team's depth chart.

As disheartened as I was by my loneliness and my injury, the toughest adjustment of all that freshman year came from the shock of my first Michigan winter. I don't know if I could have survived what seemed like an endless midwestern winter without the daily letters from Lucy and her regular care packages of my favorite Hawaiian flowers and an occasional Flamingo's banana pie.

I also owed a big part of my emotional survival to friendships with my Hawaiian teammates. I ate a lot of chicken long rice and other Hawaiian dishes at Roger Lopez's house. Despite the rivalry we'd had during high school in Hawaii, Dick and Bob became like big brothers and kept my spirits shored up that first year.

Yet my tough freshman football season wasn't without its highlights. Duffy, who I quickly came to view as an encouraging, second-father figure, named me as the only freshman to make the trip with the varsity to the 1966 Rose Bowl. And when spring finally came to Michigan that year, I made an impressive enough showing during spring drills to earn preseason consideration as backup varsity quarterback.

My second year at Michigan State was an altogether different and more wonderful experience as a member of the 1966 Spartan's national championship team. I held on extra points and field goals all season for our barefoot Hawaiian kicker Dick Kenney—including four of MSU's points in that infamous 10-10 tie game we played with Notre Dame. But the most memorable game for me was probably our 11–8 victory over Ohio State when Bob, Dick and I scored all our team's points. I tallied two of the points on a conversion after Dick faked the kick, rolled out and passed to me in the end zone.

I discovered the perfect cure for loneliness that sophomore year as well; Lucy and I got married. So while the Michigan winter seemed just as long, it didn't seem nearly as cold.

Looking back I realize many people thought we were awfully young and foolish to get married when we did. It certainly wasn't easy trying to build a new marriage while going to school, playing big-time college football, and living on a shoestring budget made possible only by Lucy's job at a local florist.

I never regretted our decision for a minute, however. While we did save a ton in long distance phone bills, we still had to eat teriyaki hot dogs and a lot of rice and beans. But I'd grown up on rice and beans. And they had never tasted better than they did in our tiny campus apartment as I looked across the table at Lucy.

Marriage certainly provided me with a sense of happiness and contentment that improved my life and my college experience like nothing else could have done. It instilled a sense of responsibility that gave added focus to everything I did, not just on the football field but in the classroom preparing for the future—our future together.

LUCY

Those years with Charlie at Michigan State were some of the most exciting and eventful times of our lives. First there was the national championship season. But the biggest highlight of 1967 for us came off the field with the birth of our first child, a healthy 8-pound, 13-ounce baby whom the obstetrician welcomed into the world with the words, 'Oh my, what a great big football player. . . uh . . . for a girl."

We called her Carri, but we also gave her a Hawaiian name, Kauiaupuehuehu, meaning "lovely, snowflake," because snow flurried the day she was born. Soon thereafter we discovered a baby complicated our lives and multiplied our responsibilities, yet we cherished our new roles as parents. I particularly enjoyed watching the relationship develop between Carri and her father. She obviously adored him and the feeling was mutual. In fact one of my biggest frustrations as a young mother was that I'd no sooner succeed in getting Carri down for a nap than Charlie would arrive home and immediately wake her up so he could play with her. No matter what hour of day or night he arrived home from football practice, class or studying, Charlie figured it was time to romp on the floor or the bed with his daughter. He was absolutely incorrigible and took great delight in the fact that Carri's very first word was "ball."

Charlie's senior football season at MSU he switched to flanker and earned recognition as the Spartan Back of the Year. But the biggest honors came at the end of the season. First, he was selected to play in the Shriner's East-West College All-Star Football game in San Francisco. Then we went back to Hawaii for the Hula Bowl where he received as much, if not more, press coverage as a hometown hero than O. J. Simpson, Mean Joe Greene, Art Thoms, Ed Podulak,

LeRoy Keys and other collegians who were better known on the mainland.

When Charlie graduated from Michigan State in the spring of 1969, we briefly discussed the possibility of his playing pro football. Several teams expressed an interest in him as a free agent. But Charlie felt his small size, and his history of knee injuries made a pro football career a long shot. He had a family to support and he didn't want to put us through the uncertainty of moving somewhere only to be cut during training camp as so many of our friends had been. So Charlie accepted a position with the Flint, Michigan, school system as a junior high teacher and assistant football coach. And he had a blast playing quarterback for the Lansing All-Stars, a semi-pro team comprised mostly of former Spartan teammates.

During his second year teaching, the Mott Foundation selected Charlie as one of fifty educators from around the nation to receive a graduate fellowship in an intern program in the field of Community Education at Central Michigan University. During the year and a half Charlie spent working on his Master's our son Kale (kuh-lee) was born. His full Hawaiian name was Matthew Kaleikapono. "Kale" after his father, and "ikapono" meaning "strong, up-righteous one." We had no idea at the time how appropriate that name would one day be.

While we wouldn't trade the memories of our years in Michigan for anything, we missed Hawaii. The island's mountains never looked greener nor the ocean bluer than when we'd leave a stark Michigan winter to go home for the Christmas holidays.

CHARLIE

Lucy and I still dreamed of returning to Hawaii one day to live. So when I took a three week internship in the Bay Area south of San Francisco at the conclusion of my graduate program, I figured California might be a big step in the right geographical direction.

I remember calling Lucy back in Flint from my hotel room phone in San Jose and asking her, "What would you think about my taking a job out here?" She answered, "I'm packing! I'm packing!"

So the day I walked across the platform to accept my Master's Degree was the same day our family began a cross-country journey with all our worldly possessions loaded in a U-Haul truck.

We immediately loved the Bay Area. The mountains and the year-round flowers felt more like Hawaii. And after a year as director of an adult education program in San Jose, when I decided I wanted to trade the hassles of administration for the joys of teaching and coaching young people again, we found Los Gatos—a picturesque, historic little town nestled in the foothills of the Santa Cruz Mountains. The high school itself had a 100-year old history with generations of rich tradition that reminded us of all that was good about Punahou—the place where our lifelong adventure together began.

part three
DEALING
WITH DISEASE

chapter six
THE TRUTH SINKS IN

Fear. Anger. Confusion. The Wedemeyers experienced all these reactions and more when their doctor's diagnosis suddenly threatened to turn their previously happy, romantic, fairy-tale story into a tragedy.

The swirl of disturbing emotions combined to create a merciful sense of numbness, which the Wedemeyers now acknowledge was some sort of defense mechanism, either a psychological response to shock or even a subconscious form of denial. Certainly denial would have been a natural reaction to a diagnosis saying Charlie had maybe a year to live—three years at the most—when he didn't even look sick.

Only slowly did reality sink in. But those first, honest glimpses into the future proved emotionally painful for Charlie and Lucy. Acknowledging and accepting the truth was even harder.

LUCY

The parents of one of Charlie's players had been bugging us for a long time to take our children and spend a skiing weekend at their cabin up at Bear Valley. So the week after

Dr. Griffin's diagnosis, we finally accepted their offer for Valentine's Day weekend.

Neither of us said as much, but Charlie and I both figured this would be the last time we'd ever be able to go skiing as a family. After spending a wonderful day on the slopes together, we went to the nearby lodge for a special family dinner. Big fluffy flakes began to fall outside the windows as we ate; so Carri and Kale finished quickly and rushed out to play in the fresh snow.

Charlie and I remained alone at our candlelit table. A fire blazed in the lodge's giant hearth. The swirling snow and winter evening scene outside the window looked like something out of Currier and Ives. When Charlie reached over to take my hand, I couldn't have imagined a more romantic setting.

As I looked into Charlie's face, I recognized in his eyes the same raw emotions I felt churning inside me. I had never felt more love for Charlie, or more loved by him, than I did that special evening. And yet I'd never in my life felt such pain. Such anguish.

Tears filled our eyes. Neither of us dared speak for fear the floodgates would open. So we just sat silently, holding hands across the table, basking in the bittersweet warmth of that moment, wishing the romantic spell could somehow make time stand still. All the while wondering how much time we had left together.

That memorable weekend served as an important milestone for us; for it was then that I think we began to learn to relish each moment together, to see and enjoy the beauty around us and and to appreciate the blessings we have. Yet neither Charlie nor I could forget that we couldn't stay in the mountains. We had to go back home to a future suddenly full of uncertainty and questions.

What do I need to say and do to help Charlie? How do you support and encourage the man you love after the doctors tell him he has a terminal disease? I would have to discover my own answers to those questions, sometimes by painful trial and error, in the months and years that followed.

A few days after we returned from our ski trip, I remember going shopping to look for a birthday present for Charlie. I spotted a shirt I knew he'd really love, but as I picked it up I was struck by the sudden thought: *What am I doing? Charlie's going to die. Why am I spending this money?* But almost as quickly, in my mind's eye, I envisioned Charlie trying on the shirt, smiling and happy. Fighting back tears, I chided myself: *For heaven's sake, of course I'm going to buy it.* In fact, I bought two.

I was beginning to realize even then that we couldn't stop living or even celebrating life just because Charlie was dying. For his sake certainly, but also for mine and for our children's, we needed to live as normal a life as possible for as long as possible. That goal became the foundation of my personal coping strategy.

Charlie and I had always been able to make each other laugh. And I think I instinctively realized, that if we were going to maintain any semblance of normalcy, we needed that sense of humor more than ever before.

One night, lying in bed, I playfully pulled Charlie's hair and teasingly said, "At least we can be thankful you don't have cancer."

Charlie turned and gave me a surprised look. "What do you mean?"

"If you had to go through chemotherapy you might lose all this thick, beautiful hair. You'd be as bald as your father."

He grinned.

"Of course that might be good. You wouldn't have to spend so much time parting and combing it to make sure every follicle is in place."

The grin gave way to a look of mock anger. "I don't. . ."

"But then knowing you, you'd probably want me to polish your head to give it a perfect, proper shine."

"That's it! Come here!" he said, grabbing me and laughing as I pretended to try to get away.

Another time I remember sitting on our bed late one evening talking and recognizing the irony in the fact that both Charlie and Benny Pierce, the coach for Saratoga High, one of Los Gatos' biggest rivals, had developed serious health problems. Benny suffered such severe spinal pain he had to use a golf cart to get up and down the sidelines.

"It makes you wonder, doesn't it?" I grinned at Charlie. "You think there might be a shortage of good football coaches in heaven right now?"

"I don't know," Charlie responded with a straight face, "Could be God's teams haven't been beating the spread."

In order to survive emotionally, we made a deliberate effort to keep laughing. But we also quickly realized we couldn't hope to cope with everyday life if we spent too much of our emotional energy worrying about the future. When my mother asked one day, "What are you going to do when Charlie can no longer walk, when he can't eat, when he can't go to the bathroom by himself?" my answer was quick, almost cursory. "I'm not going to worry about that now," I replied. "If and when that time comes we'll deal with it. We're going to concentrate on living one day at a time."

In those first months after Charlie's diagnosis, some people saw the Wedemeyer's determination to remain upbeat, and their evident refusal to worry about the future as a form of denial, of avoiding reality. While there may have been some understandable denial involved, Charlie and Lucy quickly passed beyond avoidance and actually gained a new awareness of reality. In fact, by focusing on the challenges, the opportunities and the experiences of daily living, they came to a new awareness of life's blessings.

For Lucy, this awareness quickly grew into a new sense of purpose for her life. She felt she'd been given a personal mission, a calling, to keep Charlie going just as long as possible.

CHARLIE

I drew more strength from Lucy's positive reaction than I could ever understand, let alone express. My own primary reaction, once the disbelief wore off, was determination.

Discipline and tenacity had enabled me to achieve improbable goals all my life. I'd always embraced the role of underdog. *I could beat this! I would beat this!*

This initial resolution to keep on living and prove the doctors wrong made me reluctant to want to tell people about the diagnosis. And the fact that I still looked so healthy meant that we didn't have to explain anything to most people in the beginning.

But there were those we had to tell, either because I felt an obligation or because they had known about the tests I'd gone through to try to explain the symptoms. Ted Simonson, the principal of Los Gatos High, was among the first I told. He assured me he saw no reason I couldn't continue teaching and coaching.

I asked, "What if the disease progresses to the point I can no longer walk and have to be in a wheelchair?"

Ted looked me in the eye and said, "As long as you can do the job, Charlie, you can be the head football coach here at Los Gatos High School!"

I didn't see any need to explain the details to the football team before the upcoming 1978 season. But my assistant coaches knew about the ALS and were supportive. They didn't make a big deal about the diagnosis. There was no emotional scene between us. They simply treated me like the same friends and colleagues they'd always been.

Lucy and I did share the doctors' prognosis with a few of our closest friends. And of course, we called and told our families immediately—with the exception of my parents. Since neither of them were in good health, my brothers and sisters suggested we delay telling them. But when we went home to Hawaii again in the summer of 1978, I think my father and mother both sensed something was wrong.

Family crowded into a living room filled with talk and laughter. The smell of teriyaki on the grill and the sweet fragrance of gardenias drifted in through the open jalousie windows. A mini-mob of "keikis" (*kay-kees*, Hawaiian for "children") ran in and out of the house playing. Stereo music sounded in the background and my sister Winona's son, Georgie-boy, who'd been more like a younger brother than a nephew to me, was dancing and clowning around. All in all, it was a typically chaotic family gathering.

As Mom sat beside me on the couch, quietly taking in all the commotion around her, she reached over, lovingly ran her hand down my swollen right arm and began to gently rub and massage my puffy fingers and knuckles. "What's wrong with your hand, Charlie-boy?"

I heard a mother's concern in her voice. So I tried to lighten the moment by saying, "You mean my mumu (goofy) arm?"

Her eyes didn't smile. She knew something was wrong. I looked at Lucy sitting on the other side of me; we knew the time had come to tell my parents.

I tried to be as matter-of-fact as I could. I looked reassuringly at my mother, and then at my father sitting next to her. "I have something called ALS—Lou Gehrig's disease."

There was a pause. My mother dabbed behind her glasses with a Kleenex for a moment before she asked, "What do the doctors say?"

I avoided giving the prognosis by replying, "They don't know what causes it. And they don't have a cure yet."

My mother began to cry. All she could say was, "Oh, son!" as she took my hand and squeezed it reassuringly.

"Oh, it's going to be okay," I told her.

Dad, who never seemed at a loss for words, proposed an immediate treatment. "We need to put a life preserver on you, Charlie-boy, take you out and throw you in the ocean. The good salt water will cure you."

He grinned when Mother swatted at his knee and scolded, "Oh, Dad! Stop that! Don't joke." But the tension had eased and Lucy and I felt greatly relieved to have the truth out in the open.

One result of telling our friends and family was that we were soon deluged with an incredible variety of suggested treatments people had heard about and thought we might want to try. Dr. Griffin had warned us about this; in fact the one thing that stuck in both our minds after we met with him together to talk about the prognosis was his caution, "Don't waste your money trying to beat this. There are no cures."

But his well-meaning advice didn't keep us from listening to, reading about, or checking out any ideas we heard that sounded reasonable. I certainly wasn't ready to give up without a fight.

chapter seven

IN SEARCH OF CURES

The Wedemeyers were soon besieged with unsolicited medical advice from well-meaning friends and family. One of the more unusual proposals came from Ted Simonson, the Los Gatos principal, who had read somewhere about a controversial ALS treatment program in Florida using the venom of the poisonous crate snake. Ted wanted Charlie's permission to approach the Los Gatos Lion's Club and ask them to help raise the $9000 needed to send Charlie to Florida and enroll him in this experimental program. Though Charlie refused to let him launch any public appeal for help, Lucy did make contact with this Florida group and asked for additional information about the treatment. But before any decision could be made on whether or not to pursue this costly option, the Federal Drug Administration shut down the program.

At the suggestion of various Hawaiian relatives Charlie tried traditional acupuncture treatment. But after several sessions in which he had 15 to 20 needles inserted at various points on his body, neither he nor the therapist saw any sense in continuing. Next Charlie tried acupressure which focuses on the same critical acupoints. And he even subjected himself to what proved an even more unpleasant ordeal—electro-acupuncture—in which acupuncture needles were electrically charged.

Though none of these acu-techniques seemed to help, the Wedemeyers refused to give up on nontraditional treatments.

CHARLIE

Once Lucy and I even attended something called a "Polarity" conference which friends thought might be helpful in dealing with the emotional issues raised by my ALS. During this weekend in the wine-country, the seminar leaders seemed to combine transactional analysis and the co-dependency movement—with a heavy focus of discussion on dysfunctional families and the psychological need to confront our parents with our true feelings.

Lucy and I quickly began to question the relevance of this conference for us because we felt no need to "confront" our parents about anything. In fact, the first evening, after the day's sessions ended, Lucy and I found two chairs out by the pool where we sat looking at the stars through the branches of the trees overhead and quietly reflected on the blessings we felt we'd received from our families. And the following day we skipped one of the planned health-food meals, managed a clandestine escape from the conference grounds, and discovered a nearby ice cream parlor where we enjoyed the truly therapeutic benefits of two towering chocolate-chip malts.

Still, we remained willing to consider any reasonable treatment. When my brother Earl told us about an old Hawaiian healer, Lucy and I figured, "Why not?"

We drove for miles out through the cane fields toward Waianae before we came to the old healer's dilapidated home. Broken-down, rusted out automobiles scattered around the traditional Hawaiian hut were the only 20th-century props in sight. A friendly poi dog offered a tail-wagging greeting as we got out of the car and he stood watching as we slowly climbed the rickety steps to the porch of the unpainted, weather-beaten shanty.

Inside the house, a weathered old white-haired and barefoot Hawaiian welcomed us with big friendly hugs. Earl had told "Uncle Jimmy" about my ALS diagnosis, so he first wanted to look at my hands, holding them and turning them in his own strong, calloused hands. When he finished his examination he announced, "There is nothing wrong with you. Everything will be okay."

Then he talked about the old Hawaiian ways of heal- ing—emphasizing the curative powers of the ocean and making me promise to go immerse myself in the surf after we left him.

He gave me a concoction of chamomile tea laced with aloe to drink. And finally he conducted a ceremony which seemed like a strange mix of religious ritual and ancient Hawaiian superstition. He shook bottles of Hawaiian salts and some kind of alcohol mixture over me; then, slowly running his hands over my body, he offered up a Hawaiian prayer chant that the demons would be released.

The entire time we spent with "Uncle Jimmy" he kept calling me, "My son, my son." And he talked a lot about God and how "God will take care of you, my son." So despite the fact his ceremony and his prayers provided no detectable physical relief, I came away from the experience feeling personally affirmed and emotionally reassured.

Sometime after that, Lucy's sister, Antionette, convinced me to join her in trying what was called "the lemonade cleansing diet." For twenty-one days we neither ate nor drank anything but a mixture of hot water and lemon juice fortified with maple syrup and a heavy dose of cayenne pepper. The experiment failed to cleanse the ALS out of my body. But it certainly cleared up my sinuses, rid me of fifteen pounds, and nearly cured my life-long love of lemonade.

One treatment that did provide more encouraging results was something called deep muscle massage that Lucy's brother Breck called from Hawaii to tell us about. Lucy did some additional research and found a chiropractor down in Pasadena who practiced this kind of therapy.

For months we made a weekly trek, loading the children in the car early on Saturday morning and driving the 400 miles to Pasadena where I'd receive a couple hours of rigorous massage from one or more therapists who would knead the muscles of my arms and legs all the way down to the bone. The therapy caused excruciating pain; but from the outset I noticed a marked improvement in my mobility. By this time ALS was beginning to affect my legs. I would shuffle into the therapist's office each week, my feet dragging, with Lucy holding my arm to steady me. After my treatments, my muscles stimulated by the grueling workout, I could lift my feet and walk slowly on my own back to the car for the long ride home.

But as the weeks and months went on, the positive results of this therapy lasted for shorter and shorter periods of time. Where I'd felt the effects for three or four days at the beginning, the rejuvenation lasted only two or three days, then one or two, until I could no longer discern any noticeable effects by the time we'd complete the six or seven hour drive home. This declining effectiveness, plus the time and cost, finally forced us to give up on the one treatment that had seemed to offer some initial relief and hope.

We didn't completely give up on the principle of deep muscle massage, however. Lucy would knead my muscles as long and as hard as she could before her own hands and arms and shoulders ached. Then I'd lie on my side in bed and Lucy would lie down behind me and use her feet to massage my shoulders and my back. Eventually this regular and painful ordeal no longer increased the usage of my limbs, even temporarily; yet we continued it because it seemed to help relax my muscles and reduce the frequency of the painful muscle spasms I began experiencing through-out my body. We also hoped that working the muscles in a rigorous massage might slow their atrophy and maintain better muscle tone.

The "treatment" that may well have provided the best long-term impact was the introduction of Chinese herbs into my diet. For centuries various Oriental cultures have studied the effects of thousands of plants—both their curative and preventative medicinal properties. I knew my sister Ruth cooked with herbs for her Chinese husband, Tom. And respect for that ancient wisdom was part of my own family heritage. So I was open to my sister Bridget's suggestion that one of her in-laws might have an herbal mixture that could help me.

When we first cooked up this concoction I wasn't sure but what this "cure" was worse than the disease. The stench filled the house and the green cottage-cheese like mixture looked and tasted like something you might feed a horse—a starving horse that had lost its sense of taste and smell. (Actually, alfalfa was one ingredient and a predominant flavor.)

I didn't think I could stomach it. "It looks awful! And it smells worse!" I told Lucy.

"Oh, come on," she smiled sweetly. "It can't be that bad, dear. Try it."

"Not unless you try it first."

"Okay!" She accepted the challenge. I watched as she inserted a spoonful into her mouth and fought back a grimace. She didn't actually gag until she tried to swallow.

I wanted to laugh, but she'd already refilled the spoon and was holding it much too close to my nose. "Your turn."

A deal was a deal. So I tried. When I gagged and spit the stuff out we both began to laugh.

After much experimentation, Lucy would doctor the potion with pineapple, fresh papaya, and guava juice, then blend it into a power drink that was surprisingly tasty. Though she never improved its horrid green appearance, we both drank the stuff daily for years with remarkable results. It cleared up long-time allergies, kept us both immune from colds, and even did away with Lucy's hypoglycemia. But it did nothing to arrest the slow, but steady progression of my ALS. Nothing did.

LUCY

Many times in those first months, Charlie and I recalled the doctor's warning not to "waste" our money pursuing a cure, because there was no cure. But after reading everything about ALS I could get my hands on, and realizing traditional medicine wasn't even close to finding answers, I was more than willing to try anything.

Charlie usually felt more concerned about the costs than I did. My own attitude was, *No matter what it takes. If there's any reasonable hope at all, we'll try it. Even if we have to spend our last red cent.*

Charlie's brother Herman wanted to organize a big fund raising luau for us in Honolulu. Herman was well-known throughout Hawaii as an athlete, a successful businessman, an influential politician, and also for his regular role as "Duke" on the long-running television series, "Hawaii Five-O." He could have staged quite an event. But Charlie wouldn't hear of it and asked his brother to give up the idea.

Still, we experienced a severe financial strain because insurance wouldn't cover any of the alternative treatments we were willing to try. And we knew that there would be many more medical expenses to come if the ALS took its normal course. So at Charlie's insistence I took two important steps to provide for our family's financial future by studying for and passing the state exam to become a licensed real estate agent. In what eventually proved to be another wise move, I also began training to qualify as a financial planner.

Yet another crucial event in 1978, a family tragedy, helped prepare me for the future in a way I could never have imagined at the time. While on business in the Bay Area, my father suddenly had to be hospitalized. His doctors believed he had contracted some rare, Asian disease in Hong Kong where he and Mother had been living for several years.

When I got the phone call saying Dad was in intensive care and the doctors thought he was going to die, I couldn't believe it. He'd been such an active, robust man, an athlete, an avid tennis player and a devoted weekend sailor. *He can't be dying!*

I remember rushing down the hallway of that ICU to see

my father. To be with him. But when I reached the doorway
of his room I froze.

There he was. Lying helplessly on a hospital bed, tubes
running out of his body to machines beside his bed—
machines that were keeping him alive. My father *was* dying.

I stood in that doorway, watching my mother hovering
over my father's unconscious form. I wanted to reach out
and touch him, to grab hold of him and desperately hang
on. It was as if an impenetrable glass barrier stood between
us. I couldn't even bring myself to walk into that room.

Instead I turned and retreated back down the hall to a
bathroom where I locked myself in a stall and wept. I cried
because my father was dying. I also cried that I didn't have
the strength to walk into that room. Finally I cried out to
heaven, saying, "Oh God, I'm so scared! Help me, God.
Help me touch him, please. Help me comfort my father."

Then after drying my tears and washing my face, I
marched down to Dad's room again, took a deep breath
outside the door, and walked right in beside his bed. Before
I could lose my nerve, I literally grabbed his limp arm and I
told him I loved him. A feeling of deep peace filled my heart
and I knew that Dad realized I was there with him.

My father did die two days later. His body was cremated
and the family paid for airline tickets so Charlie and I could
return to Hawaii with my mom, my brothers and my sister
to scatter his ashes in the Pacific just outside the beautiful
harbor of Malaea on Maui, his favorite island.

As difficult as my father's death was for me personally, I
felt it had strengthened me emotionally for what lay ahead
with Charlie. It had forced me to face the specter of death—
the death of someone I loved. I had learned I could deal
with it and survive emotionally. And when for the first time
in my life I'd reached the very end of my personal resources,
I instinctively realized I needed to call out to God for
strength.

Not that I was ready yet to accept the imminent prospect
of Charlie's death. My focus was on keeping him alive and

enabling him to remain independent for as long as possible. But the challenge was growing greater.

Driving had become a struggle for Charlie—his biggest problem was managing a stick shift with his right hand. He eventually taught Carri and Kale to shift for him, but one of us couldn't always go along, so we went out to find an automatic. I thought again about Dr. Griffin's warning the day we picked out a brand new Honda automatic. And I wondered if we'd made a costly, foolish mistake the next morning when Charlie went out to get in the car and drive to school. Since the salesman had started the car for us the day before, we hadn't realized Charlie didn't have enough dexterity in his right hand to reach around the wheel at an awkward angle to insert the key in the ignition and turn it to start the car. Fortunately a friend suggested a solution; we installed a relatively inexpensive switch that Charlie could simply flip to trip the starter.

That was just one of many devices we discovered in our quest to allow Charlie to continue to function normally on a daily basis and maintain some degree of freedom and independence. There were ankle braces to make it easier to walk, wrist braces to allow better control of his hands, a special gizmo for holding chalk when he needed to write on the blackboard in his classes, and even a page turning device for reading books.

Whenever Charlie had trouble doing something, we looked for a way to compensate, to make adjustments and go on living. When Charlie could no longer use his right hand, he compensated with his left. When he lost movement in his right leg, he depended more on his left. Yet we were fighting a losing battle. And that reality soon became painfully obvious as Charlie struggled with the simplest routines of daily life.

Sitting in bed in the morning and looking at the reflection in the mirror on our dresser, I could watch Charlie in the master bathroom getting ready for school. I'd see him steady his shaky right hand with his left to shave, tediously trying again and again to get the last whiskers. Watching him try to comb his hair was particularly painful. He'd have to grip the comb tightly with his right hand and then struggle to hold his right wrist in his left hand and painstakingly try again, and again and again to make a straight part.

Part of me longed to help. But I knew he didn't want that. He was absolutely adamant that it was going to be done perfectly and that he was going to do it himself.

Watching his growing frustration over the simplest tasks, I often wanted to break down and weep. But I told myself I couldn't let Charlie see me cry. I needed to be strong for him. And his dogged determination to continue living gave me strength.

chapter eight

BUMPS, BRUISES, AND EMBARRASSMENTS

No matter how determined Charlie was to beat his ALS, no matter how much Lucy wanted to help, some major concessions had to be made to enable Charlie to continue working. In his math classes he had to rely on students to write problems and instructions on the board. One of his assistant coaches, Butch Cattolico, took over most of the administrative paperwork for the football program. On the football field, his diminishing dexterity and mobility meant Charlie had to carefully explain what he wanted players to do rather than simply demonstrate a technique.

CHARLIE

I remember one of my quarterbacks, Bobby Griffin, leaned a little kapakahi ("cockeyed") whenever he took the snap from center. Because his weight wasn't distributed properly, he couldn't drop back to pass as quickly as he should have. But instead of simply showing him what he did versus what I wanted him to do, I had to try to explain exactly how he needed to position his body and move his feet.

Fortunately Bobby and I had a good relationship. Because the verbal coaching process we had to use seemed tedious. I found it much more time-consuming and frustrating to tell rather than show precisely what I wanted—whether it was getting the center to realign his hands to snap the ball long for punts and field goals or teaching the exact footwork needed by a quarterback to pull off a successful play-option pass.

But I was willing to put up with any amount of frustration necessary to keep teaching and coaching. Because as long as I could work with kids in the classroom and on the football field, life still seemed worth living.

During football season I could forget for a while any worry about doctors or disease. The long hours spent analyzing game film, working out offensive strategies, supervising practices, and playing the games seemed like borrowed time I never had to pay back.

Winning was a bonus; but win we did. The Los Gatos Wildcats went 8–3 in the fall of 1978—capturing the league championship for the second year in a row. Though we lost in the first round of the Central Coast Section championship, it was the first time in history that Los Gatos had even played in the CCS play-offs. The next year we posted a very respectable 7–3 mark. And Los Gatos, which had long been recognized as a baseball powerhouse, continued to build a reputation for its football program as well.

But winning on the football field did nothing to reduce the increasing frustration or embarrassment I experienced each time I discovered something new I could no longer do.

I remember the humiliation that descended on me one day standing in a grocery store check-out line when I realized I couldn't get the change I needed out of my own pockets. The check-out clerk waited with her arms folded as I fumbled through the coins I finally grasped in my hand. All the while I could feel the stares of the impatient people in line behind me.

I didn't have to imagine the stares in restaurants when Lucy began having to cut up my food for me. Eventually I refused to eat in public, unless we went to one nearby family restaurant that had high, wing-back chairs which shielded me from the view of curious diners.

Perhaps the only thing worse than the helplessness I felt when I needed a hand was the humiliation of having to ask for that help. As difficult as it was to have to ask Lucy's assistance buttoning a shirt, or have to take Kale with me to handle the money when I went to the store, it was infinitely harder acknowledging my needs to those outside the family.

One afternoon I shuffled slowly through the school doors and out to the faculty's reserved parking area. With concentrated effort I got my car keys out of my pocket, but I couldn't get the driver's door unlocked. I tried to use my left hand to lift and steady my right. But my hands shook so much I couldn't get the key inserted before I had to drop my arms and rest enough to try again.

A hundred times it seemed my brain sent out the orders, instructing my hands to come up and insert the key in the lock. But my arms couldn't carry out the orders. Minute after minute I stood there, picturing what I wanted to do, thinking of the thousands of times in my life I'd achieved the simple task of unlocking a car door. Still I couldn't do it. Each time I failed my arms grew heavier and heavier.

After fifteen minutes, another faculty member who must have been watching came walking up and asked, "Do you need some help, Charlie?"

"No, thanks," I lied. "I'm just waiting here for someone." I didn't think he really believed me, but I was relieved when he got into his own car and drove away. Several more minutes passed before I finally, with two hands, managed to stab the key in the lock and unlock the door. By then I was so exhausted I sat behind the wheel for several more minutes before I regained enough strength to drive home.

Humiliation comes in all shades of red. But I never saw darker scarlet than during an annual coaches' clinic up in San Francisco. A couple of my assistant coaches and I were walking down a long flight of steps to the hotel lobby. Since I had to sort of shuffle my feet when I walked, stairs were tough. And because of construction going on at this hotel, there were no handrails. So I began to descend the steps slowly and carefully. But when my heel caught on the edge of the second or third riser, I lost my balance. Instinctively I tried to reach out and grab something, anything, to catch myself. My arms didn't move. And I tumbled headlong down twenty cement steps to the landing.

Feeling more immediate pain from my shattered ego than my bruised body and head, I struggled to get up. But my assistants, afraid I might have seriously injured my back or neck, restrained me. "Don't try to move," they told me.

"Somebody call an ambulance!"

Two paramedics arrived within minutes. They first asked me, "What happened?"

I told them I'd stumbled and fallen down the steps. But by that time the ALS had begun to weaken the muscles in my throat and tongue, so I tended to slur my words together. One paramedic gave a knowing look to the other, before he asked, "How many have you had?"

They think I'm drunk! My embarrassment instantly multiplied. When I quickly explained I had ALS which sometimes made it difficult to handle stairs, their attitudes changed immediately. But as they gently probed and prodded my arms and legs in search of fractures, my eyes flicked over the faces in the gathered crowd. I couldn't help wondering how many others in that hotel lobby assumed I was simply drunk.

Despite the fact the paramedics didn't find any serious injuries, I spent another four hours sitting with my assistant coaches in a hospital emergency room. Finally I told a nurse, "I'm walking out of here and going home."

She gave me her sternest look. "If you do, we can't be responsible for you."

"I don't care!" I told her. "I'm leaving!"

"Not before you sign this," she said, handing me a release form.

I couldn't sign anything. So it took another few minutes to convince the hospital bureaucracy to let me go. By the time I got home I felt so sore, frustrated, and embarrassed I couldn't imagine that the effects of my ALS could get any worse.

LUCY

But we soon got a depressing picture of how much worse it could get when Charlie and I drove to San Francisco to attend an organizational gathering of ALS victims and their families from all over northern California. This group met in a dreary building, in a large, dimly lit room with low ceilings. Even more discouraging than the cold, confining setting were the people we saw there. Some patients lay wasting away on gurneys, others slumped over helplessly in their wheelchairs. A number of victims in rumpled clothing appeared not only sick but unkempt and uncared for.

But what hit me hardest that night was the despair and the discouragement expressed by some of the victims' family members. I vividly remember one young woman who stood up and emotionally recounted her difficult decision to place her husband in a nursing home against his wishes because she felt she could no longer care for him and mother their two small children. I could hear the anguish in her voice as she talked. I also felt the anger and the condemnation from a number of the people in the group, some of whom glared judgmentally at this woman as she spoke.

There seemed little if any "support" going on in that group meeting. The leaders themselves seemed hopelessly ineffectual, with nothing more helpful to say than a few hollow assurances that "It'll be all right" and "You'll make it through this."

Though we met several helpful families afterward, on the drive home Charlie told me, "I'm never going back to another of those meetings."

Seeing families with children at that meeting did start me thinking how we hadn't been very direct with Carri and Kale about Charlie's condition. I guess we told ourselves we didn't want to worry them. Maybe we feared they couldn't handle the truth.

They soon proved us wrong.

Only a day or two after we attended the ALS support group meeting in San Francisco I made one of my 2:00 A.M. phone calls to my sister in Hawaii for emotional support. Knowing it was three hours earlier in the islands, I liked calling when our house was quiet and Charlie would be asleep. No one would know if I let down and cried.

I was crying that night, describing for Antoinette the horrible experience we'd had at the meeting, when Carri came wandering into the family room and saw me. I motioned her back down the hall to bed. But she didn't go back to sleep; she came back out again when I hung up the phone a few minutes later.

"Were you talking to Auntie A?"

I nodded, wiping the tears from my eyes and trying to regain my composure.

"About Dad?"

When I nodded again, she asked, "Dad's getting worse, isn't he?" But without waiting for me to respond she continued, "You know, Mom, you never talk to me about Dad. You need to talk with me."

I knew the moment she said it that her ten-year-old advice was right. We talked for quite a while that night; we even hugged and cried some. But I was still at a loss for words that would comfort or reassure Carri. That sense of inadequacy haunted me and continued to keep me from consistently dealing openly and honestly with our children regarding Charlie's illness, and their own feelings about ALS.

One reason we didn't talk more openly was because we didn't have to. The people who knew respected our privacy and left most of the initiative for talk up to us—even those who tried to be sensitive and help us meet our needs.

We did get lots of support from the high school. When Charlie began having trouble negotiating stairs, the principal rearranged classroom assignments so all Charlie's classes were on the ground floor. When walking became more difficult, Charlie was assigned a classroom close to the gym. Once Charlie could no longer use his arms to write on the board, carry books or turn pages, a number of math students and football players volunteered to be his aides, to serve as Charlie's legs and arms and hands each period. And the principal did all this, because he saw Charlie's continuing desire and ability to teach. The disease had done nothing to affect his mind, nor had it lessened students' respect for him. He was just as strict and demanding as he'd ever been in the classroom; and the kids knew it.

On the football field his assistant coaches were just as supportive. In the locker room if he needed help buttoning his shirt, one of them would step over and do it for him. When Charlie no longer wanted to go out in public to a pizza parlor for the weekly post-game skull session to analyze the game and begin hashing out a game plan for the following week, the coaches and our families began getting together late every Friday night at the home of one of the assistant coaches. All the guys continued to treat Charlie the same way they always had; he remained very much the boss. And the loyalty and support of that group of good friends played an important part in keeping Charlie's spirits up in the face of his decreasing independence.

I continued to struggle with knowing when to help and when to let Charlie do things on his own. As a rule, I tried to take my cues from him. When in doubt I usually waited until he asked for help. But those occasions were coming more and more frequently.

chapter nine
INDEPENDENCE LOST

LUCY

The first time I shaved Charlie proved a trial for both of us. I was surprised how difficult it was. He always liked close shaves, so he insisted I go over his face again and again until he was absolutely sure there wasn't a single whisker left. But the process took so long that by the time I rinsed away the last traces of shaving cream, we were both feeling irritable.

And that was even before I had to trim his sideburns.

First I squared up the right side, then the left. But when I stopped and held up a mirror for Charlie to see, he groused, "They're not even!"

I trimmed a bit more off the left. Too much. So I evened it out on the right. Then a tad more on the left. With each adjustment I could see the muscles in Charlie's jaws tighten. I finally finished and carefully watched his face for a reaction as I held up the mirror again.

Charlie stared at the reflection in silence with his teeth clenched, clearly fighting to maintain his composure. I knew he was about to explode. It wasn't until he suddenly burst out laughing that I realized he'd been trying to stay mad.

He rolled his eyes and exclaimed, "I don't have any sideburns left at all!"

"Hey," I replied. "At least you can't say they're not even."

Driving may have been harder for Charlie to give up than shaving was. While I stuck to my personal policy of letting him make the decision regarding independence issues, I worried about this one because he continued to drive long after he had lost virtually all dexterity in his hands and developed difficulty walking.

He couldn't actually grip the steering wheel with his hands, so to steer he'd throw his left arm up and let his wrist drape over the top of the steering wheel. With his right hand he had just enough control to shove the automatic gear shift on the floor forward and backward; whenever the children were with him, he'd let one of them shift. Since he couldn't quickly move his right foot from the accelerator to the brake, he kept his other foot propped lightly against the brake so he could stop with a simple straightening of his left leg.

Though I knew he drove slowly and carefully on the least busy route between our house and the school, I still worried until the day he got home from school and announced, "I better not drive anymore; I don't think it's safe." He'd had a scare driving the winding route home over the mountains on Shannon Road. After making a curve to the right, he hadn't been able to swing the wheel back to the left quickly enough to negotiate the next curve. He nearly went over an embankment before he hit the brakes and skidded to a halt at the edge of the roadside ravine.

He had been frightened. Not so much for himself as at the thought that he might have lost control, hit another car and injured someone else. He said he wouldn't risk other people's lives. With that decision he surrendered a huge chunk of independence.

Driving and shaving were just two pieces in what was

becoming a clear and continuing pattern. The less Charlie could do for himself, the more time and effort was required of me to do things for him. And neither the love I felt for my husband, nor the determination I had to help keep him going, could manufacture more hours in a day or give my weary muscles extra energy.

Since Charlie now required so many of my daytime hours, I usually went in to do my office work late in the evenings when Carri and Kale could stay home with their dad. One night at the office I wearily trudged to the office Xerox machine to copy a number of important legal documents from several of my current real estate files; then I was going home to bed. But when I returned and went to set the tall stack of folders on a clear corner of my desk, the top files began to slide. Instinctively I grabbed at them, only to miss and send the entire pile sailing off the desk and across the floor.

I took a long look at the mess and closed my eyes. I didn't know whether to scream in frustration or simply sag to the floor amidst the jumble of papers and cry myself to sleep.

At that moment, my friend Barbara, who was also working late and had been behind me at the copy machine walked into the office to check out the commotion. She saw all those real estate documents strewn on the floor. She also must have seen the exhaustion and defeat on my face. Because she instinctively made the most insane, inspired show of empathy and support: She flung her own stack of files high in the air and then laughed along with me as we watched her blizzard of paper flutter to the floor on top of mine. Friends.

The constant emotional and physical drain only magnified the financial stress. The medical expenses our insurance didn't cover were eating up everything I earned—and more. Even with both of us working, we fell farther and farther behind on bills each month.

Christmas was coming and we had no money for gifts. How do you tell two young children there won't be any presents under the tree this year? I couldn't. Instead, using charge cards, I bought just as many presents as usual—but all the wrong sizes. What guilt I felt returning them all for refunds after the holidays was offset by the knowledge that *At least we all had something to open Christmas morning.*

CHARLIE

As creative as Lucy was at maintaining family morale, as hard as she worked to help me feel as independent as possible, she could do nothing to slow my growing sense of personal powerlessness. Nor could she reduce the intensity of the emotions that came with it—frustration, embarrassment, even fear.

All my life I'd been able to count on my body, relying on reflexes and coordination to achieve my goals—on and off the playing field. Now that body was betraying me as my physical condition steadily deteriorated.

The prospect of falling terrified me. Once I lost my precarious balance I didn't have the reflexes to raise my arms to catch or even protect myself. If I ever tripped, I went down like a tree cut in the forest—160 pounds of dead weight crashing to earth.

The fall down the hotel steps in San Francisco was merely the first of many. Occasionally I'd lose my balance and fall at home. Several times it happened at school.

The worst incident may have happened in the gym. Leaving my office for a meeting one day along with a football player who served as my aide, I lurched headfirst down three steps leading from the raised office into a small trainer's room. My forehead and shoulder crashed into the edge of an open glass door, the momentum of my body weight swung me around and I sprawled to the floor backwards. The last thing I remember was the sickening thud when the back of my head slammed onto the concrete floor.

I was probably only unconscious for a few seconds. When I came to and my eyes slowly focused again, I could clearly see the face of a very worried football player bending over me. I tried to smile and reassure him: "I'm okay, John. Just help me up." But he insisted I lie still and ran for help.

Grateful I hadn't been more seriously hurt, I spent the next couple of days trying to shake a horrendous headache. What I couldn't shake was the awful realization that another fall could happen anytime.

I hated having to plan my route around the high school campus to avoid steps and uneven spots on the sidewalk. I lived with the constant fear of being accidently bumped off balance in a crowded school hallway between classes. What I feared more than the prospect of more headaches and bruises was the embarrassment of having my helplessness and vulnerability so publicly displayed.

I often resented all the adjustments I was being forced to make in my life. Because I knew they ultimately affected the lives of the people around me—especially Lucy. Not only did she now have to drive me to and from school, she had to arrange her day so she could get out of her realty office at noon to meet me at school, help me go to the bathroom, and drive me to nearby Vasona Park where we would sit in private by the lake while Lucy fed me my lunch.

As frustrated as I was to be so dependent, I have many fond memories of those peaceful lunches we shared under the trees on a rolling lawn leading down to a quiet little lake. I truly enjoyed the daily opportunity to be alone with Lucy and talk. Sometimes when we finished eating we'd feed our scraps to the ducks and remember how many times we'd come there with our children when they were younger.

Accepting my growing helplessness was hard enough in private. In public it seemed far worse.

I remember one night after a ball game we'd finished our post-game coaches' meeting and headed home when Lucy realized the car was running on fumes. She turned into the first self-serve gas station we came to and quickly jumped out to fill our tank. Looking over at the pay booth, I noticed the attendant staring at Lucy. I watched him watching her until he glanced toward me. I turned and pretended to be looking straight ahead. But I could feel his eyes on me. The longer Lucy stood out there pumping our gas, the more uneasy I felt. When she'd paid the cashier and climbed back in the car I said, "Hurry up. Let's go."

She shifted into gear and began pulling away from the pumps even as she asked, "What's wrong?"

"That attendant in the booth," I told her. "He kept staring at me. I know he was wondering why I didn't get out and pump the gas for you."

"For heaven's sake!" Lucy exclaimed as she slammed on the brakes. She looked at me in disbelief and shook her head. Suddenly her expression changed and she shifted into reverse.

"What are you doing?" I asked.

"I'm going back to talk to that guy," she threatened. "I'm gonna tell him you're my prisoner and I have you handcuffed to the steering wheel. And that's why you couldn't get out and pump the gas for me like a gentleman."

Lucy laughed. But I didn't think it was funny at first. "Come on, Charlie," she chided me. "I'm sure that guy is so shocked, he'll go home in the morning and tell everyone he sees, 'You wouldn't believe what happened last night. This car pulled into the station and this gal jumped out the driver's seat and pumped her own gas while the lazy bum who was with her just sat in the front seat and let her do it.' "

"Okay, okay," I laughed. "Let's just go home."

LUCY

I always could read Charlie's emotions pretty well. I tried not to take his anger and frustration personally because I knew it wasn't really aimed at me. And when I didn't know how to deal with the resulting tensions, I often resorted to humor. It usually worked.

One morning we were already running late for school when the little Honda wouldn't start. Charlie, who had followed me out of the house, came to the driver's door window to tell me he thought it sounded like a dead battery.

"I'll get the cables and jump it from the other car," I said, opening my door. But I failed to shift back into gear before I climbed out, so the Honda began coasting down the driveway. Charlie yelled and instinctively stepped toward the car but could do nothing to stop it before the open driver's door bumped into him, sending him sprawling on the driveway, partially under the rolling car.

The second Charlie had yelled I had spun around, seen the car rolling and sprinted back down the drive. I literally jumped over his body and into the driver's seat to slam on the brake and put the car safely in gear. Then I climbed out again, shaking, to find the front left wheel of the car had stopped within an inch of Charlie's head.

The children helped me hurriedly lift Charlie to his feet. As we brushed off his clothes he snapped angrily at me, "What were you trying to do? Run over me?"

I stood silent for a moment, my heart pounding, still too frightened to speak. "If I'd planned to run over you," I told him when I found my tongue, "I'd have used the bigger car!"

Charlie got this startled look on his face.

"Or a truck. Sure. . .

"Maybe even a Mack truck. An eighteen-wheeler might have done the job."

By this time Charlie was grinning. And the tension and fear we'd both felt almost instantly drained away.

There were days when we couldn't find any humor, and we couldn't laugh. When I felt I didn't have enough left in my reservoir of determination to keep Charlie going. At times like that I was tempted by the generous offer Charlie's oldest sister, Ruth, had made back during the first year after Charlie's diagnosis.

Ruth and her husband Tom had flown over from the islands for a visit. She was outside that afternoon with me, helping do some of the yard work Charlie couldn't do anymore. "You know, Lucy," she told me with tears in her eyes, "You ought to bring Charlie home. You could live with us and let the family help you take care of him."

On my darkest days, when I felt I'd reached the end of my rope physically and emotionally I thought about Ruth's offer. But I continued to believe that Los Gatos was our home and we needed to stay here for now.

In some ways it would have been easier to pack up and move back to Hawaii. It would have been wonderful not to have to worry about paying the bills and keeping a household running. And a lot of days I'd have given almost anything to be surrounded by family, to have Charlie's sisters, who would always do anything for their youngest brother, share some of the burden of his care.

But as appealing as all that was, I feared moving back to Hawaii might possibly be the final straw in Charlie's battle to maintain his independence. As long as we could live in Los Gatos, as long as he could teach and coach he could feel needed and have something to focus on besides his illness. I knew Charlie, and I firmly believed any hope for his survival depended on his feeling useful and productive.

And if the 1978 and 1979 football seasons had been confirmation of Charlie's continued usefulness as a coach, the 1980 season was even more so. The Los Gatos Wildcats compiled another 7–3 season, tied for the conference championship, and Charlie was named West Valley Athletic League "Coach of the Year."

CHARLIE

But the most memorable experience of that 1980 season for me came not on the football field, but in the locker room after our final game. We'd eked out a tough 14–10 win over Leigh High School to clinch a tie for the league championship. I was so proud of the team for the way they had pulled together. And I was so grateful for their easy acceptance of me as they'd watched me deteriorate physically until I could no longer lift my arms to diagram plays on the board or even pat them on the back when they ran to the sidelines after making a big play.

So I congratulated the team for the accomplishment of winning the championship. I thanked them for their long hours of hard work. I expressed special appreciation to all the seniors who'd played their last game for Los Gatos. And I tried to tell them how proud and grateful I was for them. But mere words seemed so inadequate that I closed, saying, "I just wish I could hug every one of you guys. But I can't."

With that, I turned and shuffled out of the locker room before I began to cry. I had barely stepped out into the hallway before I heard the clatter of cleats clicking on the concrete floor. When I turned back toward the commotion, here came the entire team, lined up in single file, walking toward me.

Too overcome with emotion to say a word, I could only stand there, my own arms dangling limp from my shoulder sockets, as my players, one by one, put their arms around me and silently hugged me. Some of them had tears running down their faces. But that was okay, so did I.

chapter ten

GOING PUBLIC

Long before the end of the 1980 football season, anyone who saw Charlie knew immediately that something was wrong. And it was no secret in the community that he had a terminal illness. But the Wedemeyers still weren't talking about it publicly.

LUCY

One evening early in January of 1981 we received a phone call from a reporter with the *Honolulu Star Bulletin*. He told me he was calling to confirm a report he'd heard that Charlie had cancer or some other life-threatening disease. I swallowed and tried to compose my thoughts. *What do I say? What does Charlie want me to say? How much do we need to acknowledge publicly?*

I had to buy time to think, so I told the reporter I couldn't talk right then and asked if I could call back a little later in the evening. After he gave me his number I hung up and went to tell Charlie about the call.

Charlie's initial response was the same as mine: "Oh, no! We can't talk to him." I knew Charlie didn't want any attention. And he certainly didn't want anyone's pity. We both very much wanted to be left alone. But Charlie was well-known in Hawaii; if one reporter knew something, others would hear. Rather than wait for rumors to spread, maybe we needed to publicly acknowledge the ALS. We felt pressured by the reporter's call to make a decision we didn't want to make.

We postponed the inevitable by not returning the call that night. But the following day we reached the reporter and I talked to him while Charlie listened in. I explained that the diagnosis was ALS, answered a few questions about the symptoms, and told how Charlie continued to be able to coach despite having been told almost four years earlier that he had only one to three years to live. The formal interview was short, our answers brief—about enough we figured for a sentence or two at the end of a newspaper sports column.

Then the reporter told us he'd gone to school at the University of Hawaii with Charlie's nephew and we talked a while about mutual acquaintances in the islands. By the time we hung up we'd had a long friendly chat and had said much more than we'd intended.

The following Sunday afternoon my brother Tim called from Hawaii to tell us the *Star Bulletin*, Hawaii's largest newspaper, had run a front page story in its Sunday edition about Charlie and his courageous battle with ALS.

Our immediate reaction was one of horror. That kind of attention was Charlie's worst nightmare. But the reality turned out to be very different from what we'd imagined.

We immediately received an onslaught of letters and phone calls from friends and relatives throughout Hawaii— heartening expressions of encouragement, concern, and support. Even people we didn't know personally wrote or called because they remembered Charlie's playing days and they wanted us to know we had their prayers or their best wishes.

And the reaction of Charlie's immediate family to the article amused us. In talking to me about it, they seemed excited and proud about what the story said about Charlie. But they hesitated to mention it to Charlie. His mother and some of his sisters seemed alarmed that he'd even seen the article because it talked very plainly about the prognosis for ALS patients. "It's okay," I chided them. "Charlie knows."

The encouraging feedback we received from the newspaper article couldn't have come at a better time. It helped counter the emotional low which also hit us that spring when Charlie received word his teaching contract would not be renewed for the coming year.

We had both known the day was coming. In the preceding years Charlie had been relying more and more on his student aides. As his voice grew weaker and his words slurred together, the aides were not only carrying books and writing assignments and problems on the board, they were also interpreting Charlie's words and relaying instructions and explanations to the class. When even the aides began having trouble understanding him and everyone including Charlie realized he couldn't continue to effectively teach in the classroom, the principal created a new position, assigning Charlie to supervise the school's gym and locker rooms for the remainder of the school year. But there would be no such position the following year. Charlie would have to go on disability.

Knowing this time was coming didn't make it any easier to accept. Accepting it meant yet another huge concession to Charlie's ALS. No matter how valiantly he had fought for so long, no matter how many battles he'd won in beating the prognosis we'd gotten more than four years earlier, no matter how long or how well he'd continued to coach, this was an undeniable indication that we were still losing the war.

Yet the principal stayed true to his word. Ted told Charlie he could continue to coach the Los Gatos High School football team, even if he wasn't teaching. That assurance enabled Charlie to rise above the discouragement and keep going. And he immediately began watching game films and planning changes he wanted to make in next year's offense.

Bobby Griffin and some of Charlie's other football players regularly stopped by the house to talk to their coach. The stories they'd tell about things going on at school played an important role in helping Charlie feel he wasn't completely out of touch with campus life.

Lucy made her own attempt to ease Charlie's transition to being home every day. She took a leave from her job as a real estate agent to spend full time at home with Charlie. Concerned by his continuing deterioration and not knowing how much longer he had to live, she wanted to spend as much time with him as she could. But because Charlie's reduced disability pay didn't kick in for six months after his teaching contract expired, the Wedemeyers soon depleted their savings and Lucy had no choice but to go back to work.

In the meantime, they faced yet another decision about just how public they wanted to be about their continuing ordeal. An independent television producer from San Francisco called to say she'd been visiting Hawaii back in January when the story came out in the Honolulu newspaper. She and her partner were interested in videotaping an interview with the Wedemeyers for a documentary they were working on called, "Extraordinary People." She said Charlie's courageous example could inspire and help a lot of people.

CHARLIE

When Lucy told me about the call, my instant reaction was, "Absolutely not!"

Only after Deborah Gee called back several times did I even agree to meet with her. And then only because I wanted to convince her once and for all that I wouldn't be in her documentary.

I'm not sure what I expected—maybe a flashy, fast-talking, aggressive, Hollywood-type. Instead, Deborah turned out to be a young, casual, soft-spoken Chinese American woman who seemed not only down-to-earth, but sincere. We talked as much about her love for Hawaii as we did her plans for this documentary. We were able to explain that we were private people and simply wouldn't feel comfortable with television cameras following us around and exposing our lives to public scrutiny. Nor did we want to try and verbalize our emotions regarding our experience.

Deborah didn't try to argue with us. She seemed to understand our fears and accept our reluctance as natural and valid. She never tried to brush them aside. But she didn't let them stop her from gently pressing her case and repeatedly saying she thought our story could help a lot of people.

Lucy and I talked about it after Deborah left. We couldn't imagine how our story would "help others." We didn't see our experience having much relevance to a very broad audience. Maybe it could encourage someone else with ALS to keep going and not give up just because the doctors gave them a year or two to live.

It may have been the teacher or the coach in me, but Deborah's "help others" appeal continued to eat away at my resolve. I finally remember saying to Lucy, "If our experience would help just one person, maybe we ought to think about doing it."

After we told Deborah we were thinking about her project, she came back for a second visit and brought her partner, Ken Ellis. I don't remember actually saying "Yes," but before I knew it, everything was set. As much as I liked Deborah and Ken, however, I wasn't convinced we'd made the right decision.

When the door closed behind them on the way out, Lucy and I looked at each other. I saw my own doubts and uncertainty reflected on her face. I knew Lucy was thinking the same thing I was: *What have we gotten ourselves into!*

Little did we know . . .

It was a hot July day when Deborah and Ken showed up for the first day of shooting. They wanted footage of me coaching a typical practice, but preseason practice hadn't started yet. So a bunch of boys from the 1980 varsity team agreed to come out and run a few drills for the camera. In fact, almost the entire team showed up.

Deborah and Ken taped me walking on and off the field with Lucy's help and supervising a number of drills. My voice was weaker and more nasal than it had been the previous year, but most of the players still understood my slurred speech as I addressed the team. The team ran through a number of offensive plays I called. And finally Deborah interviewed a few of the boys.

One of the players acknowledged my limitations when he said, "Coach Wedemeyer can't yell at us anymore. But then he doesn't have to yell. He's got this way of looking at you. . . ."

I wasn't nearly as comfortable the following week when Deborah and Ken came back to interview Lucy and me and to videotape us, our children, our home, and our daily routines. My feelings about privacy nearly made me call the whole thing off. But I relented.

They shot footage of me sitting on the living room couch, watching and coaching Kale as he went through a brief karate workout. Then I worked out, exercising my legs by walking in place on a mini-trampoline while Lucy stood beside me to provide balance.

I felt very self-conscious being seen in my swimsuit because my muscles were so atrophied and my arms hung limply at my side, pulled down and out of their shoulder sockets. But I reluctantly allowed the cameras to roll as Lucy slipped my arms into a life jacket and helped me into the swimming pool where she moved my arms to demonstrate the range-of-motion exercise we used to keep my joints and muscles loose.

Lucy and I did draw some lines when it came to what we let them shoot. The cameras focused on Lucy in our kitchen as she started to open the refrigerator. She stopped, turned, and asked them to stop, laughing as she declared, "I don't want to see the inside of my refrigerator on anyone's TV!" When they asked to tape Lucy giving me a shave, I refused.

Seated in our living room, we talked on camera to Deborah, providing our personal background and history, then telling her about the initial symptoms, the diagnosis, and the progression of the disease. Her questions dealing with our feelings about death proved the hardest to answer.

"The dying will come," Lucy said, her voice cracking. "We know that. I think we both feel it's okay if our lives are over at any time, because we've had so much."

She went on to say we weren't about to give in to the ALS yet. "But I think it has made us realize how precious life is, how we can't take anything for granted. We've learned every second makes a difference and having a lot of love gets us through a lot . . ."

As she paused, I continued, "My wife is a very special person. And our two children help a lot. Without their encouragement and support . . ." Here I could feel the tears running down my cheeks as I thought about how much Lucy and the children meant to me, how much I loved them, how much we'd been through together. "Without their encouragement and support, it would be hard to cope . . ."

I was too choked up to go on. Lucy leaned her head against mine as we cried together. We were both embarrassed by such an emotional display and Lucy motioned for the camera to be turned off. But Deborah kept the tape rolling and talked us through the rough spot by going on to less emotional questions.

By the time the TV crew packed up and left at the end of the day, I was exhausted and didn't care to see another video camera the rest of my life. Deborah and Ken continued to assure us the show would have a powerful impact. But we never imagined how one short television program would soon change our lives.

chapter eleven

LIVING
WITH LIMITS

LUCY

We knew from the beginning that the documentary was also going to feature two other Bay Area men. When we learned they were going to be ex-Black Panther Huey Newton and the Italian owner of a famous San Francisco nightclub, Charlie laughed and said, "Black Panthers, Italians, and a terminally ill Hawaiian football coach—I guess it's a minority show."

We never saw any of the videotape Deborah and Ken's crew shot. So one early August evening in 1981 we sat with Kale and Carri, our television set tuned to San Francisco's KGO-TV, waiting with a mixture of excitement and dread, for the premier of "Extraordinary People."

There we were pictured in the introduction. The profile of Charlie would be last. But the entire second half of the show was devoted to his story.

There were old photos of the two of us in high school, and game film from Michigan State as the voice-over recounted Charlie's athletic accomplishments and talked about his ALS. There was Charlie, addressing the boys and overseeing the staged practice. There were brief scenes at home with the kids, shots of our exercise routines, and of me helping Charlie walk off the football field. Interspersed through it all were segments of our interview with Deborah; for those who might have had difficulty understanding him, subtitles were provided whenever Charlie spoke.

Toward the end came the segment where we'd talked about the prospect of death. As Charlie spoke emotionally about me and the children, the camera zoomed in for a close-up, the spotlights clearly highlighting the glistening trail of tears streaming down his cheeks. And there I was in the edge of the frame, leaning my face against his as we cried together.

When the show ended we just sat in numbed silence for a few moments, not really knowing what to think or feel, trying to imagine how others might react. We soon had our own reading on viewer reaction.

The phone hardly stopped ringing for days. Naturally a lot of friends and acquaintances called from all over the Bay Area, most of whom had known about Charlie's illness, but hadn't realized what all we were going through. They wanted to express their concern, their appreciation, and their respect for Charlie. But there were countless strangers who called and wrote us.

We were stunned by the sheer number of personal responses we received from people who wanted us to know what an impact the show had made on them. We took many calls from other ALS victims or their families who wished to thank Charlie for his inspiring, positive example. But what amazed us even more were the callers who told us they'd found help and encouragement in Charlie's example for a broad variety of personal problems—from battles with cancer, to unemployment, to divorce. One lady called to say the story had made her realize how no one knows how much time she has left; so she'd been calling the important people in her life and letting them know how much they meant to her before it was too late.

The show *had* helped people. In addition, the more

friends who told us they'd seen it, the more we realized "Extraordinary People" was doing in the Bay Area what the newspaper article had done for us in Hawaii. It let local friends and acquaintances, anyone who wondered what was going on with Charlie and his ALS, know the crucial details. We didn't have to hide anything anymore; but we didn't have to worry about awkward or emotional explanations either. People knew. And just knowing that they knew seemed a wonderful relief.

CHARLIE

Not all the attention generated by the documentary was entirely welcome however. Hollywood arrived on our doorstep in the person of one fast-talking movie producer who had seen "Extraordinary People" and wanted us to know that in his expert judgment our story had "movie-of-the-week" written all over it, baby.

He was too busy trying to wow us to hear what we told him several times: "We're not really interested in having a movie made about our story." Or maybe he just didn't believe we meant what we said, because as he left he insisted that he'd back soon with a formal contract.

A few days later he did come back, arriving in a long, black, chauffeur-driven limo and accompanied that warm summer evening by his fur-draped wife. He waltzed into our home carrying a briefcase from which he extracted a sheaf of papers he handed to Lucy. The two of us looked through the legal contract which would grant him the exclusive movie rights to the story of our lives and marriage. All we had to do was sign the contract, he would write us a check, and then he'd start working on the project almost immediately.

We told him again we weren't interested. But he kept talking. Not until Lucy finally handed back his papers and told him we didn't intend to sign the contract did he seem to believe we were serious. At that point, his facial complexion went suddenly from tanning salon cool to angry red. We didn't know what we were turning down. Our story was now public record. He could make a movie with or without our permission. We couldn't stop him. He wouldn't have to pay us anything for the rights. He didn't need us anyway. Goodbye. With that, he stormed out of our house, his wife in tow.

I had no idea whether or not he could make good on his threats to do the movie without our permission. At that moment I didn't care. I was just glad to be rid of the guy as I thought: *So much for Hollywood!*

Fortunately, the initial reaction to the documentary had time to die down in the weeks before the season started. And all the hoopla and attention surrounding "Extraordinary People" faded away until the next spring when the show received an Emmy nomination—and won. But in the meantime, during the fall of 1981, I focused on football again.

A successful 7–3 season helped offset the discouragement I felt about my continuing physical decline, which severely limited my mobility on the sidelines as the season progressed. One of my best friends, assistant coach Stan Perry, had to steady me as we walked on and off the field. He'd button my jacket, hold the clipboard with our game plan, relay my mumbled instructions to players and other coaches. He'd stand right next to my side all through the game to provide the support I needed to keep my balance. A few times during the excitement of a late-season game he'd forget and step away and I nearly fell.

Once I anticipated the other team calling a sweep to the wide side of the field which happened to be toward our bench. Even before the play began to develop I inched back. Sure enough, as the back sprinted our way I shuffled backwards a little faster, caught my foot, lost my balance and tumbled backward to the ground.

Some of my assistants and players on the bench turned to see what had happened. But I was far less hurt than I was embarrassed to be lying on the ground in full view of the stands. "Just get me up," I said to Stan as matter-of-factly as I could manage. "I'm all right."

LUCY

Charlie's decreasing mobility played a big factor the following spring when we considered another trip back to Hawaii for the wedding of Charlie's nephew, Blane Gaison, former University of Hawaii football star and defensive back with the Atlanta Falcons. Charlie and Blane had always had a special relationship; Blane stopped and stayed in the Bay Area with us for a few days any time he traveled between Atlanta and Hawaii. So I couldn't believe my ears the day Charlie told me he didn't think we'd go to Hawaii for the wedding.

When I wanted to know why, Charlie told me he didn't think he could do all the walking the trip would require. "We can manage," I told him. "There will be lots of family willing to help." When that didn't change his mind I told him, "Then we can use the wheelchair."

A friend had loaned us a wheelchair months before. Yet Charlie's stubbornness and pride relegated that chair to a corner of the garage. Charlie's mind was made up. "We're not going."

As I tried to talk to him over the next few days, I began to understand the significance of that wheelchair to Charlie. He didn't want to be seen, especially by his family, as dependent or helpless. He thought the chair would make him even more conspicuous; he didn't want the attention. Plus, he saw a wheelchair as the biggest, most critical concession he had yet made to ALS. He just couldn't bring himself to surrender.

I made lists of all the pros and cons I could think of to convince him to go. I even resorted to one very emotional argument. "Remember the time I wanted to stop and see my grandmother on one of our trips to Southern California for your deep muscle therapy? You didn't think we had time, so we drove on home. And she died before we saw her again.

"I hate to miss this opportunity to go to Hawaii and see the whole family again. There may never be another chance like this. Anything could happen. We don't know. We could die in an earthquake tonight."

Charlie would not be swayed. Until the middle of the night when the sudden shaking of our bed woke us up. I'd jumped to my feet before I realized what was happening. "It's an earthquake!"

"Okay, okay," Charlie said, struggling to sit up. "We'll go to the wedding." But in the end, it was Charlie's love for Blane and for his sister Winona, that persuaded him to go to Hawaii despite his continuing reservations.

Although the chair might have created an added awkwardness, when we arrived in Hawaii I pulled Charlie's nephew Georgie-boy aside. I asked him to make a special effort to treat Charlie like he always had, teasing him and joking with him. Boisterous laughter and teasing had always been a Wedemeyer family trademark and since Georgie-boy was the family comedian, I thought other relatives would take their cue from him in how to relate to Charlie. And indeed that's what happened. Soon no one seemed to notice the chair.

CHARLIE

I didn't want to use a wheelchair on the sidelines. But with the approach of the '82 pre-season, I doubted I had the stamina needed to stand on the sideline for an entire game. Fortunately I didn't have to do either.

A generous friend of the Los Gatos football program donated an electric golf cart for me to sit and ride in during practices and games. So in addition to serving as my right hand, Stan became my designated driver, moving me back and forth along the sidelines as play moved up and down the field. And that golf cart made it possible for me to coach yet another season.

The Los Gatos Wildcats ran up a 9–1 regular season record in 1982, going undefeated in our conference to capture our fifth league championship in six years. That showing earned us another berth in the CCS playoffs where our first-round loss seemed a disappointing end to an otherwise fantastic season.

Of course, I hated to see any season end, because once I could no longer teach, coaching became my only outlet. During the season I had things to do, practices and games to go to, game plans to make, players and assistant coaches to communicate with, daily schedules, goals to achieve. Once football season ended I had a gaping black hole in my life.

Lucy spent as much time with me as she could. But she had to work all day to earn a living for our family. Carri and Kale had school and lots of extra-curricular activities.

Unable to walk without assistance, I spent most of my lonely daytime hours propped in an easy chair in front of the TV—watching football tapes on my VCR which I controlled by a footswitch I operated with my big toe. I also watched a lot of cooking shows during those years. And whenever the recipe sounded good to me, I'd try to memorize it. Then I'd ask Lucy to pick up any unusual ingredients at the grocery store on her way home from work that afternoon so I could instruct her on how to make the dish for dinner that evening.

My fascination with new and unusual dishes nearly drove Lucy crazy. I was the kind of cook who likes to carefully follow a precise recipe, while she preferred to toss in extra things that sounded good and never hesitated to make up ingredients I'd forgotten.

But cooking shows and football tapes weren't enough most days to keep me from feeling trapped, and very much alone. I couldn't even get up to go to the bathroom by myself. So Lucy had to regularly call home, leaving her office and coming home whenever necessary to make sure my basic needs were met.

I remember one day before Lucy left for her office, she put a dinner casserole in the oven and set the timer, instructing me to have Carri check on it and take the dish out of the oven when it was done. When Carri came in I relayed Lucy's instructions, she checked, said it looked done, and pulled the casserole out. Then she left the house to go to a friend's.

No sooner had she gone out the door than the oven timer sounded; Carri had failed to turn it off when she pulled out the finished casserole. The buzzer droned on and on and on, becoming more annoying every minute. Irritation soon turned to worry as I considered the possibility of that timer shorting out and starting an electrical fire. *It might be hours before Lucy or one of the kids return. I've got to do something.*

With concerted effort, I struggled to my feet and shuffled slowly toward the kitchen. I knew I'd never get my arms up high enough to manage to turn the buzzer off by hand. *Maybe I can turn it with my teeth.* I'll never know because I only managed three or four steps before I stumbled and pitched facedown to the floor. There I lay, unable to get up, unable to shut out that awful buzzing sound, worried that our new puppy would somehow get in the house and lick me to death before Lucy came home again that evening.

I'd never felt more frustrated by my physical condition than I did lying on our floor that afternoon, unable to do something as simple as turning off an oven timer. When Lucy finally walked in the front door, she heard the timer and headed for the oven before she noticed me and instead ran to help me up. "What happened? Are you okay?"

"Forget about me," I ordered her. "Just shut off that buzzer."

After that incident Lucy made a point to call home and check on me even more often than she had before. Since no one else could understand me on the phone, I didn't want to answer unless I knew it was Lucy calling. So we worked out a system where she'd call and let it ring once, then she'd call right back and I'd know it was her.

We had a little flexible stand we could use to hold a special control right over the chair where I sat, just inches in front of my face and low enough so I could see the TV over it. When the phone rang all I had to do was lean forward and push a button with my chin to activate the speaker phone next to my chair.

I was always glad to hear Lucy's cheerful, loving voice, telling me what was happening at her office, asking how I was doing, or if I needed anything. I looked forward to her calls. But every one was another little reminder of the burden I was to her.

Countless loving friends generously helped us cope with the increasingly difficult details of life. Players volunteered to do yard work for us. Lucy's brothers and uncle helped finish up some home improvement projects. Neighbors and friends helped Lucy do things she couldn't do alone. And when she could no longer get me to football practice by herself, Bill Bowman, a teacher friend whose boys played on the Los Gatos team, would leave school during his planning period, come to our house, lift me out of bed, and then help Lucy get me out in the car.

Yet despite the generous help of so many people, I was painfully aware that most of the growing burden of my day-to-day care fell on Lucy. And it was taking a toll.

part four
STAYING ALIVE

chapter twelve

IN NEED OF HELP

LUCY

So many generous people wanted to help our family. Our good friend, Larry Petulla, a physical therapist whose two sons played football at Los Gatos came to our home two or three times a week to work on Charlie and keep his muscles and joints as limber as possible. A couple of Larry's assistants regularly came to our home on their lunch break to get Charlie into the pool and help him do his range-of-motion exercises.

It was Larry who noticed me wincing in pain one day and asked what was wrong. When I confessed my shoulders, neck, and back had been bothering me for some time, he insisted on treating me as well as Charlie—at no charge. And he warned me that the damage I'd already done to my own body would only get worse if I continued to lift and move and steady Charlie the way I had to do.

I gladly accepted Larry's therapy, though following his advice to avoid added physical strain was impossible. Charlie needed lots of help and as his body betrayed him, my muscles became his muscles. While the growing demands were exhausting and usually painful, I loved him. He needed me. Together we always found a way to do what needed to be done.

Even after we got a hospital bed that could be adjusted up and down, getting Charlie up and on his feet involved a lot of awkward lifting and pulling on my part. So Charlie insisted I wear one of those weight lifter's belts for the heaviest lifting.

Maneuvering and balancing him in the tight confines of a bathroom was especially tough. I had to stand in the shower with him and keep him upright by leaning him into a corner while I washed him and shampooed his hair. I used to laughingly tell him I wished he had Velcro skin, then I could just stick him to the shower wall.

Velcro skin definitely could have helped during one Hawaiian visit at his sister Ruth's home. The hour was late; since most of the household had gone to bed I quietly walked Charlie into the lua and flipped on the light. As I knelt down to remove his shoes and begin getting him undressed for bed, Charlie asked me to put the toilet lid down. That's when I spotted movement out of the corner of my eye. A roach scurried across the wall. Now, this wasn't one of our little North American cockroaches. No, this was one of the giant, tropical, flying, tree roach varieties. And our particular specimen looked big enough to have to file a flight plan with the FAA before taking off.

"Kill him!" Charlie exclaimed.

"How?" I'd foolishly neglected to bring a bazooka with me to the lua.

"Use my shoe!"

Clearly, Charlie didn't stop to consider the dilemma I faced—how to steady my husband while hunting down the invader. Charlie urged me on, "Kill him! There he goes!"

I propped Charlie against the wall, and quickly bent down to grab a shoe. Charlie began to teeter, but I was now on a mission.

I whirled and swatted at the fleeing monster. Missed. *Oh, no.* On my second swing I connected. Monster mash. I smiled inside. Calmly, triumphantly, I turned back to Charlie just in time to see him begin to topple sideways—in slow motion at first, like some giant sequoia felled by a lumberman's axe. I screamed as I grabbed for him. Too late. He went right on over toward the floor, wedging tightly between the commode and the wall.

Kale came rushing in to help. He'd heard my scream. The entire neighborhood had probably heard. Everyone in the house was now hovering outside the bathroom door, worried and wondering what was wrong.

"Are you okay, dear?" I was worried a little myself.

Charlie's weak, muffled reply, "Just get me up," didn't reassure me. *Had he wrenched his neck? Taken a blow to the head?*

Kale and I were still trying to gently dislodge him from his awkward resting spot when Charlie commented, "Good thing I had you put the lid down. Or I might have gone headfirst into the lua."

When I heard that quip, I knew everything was okay. By the time Kale and I got Charlie to his feet we were all three laughing so hard I wasn't sure we could keep him there. But we'd obviously survived the great cockroach safari, with even our senses of humor intact.

Getting Charlie into and out of the front seat of a car was another regular and difficult challenge. I felt certain that at least part of my shoulder problems had resulted from driving with Charlie in the passenger seat beside me. Whenever I went around corners or braked sharply I had to throw my right arm out and hold Charlie's forehead with my hand to keep his head from rolling sideways or snapping forward.

Charlie said he began to feel like one of those GM crash dummies you see in commercials. I just began to feel like a dummy.

The reflex action of my right arm whenever my foot went to the brake or my left hand turned the steering wheel, soon become a nuisance—especially for other passengers. Our children got so tired of me reaching out and grabbing them that Kale began teasing me by letting his head drop and roll in perfect imitation of his dad whenever he rode with me. I appreciated the attempt at humor. But I did worry that I'd one day embarrass myself by flinging my arm out and grab some real estate client's forehead just as I turned into the driveway of their would-be dream house.

Driving wasn't the only concern I had for Charlie's safety. It became increasingly difficult just to keep him from falling when he walked. Two people could manage if they supported him on each side and one held his head. But for one person, walking Charlie was becoming a serious challenge.

Because I didn't always have help, I eventually worked out an awkward, but effective system. I'd stand tight against his side, with my right hand I'd reach across my body and clamp tight on his right arm just under the armpit. With my left hand behind his back we could lean forward and with my left hip pressed against his right one and helping swing his leg forward, we'd manage one small step at a time.

Kale and I were the only ones who ever mastered this technique. But we both developed problems with our lower back and hips as a result.

The technique did work. Charlie never fell when I walked him like that. Though we did come close a few times; I recall one occasion at church.

Early in our marriage and through the first years of his illness Charlie went to confession and the family attended Mass every week. But as it grew harder and harder for him to walk, church attendance became sporadic and then infrequent. Charlie wouldn't think of showing up for 6 A.M. Mass on Sunday morning without having gone to confession on Saturday; and getting him to church two days in a row, not to mention getting up, showering, dressing, and getting out of the house by the crack of dawn, was more than we managed most weeks.

But one Sunday morning we made the extra effort. After taking the closest parking spot I could find, we began the slow, arduous walk into the building—one shuffling step at a time. I felt exhausted, my back hurt, the holiday service had already started. As we stepped into the narthex, the heel of my shoe caught on the doorway threshold. As I reeled back to catch my balance, Charlie pitched forward and seemed about to fall flat on his face as I jerked and tightened my grip.

I'd never been one to use strong language. And if I had been, fifteen years of marriage to Charlie with his attitude toward swearing would have cured me.

But at that moment, as Charlie lurched forward and I stumbled and caught him, further wrenching my back, I inadvertently swore. I took God's name in vain. In church. Naturally blurting it out at a moment of absolute silence.

I saw the shock register on Charlie's face. If he hadn't been so mortified he might have done like he does with his players and made me take a mile around the sanctuary. My darling children barely managed to stifle their giggles as we hurriedly slipped into our seats.

While I went to Mass with Charlie because a formal service meant so much to him, I did most of my praying outside of church. Having grown up as a devout Catholic who felt he needed to confess to a priest who then spoke to God on his behalf, Charlie had a hard time understanding the way I prayed. But in my Protestant upbringing I'd been taught I could speak to God directly, anytime, anyplace.

So when I felt discouraged or especially tired and I'd be driving my Honda, I'd roll back my sunroof which I viewed as sort of a prayer roof and talk to God. I'd tell him how I was feeling and ask for his help. Charlie knew I prayed like that. But he said he just couldn't feel comfortable conversing so casually with God, even though I told him how much I felt it really helped me.

Two times stand out when I experienced an undeniable answer to my prayers. The first came on a trip to the office of an ear, nose, and throat doctor. Charlie had begun to have difficulty swallowing without gagging and coughing; we had heard about a fairly minor operation, a crycheaphar-engialmyotomy, that might help alleviate the problem.

Kale went with me to help get Charlie in and out of a borrowed van. But as the two of us struggled to shift Charlie from the van seat to the wheelchair we'd brought to get Charlie into the doctor's office, as I stood painfully hunched over in the back of that van wrestling Charlie's immobile body, a tidal wave of emotion welled up out of nowhere. I could feel the lump rising in my throat and almost taste the coming tears.

I swallowed hard. *I can't let Charlie see me cry.* I turned away and told Kale to wait with his dad. And I jumped out of the van and rushed around behind it, out of sight. I fell on my knees right there in the parking lot and I cried out silently to God. "I can't do this anymore. It's too hard. And I'm so tired. Oh God, please, please help me!"

I don't know how to explain it except to say I felt this surge of strength I knew was from God. And I was filled completely with a sudden, calm, reassuring peace. It was like God was right there. I wiped the tears away, stood up, and went back around to get Charlie in to see the doctor. Kale looked at me a little funny as I climbed back in the van and asked, "You okay, Mom?"

I smiled at him. "I'm fine now," I assured him. "Just fine." And I knew I was telling him the truth.

The second undeniable answer to prayer was a little different . . .

There never seemed to be enough hours in a week to earn a living as a real estate agent and do everything else required of a mother, a wife, a homemaker, and a 24-hour-a-day nurse to a terminally ill husband. Fortunately I seemed to function without a lot of sleep, because a lot of days the only uninterrupted time I could find to do my paperwork— business or personal—was in the wee hours when Charlie and the children were sound asleep.

About 2:00 A.M. one morning I sat at my desk, household bills in discouraging stacks in front of me. Medical expenses and a slumping real-estate market had quickly eaten away our financial resources. I hadn't told Charlie because I knew he'd worry and feel more helpless. While I might not be able to stop the physical progression of his ALS, I at least could spare him the added stress of facing our depressing financial picture.

Though I knew we had almost nothing left in the bank, I wrote checks for the minimum amount due on just those bills that needed to be paid immediately. Then I stopped and added them up. The total came to $2000.

In utter despair, I took my arm and swept everything off my desk and onto the floor. "That's it," I told God. "We can't pay these! It's all in your hands!" And I went to bed.

The next morning when I opened the mail I found a totally unexpected check for exactly two thousand dollars. For a long time I could only stare in disbelief. Then, feeling nearly overwhelmed by this obvious answer to prayer, I went racing back to the bedroom to tell Charlie. But by the time I reached the back of the house, I was crying so hard I couldn't talk. After I finally managed to choke out the reassuring words, "It's good news!" he waited patiently for me to regain control. It was about then I realized I couldn't tell him just how good and how perfect the news was without telling him about our dire financial straits. So I simply held out the check and watched the grin spread across his face as he read what it said.

That surprise check and Lucy's desperate parking-lot prayer were two emotional and spiritual high points. But there were many low points as well. Not all news was good. Not all the Wedemeyers' prayers were answered the way they would have wanted.

Word came from Hawaii that Charlie's nephew Georgie-boy had incurable leukemia. On a trip back to the islands to see him, Charlie and Lucy had a chance to do for him, what he'd done for them. They talked openly with Georgie-boy about his illness, yet teased and joked with him in the way they always had. And they felt their attitude helped model a positive example that the entire Wedemeyer family adopted in their comfort and treatment of Georgie-boy until his death in 1983.

CHARLIE

I knew Lucy tried to protect me from as much emotional strain as she could. But I had to grieve for Georgie-boy who'd been like a brother to me. And I couldn't help worrying. Not just about our finances, but about the overall impact my condition was having on my entire family.

I could often see the pain on Lucy's face when she lifted me. Sometimes I'd feel her wince. I loved her more than ever for her faithfulness to me. Every day she said in deeds what she had told me many times in words, "This isn't just your disease, it's our disease. We're in this together." But as much as I appreciated and drew strength from that spirit, I hated what my ALS was doing to her as much as I hated what it had done to me.

I worried too about our children. Kale could never have the carefree, happy childhood I had wanted for him. He didn't even have a father who could play catch or do any of the other things a boy needs his dad to do with him.

But at least Kale maintained an openness, a transparency about his feelings. Carri reacted differently; she withdrew emotionally. That withdrawal, combined with the natural distancing so common in early adolescence, made it doubly hard to read her reactions and know how she was dealing with my disease.

When we had to ask her to transfer to Los Gatos High School from the district where we were living, because I sometimes needed her help during practice driving the golf cart or interpreting for me, I felt bad. I knew she didn't want to leave her friends and start at a new school. But I just didn't see any alternative if I was to keep coaching.

Other people began to see the growing strain my condition was creating for my family. Early in our 1983 season, two friends came to the house one day to tell me they wanted to plan a special benefit auction in my honor to help raise enough money to pay for some part-time nurses who could provide some relief.

"Lucy can't keep doing everything she's doing," Larry Petulla insisted. Joan Mathews agreed with him.

I knew they were right. But I still couldn't bring myself to accept charity. "I appreciate your concern, but you can't do it," I told them. "I don't want you to do it." I refused to give my permission and when they pressured me I told them there was no way I would cooperate.

I'm not sure I'd have agreed even if I'd known how soon—and how badly—we were going to need those nurses.

chapter thirteen

ACCEPTING HELP

LUCY

While I'd always enjoyed watching football as a player's wife and then as a coach's wife, that 1983 season marked the beginning for me of a new, deeper appreciation for the game. Because Charlie's close friend and assistant Stan Perry had made the decision to leave coaching and teaching to pursue another career, Charlie asked me to take over as golf cart chauffeur. Meaning I got not only a closer view of the on-field action, but an intimate feel for all the emotions, discussions, and decisions taking place on the sideline during a game.

Stan warned me the driving role would be tougher than it looked. And he was right. The reason being that I had a very demanding and particular passenger. Charlie constantly wanted me to move the cart to give him the best view of the action. Six inches closer to the sideline. No, a foot back. Now angled slightly to the right. A couple degrees to the left. Careful not to run over any players. Or bump that referee.

Maneuvering around the bench and in and out of a

milling sideline crowd as the action moved up and down the field would have been challenge enough. But I had a second, simultaneous role—as Charlie's interpreter. The prime reason Charlie wanted me to drive the golf cart for him was that his speech was deteriorating quickly. His throat muscles had grown so weak that his slurred words were virtually inaudible amid the sideline noise. I often had to read his lips to relay his instructions and play calls to his assistants and players.

That role taught me more about the intricacies and complexity of football in one season than I had learned in a lifetime as a devoted fan. The terminology required to call plays in Charlie's complex, multi-set, pro-style offense seemed like an unsolvable mystery to me at first. For example, when the season began I had no idea that a "Pro right, six fly, 20 nose tackle trap" was a running play where we lined up in a pro-right set formation, started the right flanker in motion past the ball, and then handed off to the left-halfback who ran a counter trap at the nose guard, while our left tackle pulled back away from his normal line position to block for the halfback as our fullback filled the gap left by the pulling tackle. I didn't have a clue as to what "Wing right switch to wing left, fake 49 down, bootleg right" was. I soon learned it was a complex pass play that began with a fake to the fullback going right of center, a second fake to the right halfback going left, and the quarterback rolling right behind his pulling right guard. Meanwhile the fullback filled the pulling guard's gap or broke through into the flat, the tight end ran a 35–45 degree crossing pattern and became the primary receiver that the quarterback would first try to pass to fifteen yards down field while the wingback would run a deep post pattern as a decoy to take the defensive safety away from the play.

Charlie used more than thirty different formations in his offense, as many as ten different plays could be run from any one of those formations, and almost every play had a zillion options depending on the opponent's defensive formation and reaction. This meant that Charlie's offense, which he never committed to paper but kept straight in his own mind, involved thousands of variations—all spelled out in what seemed to me at first to be an unbreakable secret code made up of nonsense words: Tight pro-left I, fake 59 pitch Sweep, Reverse Right Pass; Pro-right twin, three fly, fullback flood right; pro-right I, six fly, fake 31, 58 counter option; triple right flex 78, Clear wing left twin, 6 freight, 78 stop.

Eventually I learned to almost simultaneously repeat Charlie's play calls. But it seemed nerve-racking in the beginning. Fortunately, Dr. Griffin's third son, John, was one of Charlie's quarterbacks that season. And John was not only a brilliant kid and talented player, but he had such remarkable rapport with Charlie that at times the two of them seemed to communicate by mental telepathy. Sometimes before I could figure out what play Charlie wanted to call, John just *knew*.

Sometimes I'd still be trying to read Charlie's lips to tell the assistants what to call when John would hand-signal the same play from the field and Charlie would just mouth his okay. John not only respected and loved Charlie, he was always polite and patient with me when I misinterpreted a play call.

Between John's mind-reading, my lip-reading and the cooperative spirit of Charlie's assistants and players, we got the job done. The Los Gatos Wildcats played an undefeated regular season, dominating our opponents by an aggregate score of 221-49. Our lone defeat, and another sad season-ender came when we lost again in the first round of the CCS playoffs.

Even by Charlie's demanding standards, 1983 was a very successful season. It seemed especially rewarding to me because I was on the sidelines helping Charlie do what he loved most. Watching him closely during the games I marveled at his power of concentration, his ability to block out everything—the golf cart, the disease. He actually seemed more alive on the football field—as if a fresh supply of endorphins were released in his brain, enabling him to focus entirely on the football action in front of him.

Charlie's ability to see everything happening with all twenty-two players on the field at once astounded me. I saw why opposing coaches nicknamed him the "Hawaiian Eye." I also began to appreciate the subtle points of his strategy— how he'd run one play that didn't work, just to set up the defense for another play he planned to use later.

I remember a conversation part-way through the season in which an assistant coach's wife expressed her sympathy for me—having to be down there on the sidelines. She assumed, "You must feel very out of place, Lucy, with all those guys."

"Not at all," I told her. "It has been a great experience. It's given me a new, deeper appreciation for football and for what Charlie does." Indeed I counted it a privilege few wives ever have, a chance to know my husband more intimately by getting an inside perspective on his career.

But I couldn't have played the role I did if it hadn't been for the accepting attitude of the assistant coaches. In one sense they had to put up with me because Charlie was still the boss and he had made the decision to have me on the sidelines. But all his assistants respected Charlie as a coach and as a man. If having me on the sidelines was the price to be paid for Charlie to continue coaching, no one seemed to have any problems with the new arrangements. And I consciously tried to curb my naturally outspoken personality and confine myself to my appointed role as coach's assistant voice and driver.

However, there was one day early in the season when the "mother" in me took over and prompted me to make a unilateral decision during practice. I noticed in some of the drills at the beginning of practice that one of our starters seemed to lag behind his teammates. He looked listless and pale.

I called to him, "Come here, Todd."

He came jogging over. "Yes, Mrs. Wedemeyer?" he responded.

Our love story began
in high school where
I met this handsome
Hawaiian under a
poinciana tree on the
beautiful campus of
Honolulu's Punahou
Academy at the
start of Charlie's
senior year.

One of the values we shared from the beginning was a deep appreciation for family. Above is Charlie as a high school senior with his proud parents. To the right is the entire Wedemeyer ohana (family) taken in 1973. (Charlie's at far left in the back.) That's the Dangler family below right. Dad as a pilot during WWII and my mother's standing with all four children.

1964 ALL-STARS

Willis Lau
Kaimuki—B

Charley Wedemeyer
Punahou—B

Harry Knell
Kaimuki—E

Wayne Sterling
Punahou—B

At 5'7" and 160 pounds, Charlie didn't look like an imposing athlete. Yet he won all-state honors in three sports, and always loved football best. His legendary athletic accomplishments gained him recognition as Hawaii's Prep Athlete of the Decade for the 60s.

ck Matsumoto, © *Honolulu Star - Bulletin*

In keeping with Hawaiian tradition, moms, girlfriends, an other admiring femal would bestow post-game leis and kisses o players. By the time I could get to Charlie after most games, he' already have a dozen flower strands around his neck. That's Char in high school action below. He went on to earn college all-star honors playing Big 1 football for Duffy Daugherty's MSU Spartans (right) — national champs in 1966.

© *Honolulu Star - Bulletin*

Jack Matsumoto, © *Honolulu Star - Bulletin*

THE WILDCATS GREAT SEASO
1983 WVAL CHAMPIONS!

THE LOS GATOS WEEKLY SALUTES
THE UNDEFEATED LOS GATOS WILDCATS
AND COACH CHARLIE WEDEMEYER.

If we'd known Charlie had ALS he probably wouldn't have accepted the head coach position at Los Gatos High School in 1977 (left). But it was coaching that gave him purpose and kept him alive long past the time his doctors gave him.

The
Iron
Coach

Los Gatos 34, Leigh 0
Los Gatos 13, Westmont 9
Los Gatos 33, Prospect 0
Los Gatos 14, Branham 7
Los Gatos 41, Del Mar 13
Los Gatos 21, Blackford 8

LOS GATOS Weekly

Charlie soon lost use
of his hands and arms
and needed help
walking (left). When
he could no longer
stand on the sidelines
a friend donated a
golf cart. By 1983
(right) coaching was
a family affair with
me joining Charlie on
the field and Carri
and Kale pitching
in whenever they
were needed.

Even with me reading Charlie's lips to call plays, sideline communication often proved an exciting challenge. If it hadn't been for the support of his assistants (left), Charlie could never have continued coaching. But it was the players themselves who inspired Charlie and gave him the joy that made all the effort seem worthwhile.

LOS GATOS
LOS GATOS 46
LOS GATOS
LOS GATOS 88
LOS GATOS
LOS GATOS 7
5

A producer marveling at the drama of this '85 championship game said, "Hollywood could never capture this." But the CBS movie *Quiet Victory* aired in '88. Above is our family with the actors who portrayed us. Bottom right are Charlie, Carri, and Kale with the producers of the documentary "One More Season."

What no one could ever portray is the sheer zaniness of life at the Wedemeyer house. Above you see our macho son Kale (next to his dad) and some of his teammates in medical garb. Our real nurse, Linda Peevyhouse, on the far right; Craig Williams is second from left. "Any excuse for a party" should be Charlie's motto — whether it's Halloween or just a fun '50s bash.

For a guy hooked to a respirator 24 hours a day, Charlie moves in unusual circles. Here he is talking football with quarterbacking greats Y.A. Tittle and Joe Montana. Redskins Coach Joe Gibbs asked us to speak at his boys home. Bill Walsh took time out during Super Bowl week to attend an NFL banquet honoring Charlie.

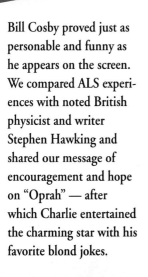

Bill Cosby proved just as personable and funny as he appears on the screen. We compared ALS experiences with noted British physicist and writer Stephen Hawking and shared our message of encouragement and hope on "Oprah" — after which Charlie entertained the charming star with his favorite blond jokes.

Dennis Desprois, © *San Francisco Giants*

Life remains full 16 years after doctors gave Charlie "maybe 12 months" to live. Four times we've been asked to throw out the first ball at a Giants baseball game. But only once could Charlie talk me into joining him, his wheelchair, and all his life support equipment on a complimentary hot air balloon adventure.

You may recognize some of the Hollywood faces who joined Charlie to raise money for ALS with a celebrity baseball game at Candlestick Park. Brandon Tartikoff (left and kneeling) told us he liked Charlie's story so much he didn't schedule any strong NBC programming the night *Quiet Victory* aired on CBS. In 1992 we flew to Washington D.C. where Charlie received the President's Trophy for Disabled American of the Year.

Here we are with our
two wonderful keikis
— Carri and Kale —
when life seemed nor-
mal back in 1970.
On that special last
family ski trip to the
Sierras right after the
diagnosis in 1978.
And finally the four
of us today.

"Are you okay? You don't look well."

"I'll be okay," he told me. But his eyes said otherwise. I put my hand to his forehead. He had a very high fever.

"You're not practicing any more today," I decided. "You need to get home and rest. And I'll drive you home as soon as you change out of that equipment!"

I left Carri to drive her dad around the field while I was gone. Neither Charlie nor any of his assistants said a word to question my decision to dismiss their star running back. And I didn't notice any of them rolling their eyes or reacting at all to my mothering instincts.

Not that I felt like anyone was merely tolerating my presence on the field. The players and coaches were always respectful and often extremely helpful to me as I tried to take care of Charlie. I greatly appreciated their sensitivity.

Getting Charlie to and from practice had become a physically exhausting chore. I'd have to hurry home from the office, help him out of bed, dress him in a clean, pressed coaching shirt and shorts, get him out to the car and into the passenger seat, and then drive him to the practice field where one or two of the assistant coaches would often help get him transferred out of the car and into the golf cart.

One afternoon as we shifted Charlie out of the car, I inadvertently knocked off his favorite Los Gatos black and orange baseball cap. I didn't realize it had come off until I slammed the car door right on it.

I heard gasps from all of the assistant coaches who saw it happen. To understand the terrible sinking sensation I felt in the pit of my stomach you have to understand Charlie and his attitude toward hats. He always wanted his cap just so—not cocked too high or pulled down too low. The brim needed to be curled a little, the peak at the front of the cap crisp and distinct. And now that he couldn't raise his arms to adjust his own cap, responsibility for maintaining Charlie's sartorial sharpness had fallen to me. And I'd just crushed his favorite cap in the car door.

I quickly retrieved the cap and tried to reshape it. No

use. The brim bent and broken, an ugly permanent crease ran through the hat itself.

At that moment it was probably just as well that Charlie could no longer shout. The angry expression on his face said more than enough. He looked ready to explode. The assistant coaches stared at the ground in awkward silence.

But in the next instant, Larry, one of Charlie's assistants immediately walked to the car door, opened it again, took off his own cap, slammed the door on it, and then pulled his own cockeyed hat onto his head and announced, "OK, let's start practice!"

The tension broke and the laughter started. Charlie was still laughing as I placed his mangled cap on his head, and he wore it proudly as we headed the golf cart across the field to where the team was gathering.

CHARLIE

One evening approaching the end of football season our doorbell rang. Lucy opened the door and greeted our visitors.

My friend Larry Petulla had returned bringing reinforcements. With him were John Lockner, former mayor of Los Gatos, and Joe Zanordi, the father of one of my players. I had a pretty good idea why they'd come, but they didn't get to the purpose of their visit right away. They filed into our family room and sat around my favorite green chair talking, telling stories, and cracking jokes for an hour or more. I laughed and enjoyed myself more than I had in ages.

Finally Larry said, "Charlie, I know what you told me last time I mentioned doing some sort of fund raiser to help cover your medical expenses. But plans are already underway . . ."

Before I could voice any protest, John Lockner jumped in to say, "We know you don't like the thought of charity. But don't be too proud to let some other people help. I'm not a poor man, but when my son had the accident that left him a paraplegic, people wanted to reach out and show they cared by giving a fund raiser for our benefit. I didn't want them to do it either, but people want a chance to help.

"The kids at school are involved, civic clubs, many of your friends, the entire community is behind this Charlie."

"And Charlie," Joe told me, "we're gonna do this whether you give us your cooperation or not. But we'd sure like to have your blessing."

I gave my reluctant okay, pointing out that "It doesn't look like you've left me much choice."

During the following weeks, the Wedemeyers began hearing details on the preparation for "We Love Charlie" night.

Snack bar profits from one of our home football games were donated to the "We Love Charlie" fund. The school's Key Club raised over $500 by holding wheelchair races around the school track. And the spirit squad sold "We Love Charlie" T-shirts during football games.

Even before the scheduled big event, Lions Club work parties came to the Wedemeyer house to do landscaping and construct ramps for the wheelchair that had become a regular part of Charlie's life. Plans were underway to enlarge the shower too so Lucy could get Charlie in and out more easily in a special shower-chair.

Yet all the prior help and kindness was nothing compared to the magnitude of response for the actual "We Love Charlie" night. The date was set for November 26 at St. Mary's Hall with the evening to include cocktails, hors d'oeuvres, dancing, and a silent auction. Tickets went on sale for $25 a person and the organizers told the Wedemeyer's the goal was to raise $50,000 to hire nurses who could be with Charlie during the days so Lucy could work full time.

CHARLIE

But as the day approached, I don't know how many times I told Lucy, "I don't think I can go through with it. Maybe I'll stay home and you can go and represent me." Wisely, Lucy didn't try to argue with me; I think she must have understood my conflicting feelings better than I did.

While I continued to feel grateful that so many people

cared, I dreaded the thought of facing them all on "We Love Charlie" night. Being out on the sidelines in my golf cart in front of thousands of people never bothered me; I was doing my job then, using my skills, and taking control. On the football field I was only one character in a larger drama.

But being cast as the central character of "We Love Charlie" night went against everything my mother ever taught me about not calling attention to myself. Even worse than the unwanted attention would be the resulting pity. For the disconcerting spotlight pointed at me would also expose my growing helplessness. I wouldn't even be able to stand up at a microphone and properly thank all my friends.

Though I couldn't admit it at the time, the heart of the issue was pride.

In the end I went mostly because I felt I ought to go. And in part because on that night, Lucy quietly got me ready as if she expected me to go all along.

We were late by the time we pulled into the crowded parking lot at St. Mary's. I've always hated being late; so that only added to my sense of dread.

I knew Lucy understood and shared some of my uneasiness when she suggested an emotional coping strategy. "If it gets to be too much, let's pretend the whole thing is for someone else and just try to have a good time."

Bobby Griffin, who'd come home from college for the weekend, pushed me through the doors into St. Mary's Hall. A capacity crowd of seven hundred people greeted our arrival with thunderous applause and Joan Mathews draped fragrant Hawaiian leis around our necks and kissed us both. It was then I truly understood for the first time in my life the difference between feeling humiliated and feeling humbled.

We were certainly humbled by the turnout and the loving response of so many people who wanted to speak to us that night. As a result, the evening proved harder for Lucy than for me, because she had the trying assignment of reading my lips and translating for dozens of conversations—all in the midst of a noisy, milling crush of people. That was a new experience for both of us.

Another new experience was being the recipients of so much warmth and love and generosity. The success of this event, the result of hard work on the part of so many wonderful friends, staggered us. By the end of the evening more than $60,000 had been raised.

But the highlight of the entire affair for me was seeing so many of my former players who'd come back home for the evening. I spent much of the night surrounded by young men I'd coached who were as eager to tell me where they were and what they were doing today as they were to recall all the memories we'd shared during their days as Los Gatos Wildcats. I wouldn't have wanted to miss that part of the experience for anything.

LUCY

One of the highlights I connect with "We Love Charlie" night actually took place a few weeks before the big event. The organizers had asked me to compile a collection of photos they could display to depict Charlie's life. So I'd pulled out and sorted through several big boxes of old photographs.

We'd driven a borrowed van to a football game one evening to scout an upcoming opponent. While Charlie sat in the front of the van watching the game and making mental notes to use in constructing his game plan, I spread out piles of photos in the back of the van and began constructing three large collages on poster boards—one from our days at Punahou, one from Michigan State, and the last from our time at Los Gatos. As the crowd cheered and the ball game went on outside, I sorted scenes from happier, more carefree times in our life together and tried not to let my tears fall on the collages.

We had so many memories, so many blessings to be grateful for. We realized that even before we experienced "We Love Charlie" night. But in the weeks that followed that special evening, there were two special groups that

Charlie wanted to acknowledge for all they had done for him and for us.

That year, Charlie and I wanted to do something special and personal at our annual post-season football banquet to express our gratitude for the way this group of boys had responded to Charlie's growing limitations and given him his first undefeated regular season. So we called our family in the islands and asked them to send us enough flower leis for the entire team. As we called the players to the front one-by-one, I congratulated the boys and draped the fragrant flower strands around their necks.

Charlie had always tried to set a fun-loving tone for our football banquets. And that tradition was continued as players gave gag gifts to the coaches and coaches made their own remarks about players as they handed out various awards. The assistant coaches surprised Carri by presenting her with a plaque in appreciation for her special assistance to her dad and to them during practices and on the sideline during the games.

But the most moving and memorable part of the football banquet for me came at the very end of the evening, after John Griffin had stood and briefly paid tribute to "Coach Wedemeyer" for his inspiring example of leadership and courage. For it was then, after the official conclusion of the banquet that the players came forward, one at a time to speak to Charlie. Most of them hugged us. Many of these macho teenage football players actually bent down over Charlie's wheelchair and kissed their coach.

My own heart swelled with emotion as I watched this tender display of respect and affection and listened as the players thanked Charlie for all he had done for them. I couldn't help but be struck and pained by the contrast between the strong, healthy young athletes and Charlie's disease-weakened form propped in his wheelchair. But I was reminded once more how important football and coaching were to Charlie's survival.

But when some of the boys expressed their disappointment and regrets to Charlie for having lost again in the first round of the playoffs and he responded by assuring them we'd do even better next year, I didn't know how to feel.

On the one hand I believed Charlie needed to focus on coaching again in 1984 just to stay alive. The heart of the 1983 team had been juniors who would be back and we had a promising crop of underclassmen moving up to varsity. Many people were already speculating next year's squad would be the strongest Los Gatos football team ever.

However, Charlie had steadily lost weight and strength throughout the season. At the rate he was declining, if he lived another year, I didn't know if he'd have the strength to coach. So I wasn't yet ready to even think about another season. For me, today seemed challenge enough.

The second group of people we wanted to do something special for was the coaching staff because they had all done so much to help Charlie continue coaching. Some years earlier, when it had become impossible for Charlie to handle the administrative paperwork of coaching, he had gone to the school administration and proposed that he continue as offensive coordinator but that Butch Cattolico be named official head coach. Ted Simonson had rejected the idea at the time, saying he wanted Charlie to continue as head coach. But he'd agreed to compensate Butch for any increased responsibility by paying him a head coach's stipend instead of an assistant coach's rate.

Whenever reporters interviewed us, we both made a point to express our gratitude for what all the assistant coaches did. But those comments were often left out of the final story. Now we wanted to do something very special, from us, to communicate our gratitude to Charlie's coaching colleagues.

After the big fund raiser, the largest individual donor who had given $10,000 to the "We Love Charlie" fund, told Charlie "I'd like you and Lucy to use that money and take a cruise." We didn't feel right about doing that, but as we talked Charlie came up with the idea of taking his assistant coaches and their families to Hawaii as a special thank you for all they had done for us. As soon as the donor okayed the plan, we issued the invitations and I began making the necessary arrangements.

A couple days after Christmas our troop of thirteen adults and five children took off from San Francisco International Airport for a week in paradise. An old friend from Punahou arranged for the use of his beach house in Waimanalo, just a couple doors down from the estate used in filming Tom Selleck's television show, "Magnum P.I."

Charlie's extended family accepted our visit as a challenge to their Hawaiian generosity and an opportunity to demonstrate a big "mahalo" (thank you) of their own to all the coaches for their support and friendship. They provided transportation, brought traditional meals for us to feast on, and even offered entertainment in the way of Hawaiian music and dance.

We spent long, lazy days enjoying the sun and the surf. At night we sat out under the palms, watching the moonlight over the ocean as we talked and laughed.

Charlie seemed in unusually high spirits the whole week, planning everything from where we should go on afternoon outings to deciding what everyone should eat, from organizing a billiards tournament for all the women at one o'clock one morning to honoring his Chinese heritage at midnight on New Years by setting off seven strings of ten thousand firecrackers each.

It wasn't until the flight home that I realized how much the trip had taken out of Charlie physically. By the time we got him wheeled into the house and into his own bed, I couldn't help wondering if Charlie would ever see Hawaii again.

chapter fourteen

THE BATTLE
TO BREATHE

As Charlie's condition had deteriorated over the years, Lucy simply adjusted to the increased demands without allowing herself to think about how hard the job had become. In the same way she determined not to try to look very far into the future; she had all she could handle today without adding the unmanageable worries of tomorrow. Although it seemed a limited perspective, maintaining a narrow, more manageable focus was the only way she knew to maintain her sanity.

Ironically, it wasn't until they began hiring nursing help for Charlie early in 1984 that Lucy began to consider the emotional and physical toll required to care for his needs twenty-four hours a day. Seeing others do some of what she'd been doing for years, Lucy began to realize what a welcome relief it would be to have someone else assume responsibility for Charlie's care. But the high expectations and the new acknowledgement of her need for help turned to frustration over Charlie's slow adjustment to what Lucy thought was a wonderful development.

LUCY

Being able to put in a full day at the office without running home a half dozen times to check on Charlie suddenly seemed a reasonable goal. The thought of sleeping more than twenty minutes at a time seemed like luxury.

But whenever I was home, Charlie would call for me to help him rather than ask the nurse. Often he'd wait until I was home before he'd "need" something and he always wanted to know where I was going to be, for how long, and when I expected to be back.

These constant demands weren't new or more difficult; I'd lived with them for years. But now, when I'd expected a little relief, they seemed all the more binding.

Fortunately I knew Charlie well enough to understand some of what was going on. I knew he seldom ever needed to go to the bathroom except when I was home, and that he always wanted me rather than a nurse to help him, because of a strong case of personal modesty. I understood that.

Another complicating factor was Charlie's demanding perfectionism. After years of combing his hair, dressing him, and maneuvering him, I almost always knew what he wanted and just exactly how he wanted me to do it. The nurses didn't. And Charlie had more trouble than ever communicating exactly what he wanted them to do. Yet I told myself this too was a matter of time. The nurses could learn, and Charlie would learn to let them.

A thornier issue was the matter of trust. As the years of his illness had passed, I'd seen and marveled at my husband's courage. But I'd also come to understand some of his fears—his fear of falling, his fear of choking to death now that his atrophied throat muscles made it difficult to swallow. And I was the one person who knew how to support him so he could shuffle without falling. I knew how to help him clear his throat when he began to cough and gag on his own saliva. Charlie had learned to trust me with his life over the years. But I was his wife and he knew how much I loved him. Could he ever trust, really trust, a part-time nurse?

There was yet one more issue, deeper even than trust, that made it difficult for Charlie to accept the nurses. And I didn't understand this one for quite some time.

The real problem and biggest reason for Charlie's reluctance to accept the nurses' help was an underlying but definite sense of loss. Seven years of fighting ALS together had drawn us closer than ever. And in the years since he'd quit teaching we'd been together at home much of every day. His only remaining outside activity was coaching and I'd become an integral part of that as well.

Our lives had become intertwined to a degree few couples ever experience. And while such extreme interdependence had its downside, Charlie and I both felt it had strengthened our bonds and enriched our love. I'd become such a part of Charlie's daily existence, and he such a part of mine, that I thought we had begun to realize what it truly means for "two to become one." This cherished closeness we both felt was the single greatest encouragement we found, the one bright and lasting ray of hope and comfort in the gathering darkness of Charlie's losing battle with ALS. Anything that reduced our closeness and interaction also reduced that hope.

My strategy for countering that was to try to be more open with Charlie about my own feelings and needs. But that wasn't easy without making myself feel selfish or making Charlie feel guilty about his demands on me. And I didn't want to do either.

I remember one of the very first times I held my ground and asserted my own needs. I'd been so emotionally wired I felt as if I would explode. So after the nurse arrived that morning I decided I would take the dogs and go for a long, stress-relieving run. I needed to do something to clear my mind and drain the tension out of my body. A good long run would burn the carbon out of my system.

Because the nurse was fairly new, Charlie didn't yet trust her and he really wanted me to hang around, ready to help if he needed anything. I understood the reasons for his fearful feelings, but I felt certain he'd be fine so I announced: "I'm gonna take Malia and Alii for a run. I'll be right back."

I saw Charlie glance at the nurse to make sure she wasn't looking and then mouth the words to me, "I need you to stay."

"You'll be fine," I told him. "The nurse will take care of you and I'll be back in forty-five minutes or so."

Charlie got his determined, bulldog look on his face and mouthed back, "I may need you!"

"But I need to do this," I insisted. And before Charlie could say any more, I called the dogs and walked out of the room without looking back. So I only sensed the intensity of Charlie's anger. While I knew he wouldn't vent it in front of the new nurse, the temperature of the entire house may have jumped a couple degrees before I ever got out the front door.

The long, slow run through the neighborhood proved the perfect stress reduction therapy. The only tension left by the time I got home was prompted by the dread of facing Charlie's simmering emotions.

I instinctively tried to seize the offensive with a cheerful, light approach. "I'm back," I called as I opened the front door. "Anybody home?" *As if Charlie were going somewhere.* But when I walked into the bedroom, I could tell by the dark look on Charlie's face he was still upset.

"The run really helped; I feel much better now," I said. And to demonstrate my improved mood, I bent over and gave Charlie a quick kiss on the cheek. (One advantage of having an immobile husband is that if you make a unilateral decision to kiss and make up, he can't very well get away.) Charlie's jaw remained set without a hint of softening around his eyes.

I sat lightly beside him on the bed. "I'm sorry I left you," I told him. "But I just felt like I had to get out of the house for a while. . . ." I studied his face for a moment, running my fingers playfully through his hair. "Maybe it's PMS!"

For a split second Charlie maintained his serious expression. But then he lost it and began to laugh. The tension had broken. And I think that was a turning point after which I felt more free to express my own emotional needs to Charlie and I sensed more understanding from him about my feelings.

I did however have to pay for my PMS joke—many times over. Charlie liked the line so much he took great delight in telling countless others that while he had ALS, I had PMS.

While Charlie gradually reconciled himself to both his and my need for nursing help, I think my "relief" continued to seem, perhaps inevitably, like "loss" to Charlie. And I suspect that "loss" seemed all the more troubling because it came at a time when we both realized Charlie remained on a steady physical decline.

For a couple of years the muscles in Charlie's throat had been getting gradually, but noticeably weaker. He and Lucy had both read enough to know that for many ALS victims, this deterioration, medically referred to as the "bulbar stage," marked the beginning of the end. When people with Lou Gehrig's disease reach the point they can no longer eat or breathe, they often die of pneumonia or malnutrition.

As it became increasingly difficult for Charlie to swallow, it proved impossible to keep meat on his bones with the almost liquid diet of juice, soups, and foods Lucy could puree for him. His weight, a solid and steady 178 before ALS, had slowly sunk over the first few years of his illness. Now the gradual weight loss was accelerating. By the end of the 1983 season Charlie weighed less than 130 pounds.

CHARLIE

When my muscles first began to atrophy I'd sometimes sit in a chair or lie in bed and look at my lifeless limbs with a deep sense of personal loss. Those same arms and legs had earned me my identity as a boy growing up in Hawaii, had paid my way through college on an athletic scholarship, had won me a black belt in karate. The skills represented in them had led me into my life's work as a coach.

By the spring of 1984, whenever I looked at myself, I hardly recognized that body. It was as if someone else's limbs, maybe those of some frighteningly frail old man or an emaciated survivor of a concentration camp, were now attached where my own arms and legs used to be. The old cliche "skin and bones" described me well. And sometimes it seemed like the bones themselves were shrinking away.

With the decline of weight came an obvious erosion of strength. The weaker I felt, the less I would eat. The weaker I became and the less I could eat . . . I felt powerless to slow the effects of this accelerating cycle.

I knew I had to eat to live. I tried. And Lucy tried to help, doing everything the doctors and her vast reading suggested. About the time I quit teaching and Lucy stayed home with me those following months we began preparing and eating all-natural foods to improve my health and cut down on possible allergies. I eventually gave up eating meat because the pieces caught in my throat; I stopped drinking milk because it caused more phlegm and made swallowing more difficult. Pastas became a staple in my diet for years.

Our friend Anna Steiner brought the most wonderful manicotti when she regularly came over to help Lucy with the housework. Even pureed it tasted wonderful. And whenever I tried to thank Anna she would shake her head and say, "Don't thank me. Thank Jesus."

Like most Hawaiians, I'd always loved to eat. So when I'd no longer been able to chew and swallow solid food and had to go on a semi-liquid diet, I missed the great variety of taste and textures, the pleasurable physical sensation of eating I'd always taken for granted. And now I had trouble even swallowing liquids without coughing and gagging and feeling as if I might actually choke to death in the process. One of life's most basic pleasures, eating, now prompted feelings of dread and fear.

The same weakened muscles that made it hard for me to swallow food, often made breathing more difficult. Because

I could no longer take long deep breaths, any exertion such as walking would deplete the oxygen supply in my body and leave me gulping for air.

Because I couldn't swallow very efficiently I sometimes choked on my own saliva. That would start me coughing, but the chest and diaphragm muscles required to cough effectively were so weak I couldn't clear my airway before the repeated coughing used what little oxygen reserves I had and I'd be convulsively coughing, choking on the saliva, and trying to gasp for air—all at the same time in a deadly, painful cycle.

The best way to describe the panicky sensation is to say it reminded me of times as a teenager when I'd been surfing on the North Shore. Once in a while I'd wipe out in a giant wave which would slam me against the bottom, squeeze all the air from my lungs, and then tumble me helplessly along the bottom in a churning wall of water. I'd be so desperate for a breath of air in the midst of all that pounding I could consciously think of nothing else.

Yet as an able-bodied teenage surfer, the prospect of actually dying in the powerful Pacific had never seemed as terrifyingly real as this fearful sensation of drowning on my own spit. The very absurdity of that prospect illustrated my vulnerability, my terrible and increasing helplessness. But that wasn't the worst of my breathing problems.

Both routine sinus drainage into the throat and common bronchial congestion are normally and instinctively taken care of by coughing and swallowing. But because I could no longer manage either to cough or swallow very effectively, my most frightening and desperate battles to breathe came whenever I experienced any kind of congestion.

My involuntary coughing reflex would be triggered anytime my throat or trachea felt clogged. I never knew how long those coughing spells would last when they started. Some lasted only a minute or two. Very often they'd continue five, ten, twenty minutes. But there were many terrible bouts of violent coughing that might go on for an hour or more, with my body temperature rising to the point that Lucy would periodically rub me down with a wet wash cloth soaked in ice water which we kept by the bed every night to serve this very purpose. We also had a big paper fan which one of the children would sometimes use to help cool me down.

During the worst of these coughing episodes, it seemed my desperation for relief and for oxygen increased even as my strength waned, until I'd be physically and emotionally wrung out, every muscle in my body aching with fatigue.

So whenever I began to cough, and anytime I realized the congestion was building to the point it might trigger a bout of coughing, Lucy would immediately employ a make-shift emergency strategy we developed. She would get a container full of steaming water so hot she couldn't hold it without some kind of hot pad, lean my head forward enough so she could place the container to my lips and tip it just enough for me to catch a mouthful. I'd swish the near-scalding water around in my mouth to try to break up the phlegm for a few seconds before Lucy would tilt my head forward again so that I could spit the now lukewarm water into a bowl.

Sometimes we'd repeat these steps for an hour with me coughing continuously and Lucy gently and lovingly sup-porting my head and maneuvering the water and the "kuha" (spit) bowl the entire time. I don't know which one of us would be more exhausted by the time the congestion finally broke up enough for me to breathe easily again. But I do know during these long grueling battles for air, it was Lucy who kept me breathing. I can't begin to express the gratitude I felt for her amazingly calm presence during those panicky, desperate moments when I felt myself hanging so precariously on the verge of death. She was always there, holding the lifeline and repeatedly refusing to let me go.

When I could no longer fall asleep at night for fear of of choking, Lucy would curl up in a chair next to me, slumped against the bed where she could keep a hand draped over my right leg. I still had enough voluntary control over the large muscles in that limb to give it a jerk and awaken Lucy if I needed her. So it was only that warm, reassuring touch of her hand on my leg that enabled me to relax and doze fitfully for a few minutes at a time.

chapter fifteen

IT TAKES TWO
TO FIGHT

LUCY

One night I nearly jumped out of my chair when the involuntary twitching of Charlie's leg signaled the onset of yet another coughing spell. Trying to shake the fog of fatigue, I looked at the bedside clock and its LED display glowing in the darkness. When my eyes focused enough to read 2:38 I groaned. *It was just 2:27 when he quit coughing last time. The time before that it was 2:11.* I couldn't remember the earlier times. *How many episodes have there been since I came to bed at 12:30? At least six. Eight? Or was it nine?* I didn't know; they all blurred together and I was too tired to count.

Thankfully, Charlie only coughed a couple minutes this time before he got the congestion broken up and spit out. As he settled back on his pillows and began to breathe easier again, I fluffed my own pillow, adjusted my neck brace, and tried to get comfortable once more. But this time, before I closed my eyes I reached over and turned the clock toward the wall, so I wouldn't be so discouraged to see the time when I was awakened the next time. Most nights after that I did the same thing, finding it somehow easier and less tiring not knowing exactly how little sleep I'd gotten.

Yet it wasn't usually the frequency of these coughing bouts but rather the duration that proved most exhausting. The longer Charlie coughed, the more he'd slump down and close off his windpipe. So during the protracted bouts I'd have to sit him upright again and again, hoisting him by the shoulders and propping pillows behind him to keep him up. With one hand I'd have to continuously support and tilt his head while I alternately held the container of hot water to his lips or positioned the kuha bowl for him to spit into with the other hand.

Anytime Charlie coughed for very long, my back would ache from the awkward strain and my arms would eventually cramp with fatigue. Frequently, when the physical exertion of his violent coughing left Charlie drenched with perspiration, I'd have to peel off his wringing wet clothes and sometimes get him all the way up in order to strip off the sweat-soaked sheets and remake the bed.

Many mornings I got up wondering why I'd bothered going to bed at all. Fortunately I discovered I was blessed with a metabolism that allowed me to survive and actually function day after day on surprisingly little sleep.

Not that I bore the whole weight of Charlie's care alone. Carri and Kale assumed a lot of responsibility. Many were the nights when we were all up during one of Charlie's coughing spells, trying everything we could to get him relaxed and breathing easily again. But the distinctive personalities of our two children, as well as the very different manner in which they dealt with Charlie's illness, was frequently evident in the way each of them responded to these often frightening, middle-of-the-night crises.

Kale had spent his entire life idolizing his dad. And whether it was in the backyard playing catch as a pre-schooler, out on the football field listening to Charlie instruct his high school players, or in the living room practicing karate moves, Kale had always hung on Charlie's every word.

No matter how many hundreds of times Charlie asked him to execute a particular technique, to catch a ball a certain way, to perform a more precise karate move, Kale never acted discouraged. He was always cheerfully willing to do whatever his dad asked him to do "just one more time."

After a lifetime spent trying to please his father and carefully follow Charlie's most detailed instructions, after thousands of hours of one-on-one coaching sessions, I guess it shouldn't have been so surprising how attuned Kale was to his dad's needs. Yet I was often amazed at Kale's sensitivity and responsiveness to Charlie.

When Charlie began to cough in the night, Kale, whose room was across the hall from the master bedroom, would sometimes be in our room, propping Charlie upright before I was fully awake. Once we started the routine with the steaming water and the kuha bowl, I'd tell him, "You need to go back to bed and get your sleep, honey. You've got school tomorrow. Dad will be fine. I'll call if we need you."

Most of the time he'd respond by shaking his head and saying, "I'll stay and help." Often I'd let him. Partly because he wanted to help so badly, but mostly because I needed it. An extra pair of hands to fan Charlie or wipe him down with ice water made the hot water routine a lot easier. And the welcome company of my devoted junior-high son on the other side of Charlie's bed kept the nights from seeming so discouragingly long.

I vividly remember one time when Charlie hadn't had a good night's sleep in days. So neither had I. Exhausted, running a low-grade fever, and fighting a terrible case of bronchitis, I could hardly hold my own head up, let alone Charlie's, when Kale heard his dad coughing and came rushing across the hall. I must have looked horrid because Kale's first reaction wasn't directed at Charlie, but at me.

"You okay, Mom?"

"I'll be okay. You need to go back to bed and get some sleep."

"I think you're the one who needs the sleep," he said. "I'll take care of Dad. You go try to sleep in my room."

I wanted to argue, but I didn't have the strength. "All right," I conceded. "But wake me up in a few minutes so you can go back to bed."

Sometime later, Charlie's coughing awakened me and I jumped out of Kale's bed and rushed into our bedroom. But as I stopped beside my own bed, I fainted and fell against the corner of the dresser, cracking a couple ribs.

I awakened late the next morning, confused and disoriented for a moment to find myself on the floor of my bedroom, under a blanket tucked carefully around me, my head resting on a pillow. But when I sat up I saw the explanation. There standing next to the bed where he'd stood for thirteen straight hours, like a guardian angel watching over both of his parents, was Kale. When he greeted me with his big "good morning" smile, I gratefully kissed my son and sent him off to bed. I didn't even consider sending him to school that day.

Carri too was up a lot of nights—always willing to do whatever was asked of her—whether it was running to get steaming water, assisting me in getting Charlie's sweaty clothes off, or helping remake the bed.

But Carri, perhaps because she'd inherited so much of her dad's personality and perfectionism, often seemed wary of doing something wrong. Having always been sensitive to correction and to Charlie's demanding expectations, she'd retreat to her room as soon as possible after any crisis passed.

For a long time we didn't really know how to deal with Carri's reactions. Of course we knew some emotional distancing from parents and family is a normal, healthy part of adolescence and we wanted to give her room to grow up and be her own person. But we also realized emotional withdrawal had become one of Carri's primary coping mechanisms for dealing with Charlie's illness. And that worried me.

I'd lie awake at night, my hand on Charlie's leg, my ears attuned to his shallow breathing, my mind and heart wrestling with the questions: *How do we allow and even*

encourage Carri's growing teenage independence on the one hand,
and at the same time maintain and strengthen those emotional
bridges and communication lines needed to help a daughter deal
with the difficult reality of a dying father? Where is the balance?

CHARLIE

Like Lucy, I appreciated the way both our children pitched
in to help—not only with my care, but with all the other
responsibilities that fell on them because Lucy was working
and I couldn't do the things I'd always enjoyed doing
around the house and the yard. Yet I couldn't help feeling a
sense of growing distance not only between Carri and me
but also with Kale.

We'd always been a physically demonstrative family—
ever affectionate, always touching, tickling, kissing, and
hugging. While both Carri and Kale still hugged and kissed
me goodbye when they left for school in the morning and
always kissed me goodnight every evening, my atrophied
arms ached to be able to reach out again to pull them tight
against me and feel the kind of closeness you only get from
a good hug.

But it was more than just my inability to reach out and
touch my son and daughter that made me lament this lack of
closeness. Some days I felt as if my own children were
avoiding me. More and more I'd be lying in bed and I'd see
or hear one of the kids in the hall going to or from their
room without coming into my room to talk, or even sticking
their heads in to say hello.

I couldn't understand why my normally loving children
were treating me like that. For the first few years of my
illness they'd been so attentive, so expressive of their
concern. Had they passed some sort of psychological
threshold where they simply couldn't continue to cope with
my disease anymore? Was there an inescapable emotional
loss that would painfully parallel the loss of physical
affection I'd experienced?

For weeks I brooded on what I felt certain was a

changing pattern, until I knew it wasn't my imagination. Finally I voiced my suspicions to Lucy.

"I don't know why," I said. "But I think Carri and Kale have been avoiding me lately. I hear them walking by in the hall all the time, but they hardly ever stop to talk to me."

I halfway expected Lucy to try to downplay my observations and reassure me that what I thought was happening wasn't really happening. She didn't say anything for a little bit, like she was trying to decide what to say, or at least how to say it.

What she said surprised me: "You're probably right. I think there may be times when Carri and Kale are avoiding you."

I doubt I disguised any of the pain I felt when I asked, "But why?"

"Well . . ." Lucy pursed her lips, sighed softly and looked me right in the eyes with what I instantly recognized as her "no-nonsense-here-it-is-Bub" look. "I suspect a big part of the reason is that most of the time when they do come in to see you, they feel like they're walking into an Inquisition. You want to know how much homework they have, whether they've started it, how long it'll take them, when their next tests are and whether or not they ought to be studying for them. You want to know if the grass has been cut, the bushes trimmed, the dogs fed, the garbage hauled out, and the garage straightened up. And if they do have everything done, you've always got some new chores to add to the list.

"Now that football's over and you're not occupied with coaching, they feel more bugged than ever. They're just kids," Lucy assured me. "You can't expect them to come looking for new chores to do every day. And no teenager ever wants to get the third degree from his parents if he can avoid it."

Part of me wanted to respond with an angry "But . . ." and give an impassioned defense of my behavior and my feelings.

Yet, in my heart I had to admit she was probably right.

And I thought I understood why. The more frustrated, limited, and out of control I felt physically, the more control I tried to exert over others. The less I could do, the more compelled I felt to make sure everything was getting done.

I'd always been a perfectionist; maybe I'd always been too demanding. Had the kids always wanted to avoid my demands? Maybe their true feelings came out only because they could avoid me now that I couldn't follow them or even call to them as they walked by in the hallway.

If that was the case, I wanted to change. I wanted to knock down any barriers between me and the children. And once again, Lucy found the right way to help.

LUCY

Charlie really worked on changing the tone of his interaction with the kids. He still asked questions, but he tried not to grill them all the time. He still handed out chores and wanted to know what had been done, but he tried to limit the number of those conversations.

I encouraged Carri and Kale to make a point of talking to Charlie every day about what was going on at school and with their friends. And I began to see a change not only in their relationships with Charlie but in his spirits, and I realized how important it was, now more than ever, for Charlie not to feel isolated but involved in the lives of those around him.

One reason our own relationship had stayed so strong was that I'd always talked to him about what I was doing. I'd tell him about real estate clients, houses, prices, and ask his opinion on various developments. I think I'd instinctively realized how important that kind of communication was between the two of us.

Now the difference Carri and Kale's improved communication made with their dad gave me other ideas. I encouraged the nurses who took care of Charlie during the day to talk to him more about their own lives—their friends, their families. And I think that played an important role in Charlie's acceptance of his nurses.

The first one of them to become a special part of the Wedemeyer family was a nursing student by the name of Leslyn. Charlie nicknamed her "Little Falcon" because she stood only five feet tall and had graduated from one of our biggest rival schools—the Saratoga Falcons. Charlie teased her mercilessly about her height, but she'd turn and give it right back to him by pointing out that she was head and shoulders above him whenever she pushed him around in his wheelchair.

Leslyn exuded a confidence in caring for Charlie that many of our earlier nurses never had. And she quickly developed an intuitive relationship with Charlie. She became so good and so fast at reading his needs and his wishes, not to mention his lips, that Charlie soon trusted her more than he'd trusted anyone but me.

And Leslyn set new standards for our nurses in other ways. With a wonderful willingness to do anything to help, she'd not only nurse Charlie but clean up the kitchen, do dishes, or even wash loads of clothes. Just as she involved herself in our family's life she allowed us to become part of hers. We met her family and she often brought her boyfriend over to visit. And soon we felt so comfortable with her that we let her take over the instruction and training of new nurses.

A few weeks after she started working for us she introduced us to her good friend Lynn who soon became another regular nurse and also a special honorary member of the Wedemeyer clan. Eventually Lynn's husband volunteered to come and help get Charlie out of bed when our friend Bill Bowman couldn't be there.

The nurses provided more than just relief for me and help with Charlie's daily care. They became a valuable social link between Charlie and the outside world. And I'd always felt the more of those links Charlie had, the happier and healthier he would be.

Not that Charlie had become a recluse. He'd maintained

close contact with family. And there was football where he had relationships with his players and the assistant coaches. Even after communication grew more difficult and the weekly post-game pizza parties to plan for next week's game became a thing of the past, we continued to socialize with Charlie's assistants and their spouses or girlfriends. The Hawaiian trip had been the biggest special event we'd staged for the coaching staff. But we'd always hosted a big Christmas party, complete with gag gifts and a crazy agenda of fun and games that Charlie planned and insisted everyone take part in.

When these relationships and social events were at Charlie's initiative, on Charlie's terms, he loved them. But when it came to new and unfamiliar territory, when Charlie wasn't in control, when someone invited us to be a part of their plans, especially if it required going out in public, Charlie assumed an entirely different attitude.

Leslyn and Lynn were good at encouraging Charlie to get out and go places. Their can-do attitude inspired him to do things he hadn't attempted for years.

Yet getting him to accept an invitation to someone's home, or even to go out to eat, took more persuasion than I could muster a lot of the time. He remained concerned about what other people were thinking, worried about being embarrassed.

I thought he sometimes carried his concern about appearance to ridiculous extreme. Occasionally I told him so.

I remember the day two of his former players who were back from college on break, stopped by the house to pay Charlie a surprise visit.

After giving them both a welcome hug and inviting them into the living room, I went back to the bedroom to bring Charlie out. I knew he'd be excited to see these boys.

But when I told him they were waiting in the living room to see him, he got this stricken look on his face and said, "I can't go out there!"

"Then they can come back here."

"No," he said. "I can't see them this afternoon."

I couldn't believe it. "Why not?"

"I'll have to change. And I'm not even shaved."

I tried to convince Charlie these boys had come to see him, not shoot a photo spread for *GQ*. To no avail. He refused to see anyone until he looked more presentable.

After a quick trip to the living room to apologize for the delay and assure the boys, "Coach will be ready shortly," I raced back to the bedroom to get him ready. I finally got him changed and convinced him the boys couldn't wait long enough for me to shave him. So, we got out to the living room for a nice but brief visit, before our visitors had to hurry to the airport.

We almost lost another meaningful opportunity that spring when John Griffin invited us to his graduation party. Charlie and John had always had a special rapport that went beyond their coach-quarterback relationship. Because his dad had been team doctor for years and his two older brothers had played for Charlie, we'd known John and watched him grow up since elementary school. His respect for Charlie and his easy acceptance of Charlie's handicap had helped set an example that carried over to the whole team during his years on the varsity. John had always had such a good grasp of Charlie's complex offense and he'd been so great at understanding his coach's worsening speech that Charlie had expressed some doubts to me about whether or not he could continue to coach the coming year without John at quarterback.

I not only wanted to go, I felt we needed to go. We'd missed the older Griffin boys' graduations, I figured we should make an extra effort for John. I knew Charlie deep down felt the same way. But the day we got the invitation in the mail and I showed it to Charlie, he responded the way he usually did to any social invitation.

"I can't go," he said. "You should go."

"We both need to go," I argued. And I went on to remind him how much the Griffin boys had meant to us and how much the family would appreciate our going, all of which I realized Charlie already knew.

My husband could be extremely stubborn when he'd made up his mind. But this time I was just as stubborn. I kept insisting we tell the Griffins we'd be coming, until Charlie eventually surrendered with a reluctant, "Okay. Okay. We'll go."

But after I thought I had Charlie won over, circumstances conspired against me. Almost everything went wrong the day of the party. One of the nurses called in sick and by the time I filled in for her and found another nurse to cover for her, I'd fallen hopelessly behind schedule.

"We're going to be late," Charlie said.

"No, we'll be fine," I assured him, knowing he was probably right.

Getting Charlie bathed and dressed took even longer than usual. Starting time for the party came and went. Contracted muscles kept Charlie's toes curled down so badly we had a terrible time slipping his loafers on without painfully doubling his toes under his feet.

In the middle of everything Charlie had one of his coughing spells and we had to break out the hot water and spit bowl. By the time we got him breathing easily and in a clean, dry shirt again, I realized the party was more than half over.

Charlie was even more aware of the time than I was. "No sense going now," he said. "It's too late."

"It's not too late!"

"The party's almost over! I'm not going."

I sensed growing resolve. "John will still be there. So will the family. We told them we were coming, they'll be counting on it. I'll apologize for being late if you want, but we have to go."

Charlie quit arguing, we loaded him in the car and we went. Sure enough, the party was going strong when we got there. John's older brother Bobby came out to the car to help get Charlie out. And the moment we rolled Charlie in the door John rushed over to greet us both with a hug.

"Hey, Coach," he said teasingly, "I think we still have a little teriyaki chicken left."

Charlie laughed and licked his lips.

"I'm so glad you could make it, Coach," John said seriously.

"Coach wouldn't have missed this for anything," I assured him, avoiding Charlie's darting sideways glance. We ended up staying and talking long after the party had been scheduled to end.

By the time I got Charlie home and in bed, we were both exhausted. But he'd obviously enjoyed himself so much I couldn't help asking, "Now aren't you glad you went?"

He scowled at my obvious I-told-you-so manner. But I knew it was only mock anger even before his face softened into a small smile and he admitted, "I had a good time."

I hated having to push, but I firmly believed Charlie needed to do things like that to feel he could still be a part of other people's lives. Even when it took extra effort. And even as it got harder, which it was about to do.

part five

CHAMPIONSHIP QUEST

chapter sixteen

BITTER DEFEAT

LUCY

Despite my earlier doubts that Charlie would see Hawaii again, we planned one more "final" visit to the islands that summer of 1984. Although Charlie had lost even more strength since our first-of-the-year trip with the Los Gatos coaching staff, our nurses, Leslyn and Lynn, made this journey seem less of a physical ordeal.

And the Wedemeyer "ohana" (family) warmth and love along with the beauty of the Hawaiian paradise rejuvenated us. We even managed to get Charlie out in the ocean for the first time in years by propping him in one of those floating lawn chairs and towing him out into the shallow water of the lagoon used for shooting the opening of "Magnum P.I."

But even in that idyllic setting, thousands of miles from Los Gatos, Charlie kept coaching. Charlie's number one quarterback prospect for the upcoming fall season was Brock Bowman, son of long-time friends Bill and Heidi Bowman. When Charlie learned the Bowmans were planning a first-time family vacation in Hawaii, he told them, "You need a tour guide. Let's all go together." And then, because his starting quarterback would be in Hawaii with us, Charlie also invited one of his leading running backs, Brock's friend Jeff, to make the trip as well.

Charlie made good use of the Hawaiian vacation time to get the boys in shape for the coming season. Brock and Jeff ran miles along the beach every day, and whenever he had a spare minute, Charlie had them practicing pass patterns until their tongues hung out. Some days he kept them going long after dark in what the boys called "moon drills" where they executed the most precisely timed pass plays—solely by lunar light in the schoolyard down the street from where we stayed.

While I had little doubt all that extra practice would pay off for those boys come fall, what they learned on that trip from Charlie didn't begin to compare with the very important lesson Charlie learned from them. Early on our second morning in Hawaii, they met me in the hallway outside our bedroom and asked, "Is Coach awake yet?"

"Yes," I reported, "but I haven't shaved him yet. He'll be out in . . ." Before I could finish, Brock and Jeff walked right into the room and plopped down on the edge of Charlie's bed to chat.

I sensed Charlie's discomfort. It was only 7:30 in the morning. He still wore the wrinkled t-shirt and shorts he'd slept in. His hair hadn't been perfectly combed yet. And then there was his stubbly beard. I knew he didn't feel presentable. But the boys didn't seem to even notice; they were excited about being in Hawaii and wanted to talk with their coach about football, plans for the day, anything. So as they talked I began to give Charlie his shave.

These early morning bull sessions became a daily routine for the remainder of our time in Hawaii. By the end of the trip Charlie looked forward to them every morning. And I've been grateful ever since to Brock and Jeff for helping Charlie get beyond his hang-up of always worrying about how he looked before he could entertain visitors.

But there were other such lessons yet to be learned. About denial, fear, and pride.

Charlie's strength waned so severely and his coughing and choking episodes became so frequent that no matter how early I planned to leave work and come home each afternoon to ready Charlie for football practice, I could never be sure we'd get to the school on time.

Some days it would take twice as long to dress Charlie as others. And if he gagged or began a coughing fit while we were getting ready, there was nothing to do but ride the incident out—whether it took ten minutes or an hour.

The assistant coaches would start practice without us when we ran behind schedule, which happened quite often. But whenever we'd drive up to find the team already at work, Charlie would be so upset and embarrassed by our tardiness that he'd plunge right in and take over practice without apologizing or explaining why we were late.

Looking back we can see it was a big mistake not to explain what was going on. No telling what the assistant coaches were thinking: that practices weren't a priority with us, that our time was worth more than theirs, or that we just didn't have the same commitment we'd had before. We were so concerned about putting the best face on things and not wanting any pity for our struggles that we didn't stop to consider the potential for misunderstanding.

And we did struggle. One day, waiting for Kale's frosh-soph practice to end, we sat in the old borrowed mini-bus we used to transport Charlie, when he began to cough and choke convulsively. Each time he coughed Charlie slid a little farther down in his chair, forcing his chin down against his chest, tightening his throat and further closing off his windpipe.

Bending awkwardly beneath the ceiling of the bus, Lynn and I tried to brace and lift him. But he slumped lower and lower with each coughing spasm. I feared Charlie was going to die right there in that bus because we didn't have enough strength to hoist him back in an upright position. But at that very moment I spotted Kale walking toward us. At my shout, he sprinted for the bus. Seeing instantly what was happening, he bounded aboard, grabbed Charlie under the arms and straightened him back up—holding him upright until the coughing subsided and he began breathing easier again.

Another day, after I'd rushed home from my office to dress Charlie for practice, we were shuffling slowly down the hall on our way out of the house at the moment another coughing spell hit. When I felt Charlie's knees begin to buckle there was nothing I could do to keep him from falling to the floor except pin him against the wall with my own body and try to hold him there until the coughing gradually subsided. By then we both felt too exhausted to move.

Finally, in a voice full of angry frustration, Charlie demanded to know, "Why do you keep making me go to practice? I can never make it on time!"

I felt like screaming, *What do you mean, "Why do I keep making you go? I'd much rather stay home and take a nap!"* But before I could say anything, Charlie's question hit me. *Why AM I knocking myself out day after day? Why ARE we pushing so hard to keep going?* I didn't know. I couldn't explain it. Yet now, when I stopped to really think about it, I realized it certainly wasn't for me. But it wasn't just for Charlie either. There was something else, something I sensed but didn't understand and couldn't put into words that was pushing me to keep going and to keep Charlie going.

I tried to explain that to Charlie. Whether he understood it any better than I did, he went to practice that day without further protest. Thankfully. Because I had no idea what I'd do if he did actually give up. For years I'd drawn inspiration and strength from Charlie's drive, his incredible spirit of determination. Some days it seemed the only thing keeping either of us going. If he lost that will to keep going, to keep coaching, I knew I didn't have enough left to keep him alive.

Yet neither Charlie's assistant coaches, nor any of our other friends, knew just how close we were to the edge physically and emotionally.

This lack of open communication helped create, or at least contributed to, a growing sense of tension within the Los Gatos

*High School coaching staff. The unpredictability and uncertainty of
a situation that had dragged on for years created stress for everyone
involved. Then there was the interference caused by the increasing
media attention on Charlie. Add to that Charlie's perfectionism and
demanding standards and the situation was ripe for staff frustration and discontent. Charlie'd want to go over plays again and
again, instructing the squad to do "One more!" so many times the
players began teasing him: "How many 'one more's,' Coach? Ten?
A hundred?" But the assistant coaches (who'd arrived at practice
on time after already putting in a long day in the classroom) were
usually ready to go home long before Charlie wanted to knock off.*

*Both Charlie and Lucy sensed new tensions, but they remained
too focused on their own survival to give it much thought. There
was after all another, logical explanation for new and greater
feelings of pressure. For on top of everything else, the 1984 Los
Gatos Wildcats, both players and coaches, carried the added weight
of the entire community's unprecedented expectations for a team
many predicted would be the school's best ever.*

CHARLIE

As head coach, I had high expectations of my own for that
talented 1984 team. I knew going into the season that we
had a good shot at going farther than any Los Gatos team in
history— maybe all the way to the California Central Coast
Sectional championship.

When we opened our season with a convincing 27–0
victory over Saratoga High School, traditionally one of our
toughest opponents, everyone's expectations climbed. They
soared even higher over the next five weeks as our potent
offense averaged 44-plus points a game and our defense
gave up but seven points total against five opponents.

USA Today ranked the Los Gatos Wildcats number one in
the country among schools our size. And while all my life
I'd found enjoyment and satisfaction in the role of an
underdog, I had to admit it felt pretty good to be the team
everyone else was gunning for. I couldn't have been
prouder of that team's performance week after week.

Because this was Lucy's second season with me on the sidelines, that arrangement seemed more natural to me. She knew more of the terminology and what to expect. So I didn't have to worry about a repeat of the problem we'd had in our very first game the year before. While sending in a first down pass play I instructed Lucy to "Call MAX." By the time I realized Lucy was looking frantically up and down the bench for some player named Max, it was too late to straighten out the confusion and change the play.

"Who's Max? There isn't anyone named Max."

"MAX isn't a player!" I told her. "It means maximum pass protection; I wanted all the backs to stay in the backfield and block for the quarterback."

"Oops!" was her only response.

"You're fired!"

"And who pray tell is going to interpret for you?"

"I don't know," I replied as the play began to unfold. But after we completed the pass for a nice gain I had no choice but to rehire her again for the remainder of the game.

Fortunately Lucy is a quick read; we never had that problem again though sideline communication remained a challenge. As quickly as possible I'd decide what to call and reel off the play to Lucy who would almost simultaneously repeat my words over a headset to my assistant coach Butch. Then using hand signals, he would relay the call out to the quarterback who then called the play in the huddle. Despite this multi-step procedure we had to go through on every play, we never (in all the time Lucy was with me on the sidelines) received a delay of game penalty.

The last three games of the 1984 regular season proved only a little tougher; we won all three by an average of almost four touchdowns. In the minds of everyone concerned with Los Gatos football—players, coaches, fans, the entire community—our undisputed league championship and undefeated regular season record was merely a necessary warm-up for the playoffs. Never before had we gotten past the first round. But this looked to be our year to win it all.

We did win the first week of the playoffs, downing Seaside with a score of 29–12. And in our second round, we eked out a 13–7 win over Wilcox after Brock was knocked out of the game with a concussion and we had to finish the game with our back-up quarterback. But our semi-final opponent, St. Francis, fielded the toughest team we'd faced all year.

The impressive record of our team, my ongoing battle with ALS, and the novelty of having a coach's wife on the sideline relaying all the plays had drawn quite a bit of media coverage throughout the regular season. But that attention was nothing compared to the media barrage that began when we reached the playoffs.

The producers who'd shot the documentary came back to follow our quest for the championship. All the Bay Area papers and several local television stations reported our team's story. And the week leading up to the semi-final showdown with St. Francis, it seemed every newspaper in California wanted an interview. While I remained very uncomfortable with all this personal attention, what bothered me most was the fear that all this hoopla would be a distraction for the team as we prepared for the biggest high school football game in Los Gatos's history.

LUCY

I remember one of the interviews Charlie granted that week at the beginning of a practice. The reporter stood alongside the golf cart at the edge of the field and repeatedly asked questions about the ALS, and about us. Charlie kept trying to redirect the interview.

"This is his biggest game ever as a coach" I told the reporter, reading my husband's lips. "But Charlie says he wants the focus to be on the players, not him. He says these boys are great; they've had a wonderful year."

Acknowledging the speculation that this would be Charlie's last season and this the last shot at a championship, the reporter asked how long he wanted to coach.

Charlie grinned at me and whispered his answer. I had to bite my lip and turn toward the practice field where the team ran through their warm-up drills.

"I'm sorry," the reporter finally said. "I didn't catch coach's answer."

"He said," I took a deep breath to maintain my composure, "he'd like to coach forever."

But he couldn't. Charlie knew it. I knew it. So did the media, which is why reporters swarmed around us all week. I think everyone sensed this was the end of the coaching line for Charlie. And what an unbelievable storybook ending it would be if he could win the CCS championship in his very last game.

Only St. Francis stood between Los Gatos and a berth in the finals. However, St. Francis was the two-time defending CCS champion. So it wasn't going to be easy.

On the morning of the game, the *San Jose Mercury News* ran a major front page story, featuring a huge photo of us in the golf cart as I was adjusting Charlie's Los Gatos hat. Charlie hated the photo and I knew why. It emphasized his helplessness and pandered to the readers' pity. We didn't like the story either. Starting with the headline, "Losing to Disease, Coach Leads His Team to Victory," and all the way to the end, the focus was on Charlie and his condition with only seemingly incidental mention of the game. This after Charlie had granted the interview with the understanding that the story would be upbeat and not dwell on his illness.

All the media attention had its impact. A capacity crowd packed the stands early that evening. And when I drove the golf cart out onto the field during warm-ups, Charlie received a spontaneous standing ovation so loud and long it nearly overwhelmed us. We'd never experienced anything quite like it.

While the San Jose paper's story upset Charlie and the sheer number of reporters clamoring for interviews and quotes that last week had been a hassle, those were mere annoyances compared to the media migraine that descended on us that evening against St. Francis.

So many press people surrounded us during warm-ups that Charlie couldn't watch the players running their drills. The situation didn't improve when the game started. A soggy turf made maneuvering the golf cart up and down the bench difficult enough, without having our way and our view blocked by the photographers and minicam crews who had obviously been assigned to cover us rather than the game.

No matter how many times I asked them to turn off their lights so we could see, Charlie actually missed seeing some of the on-field action. The St. Francis Lancers scored early on a 10-yard pass play. They kept our offense stymied by blitzing their safety—a wrinkle they'd added especially for this game. We had trouble adjusting to their surprise strategy and didn't manage to score and tie the game, 7–7, until late in the second quarter.

At half-time Charlie and I talked to his assistants about our media problems. Butch complained to a CCS official who promised to talk to the press. So the second half action was a little easier for us to see, although one obnoxious photographer persisted in sneaking right up to the cart and practically blinding us with his flash.

Early in the third period we recovered a St. Francis fumble. Brock Bowman completed two quick passes, before our leading running back, Todd Mayo, ran for a 15-yard touchdown to put Los Gatos ahead 14–7.

In the fourth quarter one of our backs intercepted a pass to give us the ball on the Lancer 25. The Los Gatos bench went wild. I could sense victory; a ten-yard gain would bring us into field goal range and we could put the game out of reach.

But the offense couldn't move the ball in four downs. St. Francis took over and launched a 56-yard bomb. Four of our backs had St. Francis's best receiver surrounded when he hit the ground and the ball fell right into his arms for a completion. Two plays later the Lancers scored a touchdown and added the extra point to tie the game at 14–14.

We failed to score on our next possession. But with only

two minutes to go in the game, a St. Francis receiver coughed up the football, Jeff Blaisdell grabbed it, broke free and sprinted down field for the winning touchdown. The Los Gatos sideline exploded. I let out a scream and began to whoop with the players as Jeff crossed the goal line. But when I looked back at Charlie I saw the grimace on his face.

He'd already seen what everyone had missed, an official running down the field and waving his arms. The referee had ruled the play dead—calling an incomplete pass. No touchdown. Two minutes later, the gun sounded with the score deadlocked.

I realized we couldn't end on a tie—one of the teams would play in the finals the next week. But it wasn't until regulation time ran out and the officials informed the benches they had a five minute break prior to overtime, that I knew anything about the "The California Tie-Breaker," which our state's high schools use to decide football games that can't end in a tie.

In this variation of sudden death, the ball is placed on the 50-yard line. Each team alternates for four downs. Whichever team makes the most yardage wins.

The coaches huddled around the golf cart to discuss strategy. But Charlie's plan was simple. "We'll pass every play," he told Butch.

Our offense took the field first. Brock Bowman completed a 13-yard pass in what looked like a great start for the Wildcats. But there was a yellow flag in the mud. A holding call, the first penalty of the game, not only nullified the gain but set us back 15 yards to our own 35.

Now everyone in the stadium knew we had to pass on our next play. Brock searched in vain for an open receiver until St. Francis's pass rush caught and sacked him for a huge loss back on our own 18. Two more desperation plays failed. So when St. Francis took possession they didn't have to do anything. The game was over.

Los Gatos lost.

I felt so stunned I almost failed to respond when St. Francis's coach came running across the field and leaned down under the golf cart canopy to squeeze Charlie's arm and tell him, "It was a great game, Coach. You guys gave us the best game we've had all year. The California Tie-Breaker is a terrible way to lose."

I remember Charlie's assistant coach and friend, Larry Matthews, coming over to hug Charlie. "Sorry, Charlie," he said. "I thought we had 'em there."

Of course the media surrounded us again to get our response to the loss. I was frustrated and upset enough about the way they'd interfered during the game that I'd have been tempted to tell them to leave us alone and drive away. But Charlie answered every question patiently and politely. He didn't complain about any of the questionable calls made by the officials, he didn't even lament the tie-breaker procedure that cost us the game. "St. Francis has a terrific team," he said. "They have a great winning tradition."

"What will you do now, Coach?" a reporter asked.

Charlie smiled and mouthed for me to interpret, "Get ready for next season."

When all the reporters had finally drifted away and the last of our supporters and friends had offered their encouragements, I started the golf cart and drove slowly off the field.

The field gradually darkened as someone extinguished one bank of lights after another even as we circled the cinder track toward the exit. Suddenly, out of the shadows a tiny figure stepped onto the track in front of us and I braked the cart to a stop.

A five- or six-year-old boy, wearing Los Gatos colors, timidly approached us. "What is it, honey?" I asked.

He held out his hand. I reached out and accepted his offering—a small, crumpled up candy wrapper. "For Coach . . . and Mrs. Coach," he added.

I opened the package and found the last two M&M candies in the bag—one for Charlie and one for me. I just wanted to hug the little guy, but I didn't. "Coach says thanks," I told him.

"You're welcome," he said. And as he turned and walked slowly away he looked back over his shoulder to add, "Maybe we'll do better next year."

So it was that we left that field after the most devastating loss we'd ever experienced with the bitterness of our disappointment tempered by the taste of M&M's and the sweet encouragement of a little boy whose name we never knew. As we reached the parking lot, the last of the stadium lights blinking out behind us, leaving the field and Charlie's championship dreams in darkness.

chapter seventeen

ONE QUIET
VICTORY

CHARLIE

While winning isn't everything, it certainly beats losing. And win or lose, you replay every game again and again in your mind, wondering which plays you should have called differently, what formations you might have changed, how you could have better anticipated your opponent's strategy. But I'd always tried not to let any on-the-field failures carry over into my daily relationships with family and friends.

That semi-final loss to St. Francis hurt more than any I had ever experienced however. And in the weeks that followed, the pain persisted—darkening my days and my spirits.

Expectations had been so high. The players'. Our fans'. The coaching staff's. Mine.

The high ranking. Our undefeated regular season. The first wins in the playoff. All the team's hard work.

All the ingredients had been in place for a CCS championship. But it hadn't happened. And though I hadn't been able to admit it, I knew in my heart: *Now it will never happen.* As weak as I was, and growing weaker every day, I didn't see how I could cope with the demands of another football season. And that sense of loss hurt more than the playoff defeat.

As long as I could coach, I'd been able to use my mind, feel a part of something bigger than myself, focus on what I could do instead of worry about my limitations, and contribute something to the people closest to me. Without coaching, I would have nothing to give; I'd lose one of the biggest reasons I had to go on living.

Lucy tried to encourage me by being her usual, upbeat, and optimistic self. But by this time my spirits were as hard to prop up as my body.

I remember the December afternoon my assistant coach Eric Van Patten and his girlfriend, Diane, stopped by to visit. After the tensions among the staff throughout the fall, I truly appreciated Eric's obvious intent to keep the communication lines open and maintain the long friendship we'd shared.

Lucy came into the bedroom to tell me our company had arrived. "I'll bring them back to see you," she said.

"No," I told her. "I'd rather go out to the living room." The bedroom always seemed too small and cramped for receiving visitors.

"Then I'll tell them we'll just be a minute." When Lucy returned she helped me out of bed.

"I need to go to the lua first," I said.

"Okay," Lucy said. She held me upright and we began a tediously slow shuffle into the bathroom. We were barely through the door when I began to cough. My knees buckled and I would have crashed to the floor if Lucy hadn't instantly tightened her grip on my arm and wedged me against the wall with her body. I felt her muscles strain and tried to stiffen my legs to help, but with each cough I could feel another bit of strength seep from my body. When the first spasm of coughing passed, it was all Lucy could do to move me over and ease me onto the seat.

Breathing hard from the exertion, Lucy said, "I'll get the hot water and the spit bowl. Sit still."

Another time I might have grinned at Lucy's attempted humor and made a snappy retort. But I hadn't the strength to do anything but cough and try to keep from sliding off the toilet seat.

Lucy returned within moments with the hot water to begin the grueling sip and spit routine. By the time the phlegm broke up enough so that I quit coughing we were both drenched in sweat.

"Okay now?"

I nodded, still fighting to catch my breath. "I just . . . need to . . . rest . . . a little."

"Sure," she replied. Bending down to hold my shoulders to keep me balanced, Lucy looked as drained as I felt.

At that moment, I sensed the utter futility of my life. While thoughtful friends waited nearly an hour in the living room to see me, and my exhausted, loving wife stood watching over me, I sat hopelessly on a lua seat, too weak to move and too discouraged to keep fighting.

Tears of humiliation and frustration welled up in my eyes as I looked up at Lucy, sighed in resignation, and said what I'd felt was true for a long time: "You and the children would be better off if I died."

I'll never forget Lucy's reaction. Later I learned my words had so startled her that she silently prayed, "Please God, give me the words to say." Slowly, deliberately, she straightened up as she gathered her thoughts and looked right at me. In an almost angry, don't-you-forget-it tone tempered by the love in her eyes, she said, "We would rather have you like this, than not have you at all."

I was suddenly overcome by emotion, overwhelmed by the love of this woman who had already been through so much with me. I'd never in my life felt so loved by her. I'd never felt so much love for her. I began to sob. She put her arms around me and we sobbed together. And after a time we regained enough composure and strength to get to the living room for a short visit with our guests.

I had no idea how long I would continue to live. But I knew I'd never forget Lucy's words that day. What I didn't know was how many times the memory of those words would help keep me alive by giving me the will to continue fighting for my next breath.

As swallowing had gotten harder and harder for Charlie his weight had dropped to 115 pounds. His body was so bony he could never get comfortable. Lucy would pile pillows around and under his elbows and his "okole" (Hawaiian for bottom) for support and comfort. But still she had to shift and move him every fifteen to twenty minutes all night long. He stayed so tired and weak that it took all the energy he had just to move the slightest puffs of air in and out of his lungs.

Whenever fatigue finally outweighed his fear of dying in his sleep, Charlie would doze off for short snatches of time. Sometimes while he slept Lucy had to watch intently just to see his chest move and reassure herself that he was still alive.

Charlie very possibly wouldn't have lived through the year, and Lucy certainly couldn't have continued to function on a daily basis, if it hadn't been for the part-time nursing care they hired through a local registry service. But those nurses were expensive.

Fortunately, some of the Wedemeyers' friends had been keeping tabs on the special medical account started with the proceeds from the "We Love Charlie" campaign. So as Charlie and Lucy approached the end of their resources, these people began talking about another, bigger fund raiser. This time they cooperated with the local chapter of NFL Alumni to plan a special, $100-a-plate dinner. But when they set the date for Friday, January 11, 1985, Lucy wondered if Charlie would live long enough to attend. The closer the time came, the more doubts she had.

LUCY

I could no longer deny the obvious.

Everyone who knew Charlie realized the end had to be near. Uncle Bud, who's a doctor, called me one day to talk because he wanted me to be prepared for what he saw coming. "You know, Lucy," he said. "You've spent most of the last eight years of your life taking care of Charlie. I don't think you realize what a huge hole there will be in your life when he's gone. It'll be a very difficult adjustment."

I appreciated his concern. But I thought to myself, *Adjustment? No problem. I'll just sleep the first three years.* But as exhausted as I felt, I wasn't ready for Charlie to die. And I certainly wasn't going to let him give up on life as long as either of us had any strength left to fight.

Some days that wasn't much.

One frightening January night in particular, I thought we'd lose him for sure. It started like just another one of Charlie's middle-of-the-night coughing spells. The night nurse and I began the usual spit bowl routine—to no avail. Soon Kale and Carri came in to help and the four of us clustered tightly and awkwardly around the bed in the tiny bedroom—ready reinforcements in Charlie's battle for breath. Using a big paper fan, Carri tried to keep Charlie from overheating while Kale helped prop his dad upright, lifting him back into a sitting position each time he coughed and slid down in the bed. For more than an hour the nurse and I bent over that bed, alternately tipping and supporting Charlie's head so he could sip and spit.

No matter what we did, the coughing continued. Charlie grew weaker, his skin grayer. Nothing helped. I felt so helpless, so inadequate as I watched Charlie strain desperately for one more breath. And then another.

The growing fear I saw in my husband's eyes I felt in the depths of my own soul. He was dying and there was nothing I could do to stop it.

"He's not breathing!" I don't know who realized it first.

"Call 911!" Carri ran to make the call.

In the sudden chaos that followed, Kale leaped onto the bed with Charlie, yanked him into a more erect sitting position, pried his mouth open and jammed the catheter end of a suction machine hose back down into Charlie's throat to try to clear any congestion and open up the airway. Charlie reflexively gagged and began coughing again. By the time the paramedics arrived he had returned to consciousness and was gasping for air.

The paramedics administered oxygen and Charlie's breathing eased a little. But when they prepared to lift him from his bed to a stretcher, Charlie had me ask how much it was going to cost to transport him to the hospital. When they told us the standard ambulance fee would be $250, Charlie said, "No thanks! I think I'll wait till I can walk."

The paramedics laughed and were very understanding. Seeing that Charlie seemed to have stabilized, they left us a supply of oxygen, told us to call again if we needed them and went on their way.

Charlie survived that terrifying incident, but he'd clearly reached an all-time low. So I began slipping from the room when nurses were there in order to call the family in Hawaii and tell them to try to come a day or two before the banquet if they could. I wasn't at all sure Charlie could last the week.

Leslyn spent most of the day Monday trying to feed Charlie a bowl of soup. I lost count of the number of times she reheated that bowl in the microwave, only to have the first spoonful gag him and trigger a coughing fit that lasted until the soup was cold again.

His breathing grew so labored that I stayed around the house all day, afraid to leave him, taking my turn trying to feed him. Leslyn didn't comment aloud about Charlie's weakening condition, but I saw the concern in her eyes.

Late that afternoon I needed to drop some papers off at Joan Matthew's home. She was hosting a meeting about final plans for the fund raising dinner. Yet I hated to leave the house; I just had this feeling something was going to happen with Charlie.

Leslyn encouraged me to go on. Though she was about to get relieved by another nurse, she said she'd stay with Charlie to back up the newer nurse until I returned. "I'll give you a call if there is any change at all in his condition," she promised. So I kissed Charlie goodbye and told him I'd be home as soon as I could get back.

When the phone rang halfway through my meeting and Joan said, "It's for you, Lucy," I knew it had to be Leslyn. I took a long, deep breath and managed to accept the receiver with a determined show of calm. But inside I trembled.

"Hello."

"Lucy . . ." Leslyn's voice broke. "Can you come home right away?"

My heart sank. "Is Char–"

"Charlie's fine!"

Then why is Leslyn crying? "What hap–"

"I'll explain everything when you get home. How soon can you be here?"

I made my apologies, hurried out of the meeting and raced home knowing something had happened. *But what?*

CHARLIE

I hadn't wanted Lucy to leave. But I knew she had to be at the meeting to hear the last details about the NFL Alumni dinner. *The dinner. How can I go to the dinner?*

Merely sitting up or going to the bathroom took its toll. Today it seemed to take a conscious, concentrated effort just to keep breathing.

Sometime shortly before Lucy had left, Ramona arrived, walking into the bedroom with a cheery, "Hi, Charlie. Howya doin' today?"

I grinned. "Okay." Ramona had only worked for us a few times. But she had such a warm, caring attitude that I had liked her from the start.

Leslyn filled her in. I don't know what all was said, but I heard mention of the bowl of soup I'd been gagging on all day.

"Want to try to eat a little soup again?" Ramona asked.

I grimaced. "No!" Evidently the human hunger drive isn't as strong as the fear drive. Because the realization that I was slowly starving to death seemed far less terrifying than the more immediate and violent prospect of choking to death on a bowl of soup.

"You need me to do anything right now?" Ramona asked.

"No," I told her. "I'm fine."

I felt so tired. I closed my eyes and tried to rest. But I didn't want to risk falling asleep and choking to death. So I forced opened my eyes again and concentrated on my breathing.

For a while Ramona watched me strain for breath. Then she came and stood beside the head of my bed. "You're having a terrible time getting air today aren't you?" she asked.

"Yeah," I conceded.

"Is it all right if I pray for you?" she wanted to know.

"Sure," I replied, surprised. It certainly couldn't hurt. Ramona had talked to me a little before about her own faith and her need to rely on God. I'd told her that I believed in God.

"I need to touch you," she said. "Is that all right?"

I didn't know what Ramona had in mind. As a nurse she had to touch me to care for me. "Okay," I agreed.

Yet I was still a little startled when she leaned over the bed to place her hands on my chest and began to pray out loud: "Dear Lord, I just ask that you will help Charlie breathe easier so he can sleep. And clear his throat so he can swallow and eat something. Please comfort Charlie and bring peace to his heart."

I watched Ramona's face, her expression prayerfully intent, her eyes closed. I saw her lips moving, I heard the words coming from her mouth, I felt the gentle pressure of her hands on my chest. And as she prayed, something began to happen. I felt a combination of power and peace I'd never known before. It coursed from my chest out to my arms and legs, through my entire being. At the same time it filled the room, a tidal wave of calm and comfort washing over me, a loving presence that held and surrounded me.

When Ramona stopped praying and looked at me, I saw tears streaming down her face. It wasn't until then that I realized I too was weeping. Not in sadness. Not really in joy. The emotion was just so intense, so tangible, so overpoweringly peaceful that it filled me to overflowing and the tears just poured out.

I looked to the other side of the bed at Leslyn. She too was crying. Later she told me that as Ramona prayed, she'd felt such a presence in the room that she kept looking around to see who had come in.

We all knew who it was. I certainly had no question. God was suddenly real to me in a way I'd never imagined before. I felt his love and his care for me. I knew he was real because I felt his undeniable presence and power in me and around me. And if I had any lingering doubts they were dispelled forever when I looked down toward the foot of my bed.

There on a hospital table was a small amaryllis plant a friend had brought me several days earlier. Lucy had watered it and even administered plant food in an attempt to get it to bloom. Nothing had happened. We'd decided something was wrong with the plant and had finally given up on it. I'd grown tired of looking at the scrawny thing and had asked one of the nurses to throw it away earlier in the day. She'd gotten distracted and had forgotten.

Now, after Ramona's prayer, when I looked down and saw the plant a chill went through me. The three buds that had been so tightly closed minutes before were suddenly in full, beautiful bloom. And as I stared in amazement at that flower, it was as if God was speaking directly to me, saying, "I've done a miracle in this plant and I want to do a miracle in your life."

Through my tears I finally got Leslyn to understand that I wanted her to "Call Lucy. Tell her to come home." I wanted her to share this experience.

When I finally quit crying I told Ramona, "I think I'd like to try some of that soup."

Leslyn hurried into the kitchen to heat it up. When she brought it back, I downed it all and wanted more. I ate two entire bowls before I finished—the biggest meal I'd had in months and more food at one time than I'd managed to get down over the last couple weeks altogether.

By the time Lucy rushed through the door, the two nurses were laughing in amazement at my appetite.

LUCY

I don't know what I expected to find when I got home. But since Leslyn had been crying so on the phone, I didn't expect to find the three of them in such high spirits.

The moment I walked through the door I felt a special presence in the room. I wanted to know, "What happened?"

Charlie started to tell me, but he couldn't get the words out fast enough for me to understand. So he let the nurses talk. They recounted Ramona's prayer and the powerful presence in the room. By the time Charlie had gotten me to look at the flower and grinned through the report about the two bowls of soup, we were all crying again.

I thought about other times when I'd prayed and felt God's presence and help. Finally Charlie knew for himself what I'd been talking about.

As we all marveled at what had happened, Ramona acknowledged that God had done something very special for Charlie that afternoon. "But you know," she said, "God wants us to be able to know his presence and help in our lives every day. We can all have that kind of personal relationship with him if we want it. And the way to begin is to tell him you are genuinely sorry for all the things you've done wrong, ask his forgiveness, then invite him to come into your heart and take control of your life."

Ramona looked at Charlie and then at me. "You could do that right now. Would you like to?"

Charlie said, "Yes." And I nodded.

Right there in our bedroom, holding tight to Charlie's hand as I knelt beside the bed, Ramona led us in a very simple prayer. We both asked Jesus to come into our lives.

That night Charlie breathed easier and slept better than he had for months.

chapter eighteen

UNEXPECTED HELP

Neither the reality nor the significance of that amazing spiritual experience sank in for Charlie and Lucy right away. Perhaps because the rest of that week was a wild and crazy blur.

In response to Lucy's phone calls, relatives from both sides of the family began arriving a couple days early for the banquet. Lucy had told them all when she called that Charlie's condition was grave. But none of them were adequately prepared for the physical deterioration that had taken place since they'd last seen him.

Although Lucy and the nurses were encouraged by Charlie's renewed ability to down small sips of soup, the simple act of swallowing continued to be a challenge. And while he seemed to sleep better the next couple of nights, breathing remained difficult. So the periodic choking and coughing spells persisted, striking without warning and threatening to wring the last shred of life from Charlie's frail frame before stopping.

These episodes could be worrisome enough for Lucy and the nurses after they'd been through thousands of them. For Charlie's family, every distressing episode seemed like the end.

And yet the laughter and affection that filled the next couple of days boosted Charlie's spirits and his energy level. So much so that by Friday morning Lucy began to believe (for the first time in several days) that Charlie really might make it to the banquet that night.

LUCY

Getting Charlie dressed Friday evening proved worse than usual. After finally maneuvering him into a suit for the first time in months, we struggled for what seemed like forever to get his feet into his shoes.

At one point in the process Charlie worked up such a sweat with his coughing that we had to strip him to his shorts, spray him with cool water, wipe him down with cold wet washcloths and begin again with a clean, dry shirt. By the time he was ready and I was dressed, I could tell Charlie was upset; it was already time for the pre-dinner reception to begin and we hadn't left the house.

Charlie's adult nephews, Gary and Blane helped Kale wheel Charlie out to our car and the remainder of the clan piled into a couple of other vehicles as I hurriedly turned off the lights and locked the house. But there was no hurrying the painful process of bending and folding Charlie into the front seat of a car: carefully supporting his head and shoulders, while bending his torso, lowering him to the seat, turning him and lifting his legs in after him.

No sooner did we get Charlie buckled in and the door closed than he began to choke and cough again. In hopes of ending this episode before it went very far I whipped out the thermos of hot water I'd packed for such an emergency and gave him a sip. It didn't help.

Charlie wanted hotter water so I sent Kale running back inside. He returned a minute later with a glass of water so hot he had to hold it with a cloth. I took the glass from Kale, but as I reached across the car to hold it to Charlie's lips, the glass slipped out of my hand and that steaming water spilled down Charlie's chest and into his lap, soaking him and his only suit.

Charlie might have screamed if he could have. The expression on his face was loud and clear. And when he looked at me angrily and said, "Take me back in the house. I'm not going!" I knew he meant it. He had been embarrassed enough at the thought of arriving late. He'd be absolutely mortified to arrive late for the banquet wearing his navy blue suit with big dark wet spots in all the wrong places.

"Take me back in the house!"

I ignored Charlie's demand as I tried to think.

"Okay!" I announced, "Everything will be fine!" (I had to say that, partly to reassure myself, and partly to buy a few more seconds to come up with a solution.) "Blane, run and get me some dry towels. Kale get the hair dryer out of my bathr . . . no, Gary, you get the hair dryer. Kale find me an extension cord."

With an amazing, almost instant military precision, those three guys completed their missions. By the time I soaked up all the water I could with the towels, Kale had the cord plugged in and I began to blow-dry my steaming husband.

"It'll be okay, dear. This is drying out just fine," I said, chattering away and refusing to acknowledge Charlie who continued to say, "I'm not going! Take me into the house!"

"Look, sweetheart, the shirt's dry already. And I can hardly see the wet spot on the jacket."

"I'm not going!"

Kale, seeing how adamant his dad was, threw his weight to my side of our verbal tug-of-war. "It'll be okay, Dad. No one will mind if we're a little late. And a lot of people will be disappointed if you're not there at all." Kale's upbeat optimism always had a way of encouraging Charlie when he was down; he could kid and cajole Charlie into doing things when I couldn't budge him. So by the time Charlie's trousers had gone from wet to merely damp, I sensed the fight had gone out of him.

When I announced, "Okay, let's go!" and the guys piled into the back seat I could see Charlie still wasn't happy. But he didn't protest either. So I backed out of the driveway and headed for downtown San Jose as fast I could go.

CHARLIE

I don't know what upset me most: being late for a banquet
in my honor; heading for the banquet in a pair of still soggy
pants; or, the fact I didn't seem to have much of a say in the
matter because my family was determined to drag me there
whether I wanted to go or not.

But the strongest emotion I felt as we approached San
Jose wasn't anger or even frustration. It was dread.

While I appreciated the effort so many friends had made
to plan this banquet, I wished they hadn't done it. Again I
didn't want to be the focus of so much attention.

The moment Kale wheeled me through the double doors
into the San Jose Hyatt's Mediterranean Room, the capacity
crowd rose and welcomed us with a standing ovation. As
we zigged and zagged through the people standing around
their tables many individual voices penetrated the thunder-
ing applause.

"Hiya, Charlie!"

"Good to seeya Coach!"

"Looking good, Charlie!" (That must have been some
nearsighted referee, but I appreciated the encouragement.)

"Go Wildcats!"

Hands reached out to pat my arms or touch my
shoulders. In the crowd we hurried through I spotted the
smiling faces of neighbors, former players, colleagues,
parents of players, and other friends and neighbors.

I neither saw nor sensed the pity I'd dreaded. I
experienced none of the embarrassment I'd expected. What
I felt, what nearly overwhelmed me before we finally
reached the table reserved for us, was a roomful of love and
support. Chills ran up and down my spine and tears welled
up in my eyes. I could never have imagined anything like it.
And the evening's surprises were just beginning.

As we took our places around our table and the crowd
sat back down, Lucy directed my attention to the nearby
dais. There to my amazement was my college football coach
Duffy Daugherty who hurried to our table to kiss Lucy and

give me a hug. Duffy, accompanied by his wife, Francie, had been flown in as one of the keynote speakers.

As those sitting around us finished their meal, a steady stream of people filed up to our table to greet us—friends, acquaintances, and many well-wishers I'd never met. I couldn't believe the number of current and former NFL players who'd come. Some I'd met before but others I'd known only by reputation: Y. A. Tittle, Ray Wersching, Leo Nomelini, Jim Plunkett, Joe "The Jet" Perry, R. C. Owens, and others.

All those guys and other dignitaries, celebrities, and coaches were introduced when the after-dinner program began. So many people said nice things about me I felt a little like Tom Sawyer when he snuck into his own funeral. Several people spoke, but Duffy was the main speaker prior to a number of scheduled presentations.

The *San Jose Mercury News* recognized the CCS High School All-Star Football team, several of whom had played for me at Los Gatos and the rest we'd played against. After the local NFL Alumni chapter presented me with a trophy, San Francisco '49er coach Bill Walsh gave me a football on which he'd written "With great respect, from one coach to another, Bill Walsh." I'd met Bill before at coaching clinics in the Bay Area, but I couldn't believe he'd taken time out of his schedule the week before the '49ers were to play the Super Bowl to come to this banquet.

The most meaningful honor and the biggest surprise of the evening however, came when the emcee said to the crowd and to me: "We have a very special honor and privilege tonight, Charlie, to have a surprise singer to offer a musical tribute to you. Ladies and gentlemen, Miss Carri Wedemeyer!"

Just watching Carri walk up on the platform brought a lump the size of a football to my throat. I hadn't had a clue ahead of time. I looked at Lucy who was grinning in pleasure at my surprise. She'd obviously known, which explained why she hadn't yet let me see the program printed for the evening.

Carri stood at the microphone, waiting for her accompaniment to begin. She looked so calm and composed. But I knew my daughter well enough to imagine how nervous she was. For Carri, a perfectionist like me who shied away from any risk of embarrassment or failure, I could only imagine how hard this was. Just her willingness to do this for me was an unimaginable honor.

As she began to sing, the pianist accompanying her messed up the music and suddenly stopped playing. I cringed for Carri, but she merely stopped and smiled as she waited for the music to start again. I couldn't believe my daughter's poise.

I recognized the song almost immediately—the beautiful theme from the movie *Ice Castles*. A love song. Sung so tenderly I cried as Carri sang it for me in front of all those people. "Please don't let this feeling end . . . knowing you're beside me I'm all right. . . ." Many people had tears in their eyes by the time she finished, including Carri. As she smiled in acknowledgment of the crowd's applause I wished more than anything else in the world I could leap out of my chair, bound onto that platform, and wrap my arms around my daughter for a proud father's hug.

What an evening! As appreciative as I was for the money that banquet raised for my ongoing medical care (the amount raised was more than $60,000), I can honestly say the special memories of that evening meant even more. The whole affair was an unforgettable reminder of how many wonderful friends I have, and how much they cared.

LUCY

A few weeks later another caring friend called us just out of the blue. Neither Charlie nor I had heard from Maria since our school days together at Punahou. But she telephoned from Hawaii to tell us she planned a trip to the mainland, would be passing through the Bay Area, and had a strong feeling that the Lord wanted her to come and see us. I told her we'd be glad to see her.

When Maria arrived we quickly set out to bring each other up to date on the details of our lives. Maria knew much more about us, having read Hawaiian newspaper accounts of Charlie's college athletic career and then the stories about his battle with ALS. She'd also been in touch with mutual friends in Hawaii.

Maria filled us in on her life since high school including some of the difficult times she'd had personally and in her marriage. She told us how discouraging her existence had become, until she'd turned to God, and how the Lord had turned her life and her marriage around.

When she finished talking about her experience with God, I recounted what had happened that day back in January, Charlie on the verge of death, the nurse's prayer, the presence in the room, the amaryllis flower, and the prayer we'd prayed together asking the Lord to come into our hearts. Judging from Maria's excited reaction I think she'd come to see us thinking God wanted her to preach to Charlie and me and convince us of our need for him.

It wasn't long however before we all realized Maria's purpose in coming to see us wasn't to preach, but to teach. Over the next five days Maria helped us understand that what we'd done when we'd prayed and asked God's help back in January was just the beginning. It had been like a birth, a new birth, but God wanted Christians to keep growing and getting stronger spiritually.

Maria told us that praying and reading the Bible regularly was essential training for strong Christians. She read a lot of Bible passages over the next few days—verses about healing, promises of God's help in difficulty, instructions on God's will for our lives. It was like a crash course in Bible 101.

In terms Charlie might have used, it was like a preseason or rookie camp for new Christians. Only instead of grueling two-a-day practices, Maria led all-day workouts. I got in on a lot of sessions, but I had to be in and out, doing business, keeping our daily lives going. Maria and Charlie talked and prayed and read practically non-stop from morning to night.

Every night Maria stayed with us was the same. I had to laugh. She'd be getting drowsy, announce she needed to be heading for bed, and Charlie would say, "How about another minute?" Or "Just one more verse before we quit?" So none of us got to bed before two in the morning.

CHARLIE

Lucy's right. I was like a sponge soaking up everything Maria said.

I'd realized something very special, very important had happened to me when I'd prayed with Ramona back in January. Though I couldn't explain what had happened in theological terms, I knew it had made one very important difference in my life. Although I'd begun having trouble swallowing food again and had my regular choking and coughing spells, I felt a sense of peace that allowed me to drop to sleep at night without that terrifying fear that I might never wake up.

Maria explained that God wanted our faith to do more than reassure us and reduce our fear about death. That it should also make a difference in how we lived our lives each day. After a lifetime of going to church, I finally understood that being a Christian really means having a personal relationship with God. And like any meaningful relationship it was going to take time and effort from me to get to know him better and make our relationship stronger.

The whole idea, the very possibility of getting to know God was so new and exciting that I was ready to do anything. While it still didn't feel very natural to me, I wanted to pray. I wanted to read the Bible because so much of what Maria was reading related so directly to my life. It made sense!

Before Maria left she wrote out a dozen pages of notes, references, and instructions. She included Scriptures I ought to read regularly, Bible promises I needed to turn to when I was discouraged, passages I should memorize. She gave me a step-by-step routine of Bible study and prayer. She even checked the yellow pages, made a few phone calls, and listed some Christian bookstores where she thought I could get some of the Christian books she listed as "must read."

Yet another important individual came into our lives late that spring of 1985. Linda Peevyhouse, a slim brunette and mother of three school-age boys, was fresh out of nursing school. She appeared very competent, efficient, and was a confident, quick study when Leslyn explained my daily routine and went through emergency procedures like the hot-water-spit-bowl procedure for clearing congestion. But I could tell little about her personality. If anything, she seemed unassuming, quiet, and reserved.

We needed more nursing help, so I offered her a chance to become a part-time member of our nursing team. What she didn't tell us until much later was that she went home after that first day of training and told her husband she didn't think she could handle the grueling, physical demands of the job—the lifting and the exhausting routine of my coughing spells. On her second day she concluded, "No way," and made up her mind to quit. Her husband, Wayne, talked her into trying a little longer, and fortunately she changed her mind.

Because in the weeks that followed, Linda saved my life. And in the years since, no nurse has made more sacrifices or had a bigger impact on the way I've been able to continue to live.

chapter nineteen

NO CODE

LUCY

One day in the late spring of 1985, Brock Bowman's younger brother Jason spent several hours at our house doing volunteer yard work and other chores after he'd been up very late working at his part-time job. By the time Charlie convinced him he'd done enough and needed to head home, Jason was exhausted. Driving home on a winding road, he hit a patch of loose gravel, lost control of his car, and crashed. Paramedics rushed him to a nearby hospital where he underwent surgery the next day to repair damage done to his hip in the wreck.

Partly because the accident occurred driving home from our house, but mostly because the Bowmans were such good friends, Charlie wanted to pay Jason a surprise hospital visit the next day.

But it was already late in the evening when Charlie posed the idea. "Fine," I agreed. "We'll go tomorrow."

Charlie wasn't planning to wait. "We could drive over there right now."

"I'm sure it's past visiting hours, dear. Let's do it tomorrow."

Charlie grinned. "I bet we could get in. Gail can go along; who's gonna stop us?"

I looked at Gail, the part-time nurse on duty that evening. She'd come directly from her full-time nursing job at another hospital, still wearing her white nurse's uniform and looking very official. *It just might work.*

A half hour later we waltzed right into Jason's room in the orthopedic ward. No one in the hospital thought to question an obviously sick man in a wheelchair being pushed hurriedly down hospital corridors by an attractive young nurse who looked like she knew where she was headed. People hardly even looked twice at the huge balloon bouquet I carried.

Jason wasn't exactly expecting visitors at 10:30 in the evening. But his face lit up when we slipped into his room and quietly closed the door. "Sorry, Coach!" he said. "I guess I won't be needing you to give me surfing lessons after all." (Another trip to Hawaii with the Bowman family had already been planned and our reservations were only a couple weeks away.)

"I talked to your folks already," I told him. "We're thinking about postponing the trip until after Coach's County All-Star game in late July."

Jason apologized for messing up everyone's plans. We reassured him things would work out, and we were all soon laughing and enjoying our impromptu surprise party. Jason particularly enjoyed the contraband snack of macadamia nuts and kahlua brownies Charlie had insisted we smuggle into the hospital.

All of us except Charlie were still eating a few minutes later when Jason's doctor stuck his head in the room and did a quick double take to find a roomful of visitors munching on a midnight snack. "And what's going on in here?" he asked with mock sternness.

Jason sheepishly made the introductions, obviously expecting the doctor to say something about the breach of hospital protocol. But when the doctor learned who Charlie was, he came in and sat down to talk. A few minutes later he walked down to the nurses' station and returned with Jason's X-rays to show Charlie where he'd inserted the pins and screws. The two of them were soon engrossed in a detailed discussion of football injuries.

When we'd finally bidden goodnight to the doctor and Jason, some of the night-shift nurses gave us curious looks on our way out. But no one said a word.

Charlie had felt honored to have been selected as one of the two head coaches in that summer's County All-Star Football game. Despite his continuing physical decline, he determined to take part in that game. So the second week of July he began directing practices with his talented squad of the past season's top high-school players.

The usual summer conditions had made smog alerts a daily routine in our area. Then a series of serious fires in the foothills above Los Gatos filled the valley with smoke that prompted advisory warnings for anyone suffering from respiratory problems. Air quality was so bad on Saturday the 13th that Charlie coughed uncontrollably on the side-lines throughout most of his all-star team's practice and on the drive home.

He struggled for breath as we helped him into the house. No sooner had Linda, Kale, and I gotten him into bed than he lost consciousness. I watched his chest but detected no movement. "He's not breathing!"

Linda immediately began administering mouth-to-mouth resuscitation even as Carri dialed 911.

By the time the paramedics arrived ten minutes later, Charlie had regained consciousness and was breathing on his own again—barely.

Remembering Charlie's feelings about an ambulance ride back in January, I thanked these paramedics and told them Charlie could use some oxygen, but we wouldn't be needing them to transport him to a hospital.

But this second paramedic crew, two women, were not nearly as polite. Obviously questioning my judgment, they refused to administer any oxygen unless Charlie went with them to the hospital. When I wouldn't change my mind, they marched out of the house and drove away.

Had I done the right thing? I didn't know for sure. Obviously Charlie had reached a new low. His weight was under a hundred pounds and dropping. He had neither the muscle tone nor the energy to even eat efficiently. He obviously needed strength from nourishment that he couldn't get because he couldn't swallow.

When Charlie seemed even weaker the next day, our doctor proposed using an "NG" tube to get some nourishment into him. While Linda tediously worked the tubing through Charlie's nostril and down the back of his throat to his stomach, I quickly set to work pureeing a big bowl of leftover manicotti into a soup we could funnel into him.

Using a stethoscope, Linda listened to make certain the tube had indeed gone into Charlie's stomach and not his lungs. Once she was sure, we began pouring in the manicotti. When we finished the first batch I quickly pureed another. Inserting an NG tube was such an unpleasant procedure (and it didn't make Charlie's breathing any easier either) that we determined to make the most of the moment and fill him up. You've heard of stuffed manicotti. That's what we did to Charlie. And it was the first time Charlie had had a full stomach in months.

The huge meal Lucy and Linda poured into his near-lifeless body gave Charlie the strength to keep breathing through a sleepless night. Yet the paltry puffs of oxygen his lungs took in weren't enough to keep his body systems working.

Lynn, one of their most experienced and trusted aides, was with the Wedemeyers that morning. But by noon, when Charlie no longer responded to her voice, Lucy decided to call Linda for help. Not just because Linda was an R.N., but because she'd been so instrumental in keeping Charlie alive during the crisis of the past couple days.

Linda hadn't been scheduled to be at the Wedemeyers until later in the day. But somehow she knew something was wrong: "Just before noon I had this feeling. Something told me I should go to Charlie's and Lucy's immediately. I stopped fixing lunch and quickly prepared to leave. I was already heading for the door when the phone rang and Lucy asked, 'How fast can you get here? We need you!'"

The moment Linda pulled into the Wedemeyer's driveway, Carri burst out of the house and ran toward her calling, "Hurry! Please hurry! My dad quit breathing again!"

Lynn was already administering mouth-to-mouth, but Linda immediately relieved her. By the time the paramedics arrived a few minutes later, the steady supply of oxygen from their resuscitation effort had lifted Charlie back to consciousness. But he still wasn't breathing on his own. So there seemed nothing else to do but to let the paramedics get him to the hospital and let the emergency room doctors try to keep him alive.

The entire time the paramedics were wheeling Charlie out of the house, Linda maintained her mouth-to-mouth routine. When they loaded him into the ambulance, Lynn and Linda climbed in alongside him while Lucy slid into the front seat next to the driver.

CHARLIE

I don't remember much from that day. When I was conscious, I wasn't getting enough oxygen to keep my mind sharp. I've heard Lucy and Linda recount the story from their perspectives. But my own recollection is mostly a hazy blur, with a few brief flashes of memory.

I remember lights and sirens. And I've never forgotten the terrible taste of fear. I don't remember getting mouth-to-mouth from my nurses. Linda told me the two of them alternated. While one breathed for me, the other one leaned close to my head and prayed for me—out loud. And the one time Linda paused in her prayer, she said I whispered, "Don't stop." So they continued the pattern all the way to the hospital.

The doctor assigned to us in the emergency room pulled Lucy aside and explained that he thought that by performing an immediate tracheotomy—cutting an air hole at the base of my throat and inserting a short tube directly into my windpipe—he could probably allow me to breathe more efficiently. When Lucy gave him the go-ahead, he made sure she understood this was only a temporary measure, a means of easing what he believed, based on my weakened condition, would be my final hours.

The doctor also asked our feelings about the prospect of hooking me up to a life-support system to keep me alive. She told him we'd talked and agreed that when the time came, if I could no longer function and interact with people and that if I went into a coma, we didn't want extraordinary measures taken just to keep my body alive. If it came to that, she told him, I didn't want to be hooked to any machine. I was prepared to die.

"Okay," the doctor said. "But you understand that I'll need to confirm what you're saying with Charlie."

I guess he did talk to me. I don't remember the conversation. About all I can recall from the hospital ER was the panic I felt as the orderlies rolled me down the hall away from my family and friends. Through Lucy, I talked the emergency room doctors into letting Linda accompany me into the operating room: "He can't speak," Lucy explained. "But Linda's a nurse and she can read his lips." Just having Linda beside me eased the worst of my fear.

But when we reached the swinging doors of the OR the staff refused to let Linda enter. I went into that operating room alone—unable to breathe, unable to communicate, and more terrified than I'd ever felt in my life. Then I remembered a Bible verse I'd memorized just the week before, "So do not fear, for I am with you; do not be dismayed, for I am your God. I will strengthen you and help you; I will uphold you with my righteous right hand" (Isaiah 41:10).

Over and over again I repeated that verse in my mind as the operating team gathered around me. The anesthesiologist suctioned my throat, but when he finished I could tell he didn't get everything. I remember desperately trying to tell him, "More. There's more." He didn't understand; or he wouldn't believe me.

The last words I heard as he administered the anesthesia, were "Don't worry. It will all be over soon." I didn't like the sound of that. But I couldn't move or speak to stop him. All I could do was cling to that promise, *So do not fear . . . I am with you . . . I am your God . . . I will strengthen . . .*

The next morning that anesthesiologist stopped by Charlie's intensive care room and as much as apologized. Charlie had been right; there had been more congestion the doctor had missed. They'd almost lost him during the operation because of it.

Even though the tracheotomy cleared his airway and an IV slowly dripped nourishment into his bloodstream, Charlie's atrophied muscles prevented him from taking anything more than the shallowest of breaths. The doctors felt he had only hours to live, a few days at most. The nurses who regularly took samples and saw the report on his blood gases marveled that anyone getting so little oxygen was still alive.

The ICU staff, knowing Charlie was at the point of death, made a number of unusual concessions. Lucy literally lived in Charlie's room twenty-four hours a day, only going home to shower and change clothes. Our own nurses were allowed to help care for Charlie. The unit nurses often ignored both the posted time and number limitations to allow a steady stream of visitors in and out of Charlie's room. They played deaf to the unaccustomed sounds of his visitors' laughter that frequently sounded up and down the halls of a normally somber ICU. They looked the other way when Lucy filled the room with balloons, decorated one entire wall with a floor-to-ceiling blow-up of the Los Gatos Wildcat football team, and proceeded to set up a temporary real estate office on a hospital table in one corner of Charlie's room so she could complete paperwork and conduct necessary business.

But it wasn't the unprecedented commotion in that intensive care unit that kept the staff buzzing with curiosity and speculation. It was Lucy's consistently positive and upbeat manner in the face of her husband's imminent death.

A veteran ICU nurse named Grace, recalled coming to work

that week a couple days after the Wedemeyers' arrival and hearing about them. "I quickly picked up the scuttlebutt about this unusual couple at the end of the hall. Word was the husband had been some kind of famous jock. Tragically, he was dying with ALS and not expected to live long. But the most amazing and troubling thing was his wife, evidently a blonde airhead who remained persistently perky and positive, laughed and joked with visitors, and actually conducted real estate business on the pay phones in the ICU waiting room. Her husband was on his deathbed, and she seemingly didn't have a clue. Because if she really had her act together, she'd be falling apart. She was obviously in complete denial."

Charlie wasn't one of the patients assigned to Grace that day. But she says everything she heard the other nurses say about the Wedemeyers intrigued her. She felt something drawing her to their room to meet them.

She says when she walked in, Charlie's appearance shocked her. He looked as pale and gray as any corpse, his skin beaded with sweat from the sheer exertion of living. Each minuscule breath he managed seemed like a miraculous victory against the odds. Completely immobile, barely clinging to the cliff at the edge of consciousness, he was battling death to the end with evident courage and determination.

"And there, on a futon on the floor beside Charlie's bed, was Lucy. I knew this was his wife by the way she looked at him. I saw the intensity of communication between them when they made eye contact. I sensed a special depth of relationship there. And in the brief moments I talked with them, I sensed no naivete, no lack of awareness on Lucy's part. She appeared well aware of the seriousness of Charlie's condition."

Having convinced herself that Lucy indeed had a healthy grasp on reality, having witnessed Charlie's fighting spirit, and having sensed Lucy's commitment to her husband, something else began to bother Grace after she left the Wedemeyers' room. All the facts didn't seem to fit.

She caught Linda in the hallway and asked, "Do the Wedemeyers understand that Charlie's medical chart lists him as a 'No Code?' We are not to try to resuscitate him."

Linda acted surprised and told Grace, "You better talk to Lucy right now!"

LUCY

I was seated at a pay phone in the waiting area, making a series of calls to update friends and family, when Grace touched me on the arm and asked if she could talk with me. I nodded and quickly ended my call.

"What is it?" I wanted to know.

She crouched down next to my seat and almost whispered. "Did you know Charlie is a No Code?" Seeing the question mark on my face she explained, "That means if he suddenly quits breathing, we are not supposed to try to resuscitate him. We are just to let him die."

"NO!"

"That's what his chart says."

There must be some mistake. I explained what I'd told the doctor in the emergency room, that Charlie didn't want his life prolonged if he couldn't be alert and interact with friends and family. He didn't want to be a vegetable. Since he felt prepared to die, we'd agreed rather than prolong his suffering that if he slipped into a coma it would be better to let him die peacefully.

When I finished explaining, Grace asked, "But do you realize Charlie could quit breathing and die at any moment?"

"You mean while he's still conscious? Still trying to breathe?"

Grace nodded. "I don't think it's very likely he'll go into a coma. Not the way he's battling. But I don't think he can keep fighting much longer. And I wanted to make sure you understood the No Code instructions."

"You're saying it means you won't do anything if he stops breathing? Nothing? Not even mouth-to-mouth?"

She shook her head.

"Even if he's conscious and trying to breathe?"

"That's right."

"No! That's not what we wanted. The doctor didn't understand." As long as Charlie had any fight left in him, I had to help him fight. I could never just let him die like that. We had to change that No Code.

When I asked Grace what alternatives we had, she asked if we'd considered the possibility of a respirator.

I told her one thing I knew for sure was that Charlie would choose to die rather than to be hooked up to any machine that confined him to a hospital room the rest of his life.

"Then no one's talked to you about the option of a portable ventilator?"

I shook my head.

Grace told me she'd known several patients who'd gone home on portable ventilators. "I hear one of them even gets out to do her own grocery shopping."

If someone on a respirator can go shopping, maybe Charlie could get out to a football game. I said to Grace, "You've got to tell Charlie everything you just told me."

She agreed to do that in just a few minutes, as soon as her shift ended. Meantime I made a call to Dr. Norris at the ALS Research Center in San Francisco to verify what Grace had said and find out what they could tell me about ALS patients on portable ventilators. I spoke to the doctor's wife, Dee, who worked as a nurse with her husband. She told me she personally knew of two people on respirators who'd traveled to Europe.

Hawaii's a lot closer to us than Europe! I had to tell Charlie.

chapter twenty

INTENSIVE CARE
COACHING

When he heard the options from Grace and Lucy, Charlie quickly agreed to be hooked to a ventilator. But making that decision proved far easier than cutting through the red tape to make it happen.

At Lucy's prodding Grace tried in vain to reach the staff internist Charlie had been assigned to when he checked in. She left a message saying the Wedemeyers wanted a respirator. Then she tried to find an ICU supervisor who would take the No-Code designation off Charlie's charts.

The doctor arrived a short while later, obviously upset by this new development on his case. He demanded to know how the idea of a portable respirator had come up and when Lucy didn't answer except to make a vague reference to her conversation with the ALS Research Center, he grew visibly angry.

He told Lucy he would not recommend the respirator option. He said putting Charlie on a respirator would make him susceptible to infections, recurring bouts of pneumonia, continued suffering and a variety of added complications. "He's going to die soon anyway," he concluded. "Why go to all that bother to simply prolong the inevitable?"

LUCY

I was made so angry by his disregard for our feelings, that by the time the doctor finished presenting his rationale for why Charlie would be better off to simply give up and die, it was all I could do to keep from screaming at him.

Instead I told him as firmly as I could, "We thought we were talking about Charlie going into a coma. We didn't understand our options before. Now we do. And we would like you to change Charlie's No-Code status and get him on a respirator IMMEDIATELY."

He still tried to argue. I couldn't believe it. I looked at Charlie who mouthed the words, "I think he's a 'lolo' (Hawaiian for dum-dum)." I almost laughed. When I refused to budge, the doctor finally gave up. But as he left to order a machine from the respiratory therapy department, he clearly seemed to think we were making a big mistake.

However, within minutes after the therapist turned on the machine and hooked the respirator hose over the cuff of Charlie's trache tube, I knew we'd made the right decision. The steady supply of oxygen had an immediate, almost intoxicating effect on Charlie's body. His complexion noticeably brightened. And so did his spirits.

And that night, all night long, I sat beside Charlie's bed, listening to the mesmerizing rhythm of the respirator and watching in amazement as my husband slept. He never awakened, stirred, or even coughed until early the next morning.

We soon received encouraging support from other segments of the hospital's medical staff. Since Charlie could no longer take food by mouth, the insertion of a feeding tube was the next step. Two doctors with refreshingly positive attitudes showed up that afternoon to perform the gastrostomy on Charlie right there in his ICU room.

Since both these physicians lived in Los Gatos, they knew all about Charlie. They talked for a while about football and then carefully, respectfully answered all the questions we had and explained each step of the procedure before they did it. They even allowed Lynn, Linda, and me to stay with Charlie while they worked on him.

Step one was to run what looked like a garden hose with a bright little light on the end into Charlie's mouth, down his throat, and carefully into his stomach. The first touch of the hose against the back of his throat triggered Charlie's gag reflex and he unintentionally chomped his mouth closed on the doctor's fingers.

"Hey, Charlie!" the doctor exclaimed. "Remember that old saying, 'Don't bite the hand that feeds you.'" Charlie grinned.

Once they got the end of the hose down into the stomach the one doctor fished it back and forth while the other one watched the light glow from inside the abdomen. "There. Hold it. That's it." And she marked a spot just under Charlie's bottom left rib. "Right there's where we'll make the incision, Charlie."

"Wait a minute. Charlie's saying something." Linda and I tried to read his lips; an extra challenge with the hose still in his mouth. "Charlie says, 'Can you go . . . a little lower? Don't want to . . .'" "What? 'R-u-i . . . oh, ruin. Don't want to ruin my . . .'" "What? You don't want to ruin your tan line?"

The doctors laughed. "You'll just have to quit wearing those skimpy Speedo swim suits."

The banter continued back and forth between Charlie and the doctors through the entire procedure. The incision made, the doctors were ready to insert the tube when Charlie asked if they had a wide-mouthed version. He wanted them to understand that Hawaiians don't just eat till they're full, they usually eat until they are tired.

When they finished, a nurse gave Charlie his first meal through his new stomach tube. An eight-ounce can of Ensure, a milky protein drink. Later in the evening when she brought him another can, Charlie rolled his eyes and said he'd rather have teriyaki chicken. So the next time she came in to feed him she had a magazine recipe photo taped around the can. "Here's your chicken, Charlie."

Charlie grinned and licked his lips.

CHARLIE

I can't adequately describe how wonderful it felt to be able to fill my lungs and my stomach without choking. I suddenly felt alive again.

I could no longer speak at all, even in a whisper, because breathing through a trache completely bypassed my vocal chords. But compared with the wonderful new freedom of breathing, the loss of my voice didn't seem like a significant problem. My speech had grown so weak and distorted in recent years that everyone close to me had been doing a lot of lip-reading already. In the hospital I discovered I could click my tongue against my teeth, and do it loudly enough to be heard across the room.

All in all I was so encouraged and feeling so much improved after only a couple days on the respirator that I began to hope I might be able to make the All-Star game the following Thursday after all.

When the pulmonary specialist on my case made his rounds, I had Lucy ask him about the possibility of going to the game. The doctor, a cheerful Indian gentleman, smiled and shrugged: "I do not see why not. You can do anything you feel strong enough to do. You would need to find a respiratory therapist who would go and monitor your machine. But an ambulance could take you to the game and bring you back to the hospital afterward."

That was all the encouragement I needed to start making my plans. Lucy checked with the therapists; every one on the hospital's staff volunteered to go if I needed them. The ambulance looked to be no problem either.

After Lucy made a few calls, the entire crew of coaches who'd been helping conduct All-Star practices in my absence assembled in my ICU room for a strategy session. They reported on what they'd been working on that week, and we agreed on some additional wrinkles to add.

One of the older nurses came into the room as we were

talking about the game plan. "It's time for your bath," she announced.

"Later," I had Lucy tell her. "We're in the middle of a meeting."

"I'm supposed to give you a bath now," she insisted. "I can't do it later."

"Then I'll skip a bath today."

"This is not a hotel!" she harrumphed as she bustled out the door. But the coaches' meeting continued.

Unfortunately my doctor became aware of my intention to go to the All-Star game. Early in the week he came and said, "Mr. Wedemeyer, I'm your doctor, and there is absolutely no way I'd give my consent for you to leave this hospital to go to any ball game this Thursday night."

Turning his attention to Lucy he said, "Mrs. Wedemeyer, may I talk to you outside for a moment?"

I clicked for Lucy's attention. I wanted to tell the good doctor anything he had to say to her, he could say in my room. But Lucy gave me a quick look to indicate everything would be all right.

LUCY

The doctor led me out of Charlie's room and down the hall to a tiny office. The moment he closed the door he began to tell me how foolish he felt this entire idea had been. "Don't you realize your husband has a serious illness?"

I felt like feigning shock and saying, *He does? I wondered why he was here in the intensive care ward. That might also explain those tubes sticking out of his body.* But I merely assured him that "I realize that."

"Don't you understand he could die out there trying to coach a football game?"

"Yes. Of course I know that. And wouldn't it be wonderful for Charlie to die on a football field doing something he loved to do, rather than wither away, cooped up in some sterile hospital room?"

The unchanging expression on his face told me his

answer even before he said, "Well, he can't do it because I simply won't permit it. I'm just not willing to take that responsibility."

Realizing the doctor would never change his mind, we seriously considered going AWOL and simply sneaking out of the hospital to go to the game. But we knew anyone who helped us would be in very deep trouble. So Charlie moved to Plan C. "I'll just have to coach the game from here at the hospital."

"How?"

"The game's going to be on local TV. I could watch it here in my room. All we'd need to do is find a way for me to communicate with the stadium and I could still call the plays."

Charlie thought short-wave might be a workable possibility. But a few quick phone calls revealed two problems with that idea. There was a big hill between the hospital and the stadium which would hinder reception. And then there was the danger that any short-wave transmission out of the ICU might interfere with some patients' pacemakers. Charlie grinned when he heard that. "No problem," he said. "They could turn up those pacemakers and let them beat double-time for a while before the game and shut them off at kickoff. Surely they could coast for a couple of hours."

Since the hospital staff didn't go for that idea, some sort of phone hookup looked like the only alternative. But there was also one major hitch with that idea. The ICU rooms didn't have phones; there wasn't even a jack.

When we asked about running a line in, we were told it would be against hospital policy. But with a little badgering and a lot of begging, we got special permission to run a temporary phone line into Charlie's room so he could maintain direct communication to the stadium during the game.

The unusual arrangement attracted quite a bit of attention in the local media and reporters from several television stations asked if they could film and interview Charlie about his plans. The hospital refused them access; there would be no cameras in ICU.

A half hour before kickoff the hospital finally agreed to let me meet with reporters in a room downstairs. But by then it was too late to leave Charlie.

I couldn't believe how excited he was about the game. Although we didn't know how well the makeshift communication plan would work, Charlie was absolutely thrilled to be doing it.

But minutes before the game was to start, Charlie's doctor walked in. "I had to come and tell you that as your doctor, I don't think you should be doing this tonight, Charlie. You've got to realize you're on life support. You're going to be on it the rest of your life and you're just going to have to adjust to the fact that you can no longer do all the things you wish you could do. You will have to accept the reality of your limitations. . . ." His speech dragged on and Charlie and I were both nearly in tears by the time he gave up and left the room.

However, we were cheered up a few moments later when Deborah Gee and Ken Ellis, our documentary-producer friends, slipped into the room looking overweight and overdressed for a warm July evening. Then they slipped off their bulky jackets to reveal a pair of 35mm cameras they'd smuggled in to document the events of the evening. Suddenly we were laughing again.

CHARLIE

Long-distance coaching proved harder than I thought it might. For one thing, the television cameras followed the ball every play, making it impossible for me to see the entire field as I could have if I'd been on the sidelines. So I seldom had the kind of broad overview a coach needs to make confident decisions.

Plus the communication system felt awkward. When I called a play, Lucy had to relay it over the phone lines to Bill Bowman in the stadium press box. He passed it down the sidelines through the headset of my Los Gatos assistant coach, Eric Van Patten, who gave the word to the acting coach. He either sent a player with the message into the game or signaled in the play directly to the quarterback in the huddle. The whole process took so long and passed through so many steps that we didn't run a lot of the plays I wanted.

Our team ended up losing the game. But the final score didn't matter. Just being able to take part in that game gave me a new measure of hope for the future. A nice bonus was that the Los Gatos boys who played on the all-star team snuck into my room for a visit after the game—I'd instructed Lucy to jimmy the doors so they could slip into the locked ward—and we talked about football long into the night.

By the time I finally fell asleep, I judged the entire evening a successful, exciting, and memorable experience. And evidently not just for Lucy and me. We found out later that despite hospital "policy," most of the ICU staff had spent the entire game in an empty room down the hall, huddled in front of a TV set, cheering for our team.

Another heartening experience took place one evening when Michael Scialabba, one of the juniors from the 1984 team, dropped by the hospital with his girlfriend to pay me a visit. We talked till midnight about a variety of things, including the painful loss to St. Francis. Before he left he came over beside my bed and laid his hand on my shoulder. "Coach," he said. "It's going to be an awesome season this year. But we're not going to be able to do it without you." The sincerity with which he said that along with each day's increasing strength started me thinking. Maybe it could happen. Maybe I could coach again. I knew I wanted to try.

With my condition improving noticeably each day, and the All-Star game over, I began to think about the trip to Hawaii we'd been planning with the Bowmans. We still had our reservations for that next Friday.

Lucy began making lists and asked the most helpful ICU nurses for advice on what was needed to travel with a portable ventilator. But my doctor dropped by for another chat. "You're a sick man, Charlie. Don't even think about anything so absurd." He clearly wasn't going to release Charlie until we gave up the idea.

"Okay. You're probably right," we told him, acting as meek and contrite as possible. We then let it be known on the hospital grapevine that we'd definitely abandoned our plans for the trip. On Wednesday, I was released from the hospital on my doctor's orders and went home "to die." Lucy packed madly all day Thursday, and Friday the Bowmans and our family, plus two nurses, boarded a plane for paradise.

The first thing I did when we landed in Honolulu was send Lucy to the airport gift shop to buy one of those post cards with a beautiful tropical beach scene and the message on the front saying "Wish you were here." Then we mailed it to my doctor.

chapter twenty-one
LIVING ON
LIFE SUPPORT

LUCY

Only in retrospect can we see how insane it was for us to have made that trip to Hawaii. And how important.

By the time we landed in Hawaii, we had seen the kind of unpredictable challenges we'd face when traveling with someone on life support. The very first hurdle had arisen in our own driveway.

A friend loaned us a wheel-chair accessible van to make the forty-five mile trip up to San Francisco International. We'd nearly filled the vehicle with luggage and equipment before we finally wheeled Charlie out and rolled him onto the electric lift. Up he went. Not until Leslyn and Lynn tried to back the chair into the van did we realize that because Charlie couldn't bend his neck or duck his head, we couldn't get him into the van.

The simplest solution might have been to cut a sunroof to accommodate the top two or three inches of Charlie's head. But since I didn't have my blowtorch handy, we spent the better part of an hour repacking the van, then tipping and turning Charlie until we could get him and the wheelchair inside. By the time that our equipment-laden entourage—including our family of four, the five members of the Bowman family, a friend of Kale's, plus our nurses— arrived at our gate the attendants were making their last boarding call.

Now there's a very good reason why airlines like to board "families with small children and any passengers needing special assistance" *before* anyone else gets on a plane. Our aircraft was already loaded when our party marched single-file into the cabin carrying what looked like enough equipment and supplies for an eight-day space-shuttle mission. I felt like we ought to break into a rousing chorus, singing "Hi-ho, hi-ho, it's off to work we go." We certainly couldn't have gotten any more curious stares if we had.

As most of the flight attendants began frantically searching overhead compartments for space to stow our mountain of gear, the nurses and I tried to figure out the best procedure for getting Charlie and his life-support equipment from the jet way back to his seat. We'd never done this before; so everything was trial and error, start and stop, chaos and confusion as we tried to hurry and not hold up the flight any longer.

I can only guess what the flight crew and passengers must have been thinking as they watched us march back off the plane and return wheeling Charlie's emaciated body down the aisle, bagging him all the way (manually giving him air with a bellows-like device), then lifting him into his seat and hooking him up again to a portable respirator. I didn't have to guess how Charlie was feeling about being the center of such an incredible commotion. If he could have raised his arms I think he'd have covered his face like those Mafia guys you see sometimes on the news.

Fortunately embarrassment is seldom terminal. So Charlie survived the experience—though the batteries on his suction machine conked out and we spent the last part of the flight praying his trache wouldn't become so congested he'd choke to death. By the time we landed Charlie was too excited about seeing his family and having me buy the card to send the doctor to worry about a little thing like breathing.

Today when I think back to that two-week trip to Hawaii, I don't know whether to laugh or shudder at our naïveté. I'd taken every emergency phone number I could imagine needing. But Charlie had been on a respirator for all of two weeks. And he'd been in the hospital with intensive care nursing until two days before our trip. Because none of our regular nurses had had experience with respirator patients we took one of the hospital nurses along; but she'd never worked with a portable respirator. So no one in our party really knew what to expect. We took a two-year supply of some unimportant items and none of some essentials. We had no back-up respirator, no extra suction machine, and very little understanding of how susceptible we could be to some minor mechanical breakdown.

The first serious problem came one evening when twelve of us were squished into a van heading to a restaurant for dinner. Suddenly Charlie wasn't getting enough air. We turned up the respirator. That helped, but something still wasn't right. We didn't know whether the machine was malfunctioning or what, so we rushed Charlie to the nearest hospital.

The emergency room staff eventually identified the trouble. It seems the plastic trache tube in Charlie's throat had developed a slight crack. Although the respirator was operating properly, a portion of each puff of air was seeping out through the tube instead of making it into Charlie's lungs. If the crack had been worse, or if it had gotten worse, Charlie could have had a very dangerous problem. But as soon as they inserted a new tube, Charlie began breathing normally again.

The doctors were amazed Charlie was doing so well. But because we'd all been packed like sardines into the van when we'd arrived, they recommended we let one of the hospital ambulances transport Charlie back to the house where we were staying.

That suggestion got no argument from Charlie. But as the ambulance raced us through the streets of Honolulu with its lights flashing, Charlie began mouthing a message. Linda and I tried to read his lips. "We have to stop . . . "

"Why Charlie? What's wrong?"

"We have to stop . . ." We couldn't figure out his next words.

"What do you mean?"

Charlie began to spell. "L . . . I . . . K . . . E . . ."

"Like?"

He made a negative face and began spelling again, "L-I-K-E-L-I-K-E" and mouthed the words again.

Finally I understood. But I didn't believe it. "You want to stop at the Like-Like (pronounced leekee-leekee) Drive-In?" It has been one of our favorite places to eat since we were kids. I laughed.

But Charlie said it again. He wasn't kidding.

"We're in an ambulance on the way home from the emergency room!" While Charlie was no longer in distress, I wanted to get him back to the house where we were staying. Besides it was now the middle of the night and everyone was exhausted.

But Charlie was afraid everyone was hungry after the long wait at the hospital. So he insisted, "Tell the driver we have to stop."

I can't imagine what the driver thought when I called to him and asked, "Do you think we could stop for a minute at the Like-Like Drive-In? Charlie wants to get something to eat."

Here's this skin-and-bones man in the back of an ambulance, perhaps at the point of death, hooked up to a life-support system, unable to talk, who can only take nourishment through a stomach tube, having just been rushed to the hospital with breathing difficulties, and his wife says he wants to stop the ambulance at a drive-in at one A.M. to pick up some Hawaiian fast food.

I have no idea what convinced the driver to do it. Maybe he thought of it as granting a dying man his last request.

"Okay," he sighed, "we'll stop." Shaking his head in disbelief, he added, "But I'm turning off the lights and siren." Ten minutes later we were back on the road again with plate lunches for everyone, including—at Charlie's insistence—our paramedics who were now laughing along with the rest of us.

This first real "emergency" with the respirator system provided a number of lessons. We never again would go anywhere without a back-up trache tube. But I couldn't help wondering "What if" and feeling vulnerable realizing how many things could go wrong and how little we knew about what we'd gotten ourselves into.

At the same time I felt a measure of reassurance in both this emergency's outcome and in the doctors' reaction. I'd seen the urgency with which they'd begun working on Charlie, obviously alarmed to find themselves faced with an emergency-room patient in his condition. But as they'd examined him, checked his vital signs, and identified the problem, they seemed almost amazed to see everything else was okay. They clearly felt Charlie was being properly cared for, that we'd done the right thing in bringing him in, and that Charlie could reasonably leave the hospital without any argument from them.

Maybe we weren't so crazy to make this Hawaii trip after all. We'd handled what could have been a major problem with a minimum of trouble. And it gave me a needed sense of confidence that we'd be able to find a way to deal with the next crisis as well.

That entire trip was a crucial confidence-builder for all of us. It proved to Charlie that life wasn't over. If he could get out of intensive care and go to Hawaii on a brand new life-support system two days later, no telling what was possible once we figured out what we were doing. If we hadn't done it when and how we did, I'm not sure that Charlie would have ever gone anywhere again. Without his determination to make that trip, I think it's very possible that he might have gone home and lain there until he died—as his doctor had expected him to do.

CHARLIE

I didn't make the trip to defy the doctors or just to prove I could do it. My prime motivation was to see my family, especially my parents, one last time.

My mother had not been in good health for some time. And we'd just learned my dad had been diagnosed with terminal cancer. I wanted to see them again. I wanted to tell them about the new peace I'd found in trusting God.

If they, too, were facing the end of their lives, I wanted them to have the same strength and peace my faith had given me. I wanted them to know God the way I now did, to feel his comfort and presence as they faced the fears and uncertainties of the future. But I didn't know how to tell them. I didn't know what words to use.

One afternoon our friend Maria who'd come to Los Gatos to see us in the spring stopped in with her husband Neal for a visit. I remember my parents sitting together down by the foot of the bed. Maria and Neal sat off to the side. Lucy and Linda were beside me. Kale was in the room, too.

I knew the time had come. So I told my parents there was something I wanted to tell them. Through Lucy I recounted that day back in January when Ramona had prayed for me and I felt God's presence with me there in the room, how at that point I no longer feared dying the way I had before. And how comforting it was to know there would be a better place for me in heaven.

Even as I talked I worried about my parents' reaction to what we were saying. Especially my mom. She'd been such a devout Catholic all her life I worried that she'd dismiss our talk about such a personal confrontation with God as some strange Protestant teaching. But as we talked I saw tears trickling down her face.

We read some Bible verses and then I asked Maria to add to what we'd said. Not only did my parents listen intently, but they both began to weep as Maria talked about how she could see, and they probably could too, that I'd been able to find joy and peace in spite of the terrible struggles I'd been through the past few months. She told them that was the difference God was making in my life.

When Neal asked my parents if they'd like to pray to accept the same blessings I had and to have the same kind of relationship I had with God, they both said "Yes." By the time Neal finished praying with them everyone in the room was crying and I knew beyond a shadow of a doubt why the Lord had given me such a determination to make that trip.

It didn't matter that I could no longer wipe away the tears of joy streaming down my face. In fact, if my respirator had suddenly stopped, I would have died a happy man. The two people who had given me life had made the most important decision of their lives.

Yet despite the wonderful success of that trip to Hawaii, the airport goodbyes were painfully wrenching. I kissed my family goodbye knowing even if my new respirator enabled me to live a little longer, neither of my parents had long to live. And my sisters wept openly as they hugged us, draped leis around our necks, and loaded us down with their usual parting gifts of banana pies and guava chiffon cakes. For while I'd found a large measure of relief through the machine that now breathed for me, my family saw my emaciated body and viewed the respirator as yet another painful step, one of the final steps, in my physical decline. To them, my death had never seemed so inevitable, so close.

There was little time to dwell on the poignant pain of those "final" goodbyes. Fall was fast approaching. And as I began to feel a bit better with each passing day, I began to focus on the coming football season.

However, that Bible verse about the spirit being willing but the flesh being weak pretty well described my situation over the next few weeks.

While the flight to and from Hawaii had been quite a physical ordeal, I'd spent most of my time in the islands lying in bed. I'd been up and out on only a couple of occasions; the rest of the time family and friends had come to see me. So I wasn't really prepared for the grueling physical challenge required to make football practice every day.

There seemed a million details to work out. How much help would we need to get me and my life-support equipment to practice? How would we fit the new medical equipment on the golf cart? Where would the hoses go? Would a headrest work? What supplies did we need to take along? What nurses could help Lucy get me to practice? What's the most efficient way to get me out of bed and into the chair? What kind of clothing best accommodates the new tubes sticking out of my body? Can I get my Los Gatos sweater on over my trache?

For a time Lucy experimented. She altered my shirts by slitting seams and using Velcro fasteners to avoid the hassle of pulling clothes over my head. But the Velcro was prickly and painfully pulled body hair. My clothes bunched up uncomfortably and sometimes looked like I had them on sideways. So we abandoned that idea.

Slowly, surely, we began to find solutions to some problems by trial and error, but not before everyone involved paid the price in exhaustion—especially during the two weeks in August when we had two-a-day workouts. Yet even as I began to feel physically stronger, I continued to struggle with the psychological adjustment to life on a respirator.

I was suddenly forced to trust my life to a machine, an inanimate object whose constant whoosh and whir was now my second heartbeat. If something went wrong, if anything went wrong with that machine, I could die. I needed someone with me every second. If Lucy or one of the nurses had to leave for a few seconds to run to the bathroom I'd get panicky. My imagination worked overtime. *What if there's a storm or an earthquake and the power goes off? What if the night nurse falls asleep and doesn't hear the alarm indicating something is wrong? What if the nurse had a seizure or passed out? What if we were in a wreck and the hose came off? What if the swivel*

*popped off my trache cuff during the night? What if . . . ? What if
. . . ?*

The difficulty I'd had learning to trust nurses with my
life now seemed far simpler than trusting my survival to a
mechanical contraption created out of metal, circuits, wires,
and hoses. Some nights I'd lie awake for hours, listening to
the inescapable beat of that respirator, trying to recognize
every nuance of sound in hopes I could then diagnose
danger in the slightest shift of the machine's pitch, whirr,
and whine.

What if . . . ?

*There were other adjustments, other hurdles the Wedemeyers had to
overcome for Charlie to continue to coach and live the life he hoped
to prolong. Lucy tried to protect her husband from some of these.*

*Just before he'd been admitted to the hospital in July, Lucy had
been asked to come to the house of one of Charlie's assistants. She
arrived to find the entire staff assembled along with wives or
girlfriends. Lucy felt as if she'd walked into an inquisition.
"Practices are too long. You're always late. We don't want to do
offense first." They had quite a list. This was going to have to
change this year. That needed to change.*

*No one came right out and said it, but the intent was clear.
They obviously hoped their demands would prompt Charlie's
resignation.*

*Lucy didn't know what she could say to quell the resentment
she felt in that room. She explained that Charlie was having so
much difficulty breathing she didn't think he was going to make it
much longer. "You always say that," someone responded angrily.*

*"Well," Lucy said, fighting to keep her own anger and tears
under control, "I believe it's true. And I've got to get home now."
With that she hurried out of the house and drove home, determined
not to upset Charlie by even mentioning the distressing meeting.*

*Another new burden she didn't share with Charlie was the
family's precipitous financial decline.*

LUCY

Not that it would have changed our minds, but no one had explained before Charlie went on the respirator the stagger-ing financial implications of that decision. Renting the machine was costing over a thousand dollars a month. The first quote we were given for purchasing a respirator was $32,000. Then there was the suction machine and other necessary supplies. But the real back-breaker was the cost of twenty-four-hour nursing care. And our insurance, which would have routinely paid thousands of dollars a day if Charlie had chosen to remain in the hospital, refused to pay any of the bill for at-home medical care.

The $600 a day needed to pay for nurses provided by a local nursing registry recommended by the hospital placed a terrible drain on the trust fund established to help with Charlie's expenses. So seeing our finances fast approaching the bottom, I called the registry's management to inquire about alternatives.

"We're getting desperate," I told her. "The money we have left in our medical fund will pay for less than a week's worth of nurses."

"We know how much is in your account, Mrs. Wede-meyer," she told me.

"Then you know we can't keep paying $600 a day. Isn't there some alternative? Could we use LVNs instead of RNs?" I knew LVNs sometimes take care of respirator patients in hospitals. And LVNs would be cheaper.

"No," she told me. "State regulations require us to use registered nurses for all respirator patients." She said she was sorry, but she suggested no alternatives.

Not until I'd placed numerous calls to the state regula-tors did I discover those costly restrictions only applied to nurses provided by a registry. If we hired nurses ourselves, we could often get RNs at a much lower rate than the registry charged. We could also use LVNs or even nursing students we could train ourselves to provide the basic care Charlie needed.

CHARLIE

Lucy and I agreed that Linda was the most logical person to help us train new nurses because she'd been with us in the hospital learning the respirator procedures from the hospital staff. In the few short months since she'd begun working for us, she'd graduated from nurse's training, assumed responsibility for my primary care, and proven herself to be a reliable and efficient medical person.

Unfortunately, Linda's goal was to find a hospital nursing job as soon as she got her state certification. She'd been open with us about her plans from the beginning. But that didn't soften our disappointment when her license came through and she immediately accepted a full-time position at a nearby hospital. We knew she wouldn't be easy to replace.

We learned later that during her first full day of orientation at the hospital, Linda kept worrying and thinking, *I wonder how Charlie's doing today.* On the second day of orientation when a supervisor briefed the new nurses on respirator care, Linda got all choked up. And that night she came to the house to say she'd decided to nurse at the hospital only three days a week and wanted to keep working for us as much as possible. What a blessing that was! Not just because she's sacrificially served as my primary nurse for seven years now, but also because she quickly became a valued and caring friend.

chapter twenty-two

ONE LAST SEASON

The 1985 football season for the Los Gatos High School Wildcats didn't exactly begin with a bang—unless you count the sound of the bubble bursting—because Charlie's team dropped the opening game of the season to Seaside by the score of 10–3.

That defeat ended the Wildcat's regular season winning streak of twenty-six straight victories stretching back over three years. It might also have added credence to the opinions of those who felt the time had come for Charlie Wedemeyer to step aside.

Only later, looking back, could Charlie and Lucy see that that opening season loss may have been a blessing in disguise. With any hopes for another undefeated season dashed so early in September, expectations evaporated. Much of the pressure the players might have felt from their classmates, from the community, or from each other to keep the streak alive was suddenly gone.

Charlie saw the obvious change in attitude—even among the assistant coaches. Back in 1984 each week of the season, each victory had brought the top-ranked Wildcats that much closer to their goal of an undefeated, championship season. Which meant each week, each victory had also raised the stakes, the expectations, and the significance of each game a little bit higher.

The staff had obviously felt the pressure building. They rode the players harder, yelling more and louder in practice than at any time during Charlie's coaching career. But after losing the 1985 season opener, the assistant coaches seemed to let down; at least the yelling eased up. And that relaxing of pressure may have been just what the 1985 Los Gatos team needed to beat arch-rival Saratoga 19–7 in the second game of the season and launch a new winning streak of their own.

LUCY

While losing that first game of our season may have reduced some of the pressure on the team, it only added pressure for Charlie. After all he'd been through, after all he'd lost, he had not lost his driving perfectionism. He still pushed his team to play its best each week. After such a long winning streak, he determined not to begin a losing streak, which was one factor making the Saratoga victory so important to him.

Winning also proved Charlie capable of continuing to coach. While I'd not told him all the details about my preseason confrontation with the assistant coaches, he felt the negative attitudes among the staff. Their uncharacteristic letdown after we lost the opener seemed almost like an oh-well-we-knew-this-wasn't-going-to-work-and-we-said-so resignation. Even after we bounced back to beat Saratoga and began to improve in the weeks that followed, underlying tensions grew into obvious expressions of discontent.

No longer did the assistant coaches walk across the field to help Linda and me get Charlie out of the mini-school bus and into his golf cart before practice. And after practice on Thursday afternoons, when the players sprinted over to get my traditional weekly snack of cookies and special brownies, the rest of the coaching staff would turn and head for the locker room.

I knew the unspoken resentment bothered Charlie; he worried that it would eventually hurt the team. Neither of us had any workable ideas for solving the problem, although Charlie threatened to follow the lead of the Chicago

Bears' colorful quarterback, Jim McMahon, who'd created a recent flap with some controversial messages on his headband.

"Maybe," Charlie said after another snub made him feel he'd outlived his welcome, "I should wear a headband that says EXCUSE ME FOR LIVING."

What upset me most was realizing that Charlie still didn't have either the physical or emotional energy to tackle complex interpersonal problems. Although he was breathing easily for the first time in years and was actually gaining weight on his new liquid diet, his continuing adjustment to twenty-four-hour-a-day life support and the accompanying life-and-death details of daily living took all the strength we could muster most days.

Just making sure we had nurses covering for us twenty-four hours a day could be a logistical nightmare. When some nurse would call at the last minute and say she was sick or couldn't come for whatever reason, I filled in.

On nights I could have slept, the noise of the respirator would often keep me awake. About the time I'd get soundly asleep, the alarm would go off and I'd have to get up and make sure the night nurses could take care of the problem.

Like Charlie, I too now had to learn to trust a machine to keep him alive. But I felt the added responsibility of knowing what to do when something went wrong with that machine. And as happens with anything mechanical, things did go wrong.

I remember one time when the respirator went out at the beginning of practice. Lynn bagged Charlie manually for two straight hours as I sat behind them with a simple screwdriver, frantically fiddling with switches, hoses and clamps all the while trying to keep Charlie calm and reassured by regularly announcing in my most confident voice, "I think I see the problem here. We'll have everything working again very shortly now."

Charlie didn't miss a breath or a minute of that practice. But by the time I finally found the problem, a tiny crack in the thermometer case that was letting the air escape, it was time to head home.

But even as we gained a measure of confidence in our new machine and in our ability to deal with emergencies, each of those emergencies was an unsettling reminder of Charlie's continued vulnerability. When it came to the big event of every week, our Friday night football game, I often recruited more help than we could possibly use.

While there was comfort in having a houseful of nurses and friends to help get Charlie up and out to the game, chaos was an inevitable byproduct of too much assistance.

I remember one crazy night when a half-dozen people bustled around our tiny bedroom, bouncing off each other like so many billiard balls and looking like some speeded-up clip from an old Three Stooges' movie.

"Excuse me."

"Comin' through."

"Can somebody help me get Charlie's sweater on him?"

"Just as soon as I find his other shoe."

"Who picked up the play list? It was here just a minute ago."

"Maybe Carri took it to the car. Somebody go ask."

"There it is over there. Somebody hand it to me."

"What? Where? I don't see it!"

"We should have left fifteen minutes ago!"

"Who's got the ambu-bag? Somebody call Bill and tell him we'll need to lift Charlie into the chair in just a minute."

In the midst of all this madness and tension, someone noticed Charlie's lips were moving. "Lucy, Charlie's trying to say something!"

"Yes, dear?" His eyes were so intent. "What are you saying?" Linda and I both tried to interpret as everyone in the room stopped to watch and listen as in one of those E. F. Hutton moments.

"It's a . . . what?" I couldn't follow him.

Charlie calmly began again, slowly and distinctly mouthing the words "It's a beautiful day in the neighborhood, yes,

a beautiful day in the neighborhood . . ." from the Mr.
Roger's theme song.

Whenever things got too tense or too crazy, Charlie had
a way of making light of the craziness, of relieving tension
and setting everyone at ease. He had a number of pranks he
reserved for new nurses.

Most of the people we interviewed and trained to care
for Charlie during the night when he didn't need much
attention were nursing students who had had limited
experience with patients in Charlie's condition. They were
naturally a little uneasy and tentative at first about caring for
this terminally ill patient hooked up to a complicated
machine. So sometime in their first day or two on the job, as
they'd be bending over the bed, leaning close to Charlie to
check his trache or stomach tube, trying to be ever so careful
lest they do something wrong or hurt this poor helpless
man, Charlie would suddenly jerk his body and make the
most horrible facial expression. The nurses always screamed
and jumped. A couple of them actually had to sit down for a
few minutes to recover their composure. All the while
Charlie literally shook with silent laughter.

Charlie was an incurable prankster. He had one elderly
nurse he didn't try to scare; he didn't want to give the poor
lady a heart attack. So he came up with another joke to play
on her.

At that time, Charlie still had enough muscle control in
his left leg, that he could sometimes move it just enough to
cross or uncross his legs. Linda stood at Charlie's bedside
giving orientation instructions when Charlie crossed his
legs. Startled, the new nurse looked down at Charlie's feet
and then back to Linda.

Noting her reaction, Charlie waited until she wasn't
looking and uncrossed his legs. A moment later the woman
did a quick double take and exclaimed, "How did he do
that?"

Linda looked from the nurse to Charlie who innocently
mouthed, "Do what?"

"Never mind," the befuddled woman replied.

Charlie watched for his opportunity and when the woman looked away, he shifted his leg again.

"There! Do you see that?"

This time Linda suspected what was happening. One look at the mischief in Charlie's eyes confirmed it. "See what?" she asked with a straight face.

The poor lady simply shook her head. For the next hour, Charlie watched the nurse watching his feet out of the corner of her eye. And every time Linda's instructions drew her attention away, Charlie crossed or uncrossed his legs until the sweet elderly nurse was shaking her head, muttering under her breath, and questioning her own sanity.

The same nurse had an extremely difficult time reading Charlie's lips. No matter how many times he and Linda went over the basic communication he needed to have with all his nurses, this lady always struggled to know what Charlie was saying.

One day soon after she began working for us, she was alone with Charlie when the swivel connecting his respirator hose with the protruding "cuff" of his trache tube came off. Immediately realizing he'd become detached from the machine, Charlie clicked his tongue loudly to get her attention. When she stood up and leaned over the bed he mouthed the word, "AIR," the simple one-word instruction he and Linda taught every nurse to mean something was wrong and he wasn't getting the proper supply of air from the respirator. Step One, also taught to every nurse, is that when Charlie says, "AIR," you immediately check the swivel and then grab the ambu-bag and begin manually giving him air until you can figure out what's wrong with the machine and can get him breathing normally again.

But when Charlie mouthed, "AIR," this nurse simply stood there, saying, "What?"

"AIR!"

"Say it again, Charlie?"

"AIR! AIR!"

"I'm sorry, Charlie. I can't underst—"

"AIR, AIR, AIR, AIR!"

The more desperate Charlie got the more flustered and upset the nurse got.

"AIR!" he mouthed as slowly and distinctly as he could. "AIR!" She was beginning to panic. If she did, he could die.

He instantly changed strategies. "FIRE!" he screamed silently.

"FIRE?" That brought her up short. But as she looked at him in absolute disbelief she noticed the tube was off and quickly slipped it back in place.

Once he could finally breathe again, Charlie began to laugh. And from that day on, whenever he needed air, all he had to do was say "FIRE!" and that nurse would check his air supply.

Charlie had a remarkable ability to see the humor and laugh off a lot of the bizarre things that happened. For a while we had a "lolo" hat (Hawaiian for dumb-dumb) that he required his nurses or even his football players who came to the house to wear when they made a foolish mistake, said something particularly silly, spilled his dinner, or were simply gullible enough to fall for one of his tricks.

But there were some incidents that were too frightening to laugh off. Like the time one nurse went to shake out the water that condenses in the respirator hose. But instead of unhooking the end at Charlie's throat first, she began by removing the end attached to the machine. When she lifted it into the air, all the water drained down through Charlie's trache tube and nearly drowned him before she could get the catheter down into his lungs to suction it out.

Then there was the night I heard the respirator alarm going off and came running from the other end of the house to find Charlie all alone and turning a rather unhealthy shade of blue. Once I got his air restored I went looking for the nurse and found her asleep next to the heater vent on the living room floor oblivious to the world. I sat up with Charlie the rest of the night. But when the morning nurse arrived, "Sleeping Beauty" got up, reported that Charlie had an uneventful night, and walked out the front door to go home. We never called her again.

We made a lot of mistakes those first few months on the respirator. Some could have been tragic. Like the time we arrived at an away game and discovered we'd left Charlie's ambu-bag at home. While a friend raced home for our only back-up system, I drove Charlie up and down the sidelines in the golf cart, alternately relaying his play calls and praying that nothing would go wrong with the respirator.

Charlie somehow survived the season. And just as incredibly, the Los Gatos Wildcats won all but that first regular season game, clinching the league championship for the fourth straight year and winning another berth in the CCS Championship playoffs.

CHARLIE

I'll forever be proud of the 1985 Los Gatos Wildcats. The preseason polls had them picked for third in our league. Yet despite losing their first game of the season, or maybe because that loss gave them something to prove, those boys practiced as hard each week as they played on Friday nights. Week after week they improved and gained a higher level of confidence and determination.

Once again I worried that the growing media attention might distract them. We'd attracted more than enough attention in 1984 with our high ranking and Lucy's presence as golf cart driver and sideline interpreter. In 1985 we became an even bigger novelty and I guess a more dramatic story because of the respirator which kept me alive.

Where we'd gotten lots of local and statewide attention before, now we were drawing national coverage. Ironically, coaching the 1984 season had been much more of a physical challenge for me because some days I'd had to fight just to keep breathing and I steadily lost weight and strength even as the winning season had progressed. While the logistics of life on a respirator took some adjustment, I actually grew stronger and added weight with each week of the 1985 season. But I guess the "coaching on life-support" angle created some extra human interest.

For whatever reason, Lucy and I had many more interviews going into the 1985 playoffs than we had had the year before. Deborah and Ken, our producer friends, put together a short feature, which PBS used on the "McNeil-Lehrer News Hour" the week prior to our semi-final playoff game. They got so much response to the story that when we won that game, they did a follow-up story to let people know we were going to be playing the championship finals. And then they sent a camera crew to the game to follow the story to its conclusion.

What a night that was.

By the time Lucy and the nurses got me dressed in two layers of thermal underwear, I thought we'd never make it to the game on time. When the media mob ambushed us from the shadows behind the stands at San Jose State's Spartan Stadium, all I wanted to do was get down to that field and coach the game.

I squinted into those television floodlights as questions blitzed me from all directions:

"What does this game mean to you after last year's heartbreaker, Coach?"

"Is your team ready for this one?"

"Planned any surprises in your offense tonight?"

"Any predictions about the outcome?"

"Is St. Francis the toughest opponent you've faced this year?"

"Do you consider this the biggest game of your coaching career, Charlie?"

Lucy slid into the golf cart beside me and raised her hand to silence the crowd of reporters. Then she leaned over where she could read my lips and relay what I said: "Charlie just wants to say that this is what our football team has been working for all year. This is the game he's always wanted to coach. Our opponents have an outstanding team and a great winning tradition. So Charlie expects a tough, competitive game tonight. We'll be glad to talk to each of you and answer all your questions later. But right now, if you'd clear the way, we need to get down to the field and join the team for warm-ups. We have a game to play."

With that, Lucy pulled my seat belt tight and eased the cart through the parting crowd and onto a narrow paved path sloping down to field level. Finally alone for a moment, Lucy stopped the cart at the top of the incline. On that cold December night, the stadium lights made the dew sparkle like diamonds on a field of incredibly green grass as a heavenly mist drifted dreamily over the entire scene.

No words can adequately express the feelings we shared as we soaked in that moment. The rich fantasy feel of the scene magnified our emotions. It was all so unbelievable. All too good to be true.

The 1984 season was supposed to have been the one. That was the team with championship potential. So much had happened since that dream had ended with the overtime tie-breaker loss to St. Francis. Accepting the Lord, the NFL Alumni banquet, the hospital, life-support, Hawaii, another whole season.

And here we were again, where no one expected us to be. Amazingly, playing the St. Francis Lancers again—this time in the finals, the CCS championship game. Just being there felt like we'd been given some unimaginably extravagant and unwarranted gift.

As we drove down that path and out onto the sidelines the crowd on both sides of the field began to stand and cheer. While I tried to block out thoughts about anything but the game about to start, I couldn't help hearing the chant going through the stands, "We love you, Charlie. We love you, Charlie."

The game started. St. Francis scored first on a 22-yard first quarter run but failed to convert the extra point. We scored early in the second period and also missed the extra point to leave us tied 6–6.

Late in the same quarter we intercepted a St. Francis pass and returned it deep into Lancer territory. Shortly thereafter our running back Jeff Borgese sprinted into the end zone for Los Gatos's second TD. And this time we followed up by completing a pass to Mike Scialabba, for a two-point conversion to give us a 14–6 halftime lead.

Neither team scored in the third quarter, but St. Francis mounted a drive at the end of the period and scored in the opening seconds of the fourth. They went for two points after the TD but missed again and we clung to a meager 14–12 lead.

When we regained possession, we tried to eat up some clock. But our drive stalled and we were forced to punt. In our subsequent defensive series—what should have been the most crucial play of the game—we sacked the St. Francis quarterback, he fumbled, and we recovered the ball on the St. Francis 8-yard line. Eight short yards from a touchdown that would put the game out of reach in the closing minutes.

Three running plays later we had reached the two. Fourth and goal. Time out!

Figuring St. Francis would expect another run, I called for a bootleg, giving my quarterback the option of running or throwing. If the play worked and we scored a touchdown, the game was over. If we didn't make it, St. Francis would have to drive ninety-eight yards in the closing minutes.

But someone misunderstood my play call. We had two bootlegs, and when the assistant coach signaled in another play, I tried to scream, "No, no!" And Lucy called out, "No wait. That's not right." But in the resulting confusion between the quarterback and the assistant coaches I didn't want to risk a foul up, so I changed my mind and sent in the field goal team. But the kick drifted wide. So instead of starting at the two yard line, St. Francis took over at the twenty with room to maneuver.

We tried to limit them to short-gain pass plays, but one of their receivers got past our secondary, and the quarterback heaved a Hail Mary. My heart tumbled end over end as that ball spiraled long, sailed over the head of the Wildcat defender, and settled into the hands of the Lancer receiver.

The joyful eruption on the St. Francis sideline flashed me back to the crushing playoff loss the year before. *Not again!*

Three quick plays took St. Francis to our eleven, well within field goal range; the Lancers had the best field goal kicker in the county. Fourth down. Forty seconds to play in the game. And here came their kicking team for a short twenty-eight yard attempt that would mean the game.

Butch called time-out to try to psych the kicker and to set up a defensive rush. Our strategy was simple. Rush everyone and put Borgese (our fastet man) out at the end.

I felt Lucy's fingernails digging into my arm as we waited. During the time-outs the Los Gatos fans began to chant, "Do it for Charlie! Do it for Charlie!" And Lucy learned later that a Hollywood producer who'd been among the media on the sidelines looked up into the crowd and said, "You could never capture all this on film! No one would ever believe it."

I was oblivious to everything, however, but the action about to unfold on the field. As the two teams approached the scrimmage line, the entire stadium fell deathly quiet. Next to me Lucy pleaded, "Come on defense, you can do it. Come on defense! Don't let 'em get it! Don't let 'em get it! Don't let 'em get it!"

Seeing the St. Francis kicker make the sign of the Cross, I thought, *Lord, don't answer his prayer* and hoped for a miracle of my own. The center snapped the ball . . . a little low . . . the holder bobbled it then got it down . . . the kicker planted . . . and I saw Jeff Borgese shoot past the blocker, leave his feet and extend his body parallel to the ground. Never in my life had I heard a sweeter sound than the thud of that football ricocheting off Jeff's body. Maybe I only heard it in my mind—that stadium suddenly exploded as we took over the ball, ran out the clock, and won the 1985 California Central Coast Sectional Championship.

LUCY

Players hugged and rolled deliriously on the field. Our nurses screamed and embraced each other. And as the initial wave of celebration died down along the sidelines, the team swarmed around the golf cart to hear Charlie's words. While the boys knelt quietly around us, I had to practically shout to be heard over the continuing celebration throughout the stadium. "Coach says he's so proud of you guys," I told them. "You all played like champions tonight. You've accomplished something no other Los Gatos football team has ever done and you're going to remember it FOR THE REST OF YOUR LIVES!"

With that the boys leaped to their feet and the whooping, hugging, and backslapping began all over again.

The St. Francis coach worked his way through the wild crowd, and leaned under the golf cart's canopy to say, "Congratulations Coach. You're an inspiration to us all!" I thanked him for Charlie and a couple minutes later I looked over to see that the respirator hose had popped off when the St. Francis coach had patted Charlie on the back.

"You're not even breathing!" I exclaimed as I hooked him back up to his life support.

Charlie just grinned and mouthed the words, "I don't care!"

part six

LIVING ON

chapter twenty-three
SIDELINED

Congratulatory letters and calls flooded in from all over the United States. People sent clippings from dozens of papers, which ran articles about Charlie's courageous coaching feat. President Reagan wrote to commend him on his inspirational example. The town of Los Gatos named him Grand Marshal of its annual Christmas parade.

In the wondrous afterglow of that championship game, no one could have foreseen just how quickly Charlie's greatest football victory would be followed by a most devastating loss. Yet it didn't come as a complete surprise.

Early in 1986 the Los Gatos principal, Ted Simonson, asked for a meeting. He informed Charlie that Butch, the assistant coach who had performed the head coaching responsibilities Charlie could no longer handle, was planning to resign—presumably to pursue the head coaching job at some other school. Evidently Ted expected this news to discourage Charlie. When Charlie began suggesting the names of potential new assistants, the principal seemed surprised.

In the days that followed it became obvious the school administration was now ready to see Charlie go. The Wedemeyers saw the handwriting on the wall even before they received the official letter from the school telling them that Charlie would not be head coach of the Los Gatos Wildcats the following season. That decision, once it became public, prompted a firestorm of controversy that quickly spread from the high school campus, through the business community and onto the pages of the Los Gatos and San Jose newspapers.

LUCY

Without football to focus on I knew Charlie wouldn't still be alive. And now they were taking it away!

No one seemed to understand how important coaching was to Charlie. We realized that even before we saw the editorial in one local paper that supported the school's decision. That article noted that because Charlie had now coached the Wildcats to the CCS championship, he could achieve no greater success as a high school football coach, there was nothing left to accomplish, and therefore it was time for him to retire.

Charlie laughed when he read that. But there was no humor in his response. "If they think I've kept coaching because I just had to win that championship, they really don't know me!" While Charlie always saw "winning" as a measure of achievement, it was never his primary motivation for playing or coaching football. He wanted to continue coaching because he was a born teacher who frequently said, "Football is one classroom that teaches kids about life—about handling victories and defeats." And we believed Charlie would be just as capable of coaching and teaching these lessons in 1986 as he had been during Los Gatos's championship 1985 season. In fact, because he had regained some weight and stamina since he'd been on the respirator, and he no longer struggled just to breathe, Charlie's overall health seemed better than it had for years.

When reporters called us or friends asked, we admitted our disappointment about the school's decision and expressed our belief that Charlie could continue to coach. But as much as possible, we tried to avoid the public controversy swirling around us.

Charlie inquired about the chance of his continuing without the "head coach" title, as an assistant with responsibility for calling the offense, the same plan he himself had proposed five years earlier. But that idea was instantly rejected. Even though the plans were to maintain the offense Charlie had designed and implemented, he was told "It's no longer your show."

I don't think I'd ever seen my husband emotionally lower than he was at that point. In many ways this final blow of losing his job seemed more distressing for Charlie than losing his health.

Seeing how distraught Charlie and I were, Linda asked her pastor to come by our house. He brought a minister friend and the two of them listened to our feelings, and shared some comforting Bible verses. They also cited the example of Eric Liddle in *Chariots of Fire* and talked about how God always has plans for people that are so much more important than our own human goals and ambitions. How we need to trust God and seek first his will for our lives.

In a simple, but very definite way, that's what Charlie and I did that evening. It was a major emotional and spiritual turning point in our lives. And as the two ministers prayed with us, the anger and the bitterness we'd felt about Charlie's firing was replaced by an immediate and overpowering sense of peace. So by the time our visitors left, Charlie and I had begun to believe that if Charlie could no longer be the coach of the Los Gatos Wildcats that only meant God had some greater purpose in mind for the rest of his life. And we'd just have to trust him to help us find out what that purpose was.

Some of our supporters talked angrily about pulling their sons out of Los Gatos and transferring to some rival school to play football. Indeed we received several inquiries from other schools around the area wondering if Charlie wanted to help with their football program. But we nixed both those options.

The Los Gatos community had been so good to us over the years, we didn't want to leave. In talking about what to do, Charlie and I agreed we didn't want to simply run away because we'd been hurt. We thought we could be a better example if we stayed.

Another important factor in our decision was Kale. He'd spent his freshman and sophomore years attending Los Gatos High School. His best friends played football for the Wildcats and he wanted to play with them. After spending years at Charlie's side for every practice and every game, Kale knew the Wildcats' coaches as well as he knew the offense they intended to use. He recognized the potential for tension and awkwardness in his relationship with the coaching staff, but he felt he was emotionally strong enough to handle those problems.

In recognition of his years of service at Los Gatos, or maybe in concession to all those who protested his firing, Charlie was given the honorary position of "Coach Emeritus." While this new role gave him absolutely no authority, it did entitle him to attend practice and be on the sidelines during the game. That was some consolation for Charlie who said, "At least I'll be able to be out on the field every day to watch Kale play!"

And play he did. Kale not only won a starting running-back position as a junior, he went on to have such a tremendous season he was named the team's Most Valuable Player. Kale's success, and the excitement we felt for him, did much to ease Charlie's adjustment into retirement.

CHARLIE

One of the greatest regrets I felt when I was diagnosed with ALS and told I didn't have long to live, was realizing I'd probably never get to see my son play high-school sports. So even though I'd lost the chance to be his coach, I kept reminding myself that just being there at practices, and watching from the sidelines was a dream come true.

The joy I experienced during Kale's two great years of varsity football, and the pride I felt when he was awarded a football scholarship to the University of California at Berkeley did indeed take some of the sting out of losing my coaching job. And as I outlived the medical predictions and had the privilege to see both my children enter adulthood, I began to focus more on the future and less on the past. In the process, other opportunities arose and I began to see the beginning of God's new plan for my life unfold.

The documentary plans were in the works. Producers Deborah Gee and Ken Ellis had followed our story with periodic visits and taping sessions ever since they'd done their original "Extraordinary People" show back in 1981. They'd videotaped the playoff loss to St. Francis in 1984 and come back to follow our playoff bid again in 1985. In the months after Los Gatos won the CCS championship they began putting together an hour-long documentary titled "One More Season," which they hoped to market to the networks.

At our nurse Linda's request, we took a video copy of "One More Season" to show her pastor when she invited us to a couple's retreat sponsored by her church. But we were caught by surprise when the pastor proposed showing the tape to the entire group in one of the general sessions.

Embarrassed by this turn of events, I sat in the back of the room wearing sunglasses and feeling extremely ill at ease while the video played. I needed a better disguise. Because, when the video ended, the retreat leaders introduced Lucy and me and invited us down to the front of the room to answer questions about our experience.

I couldn't think of any gracious way to decline. So as Lucy wheeled me forward I thought, *This is going to be a horrible, embarrassing experience.*

It wasn't. In fact, as I began looking around that roomful of people I realized many of them, men as well as women, had been moved to tears by the documentary. And as we answered questions with Lucy talking and alternately reading my lips, I watched the expressions of interest and acceptance on our listeners' faces. After we finished they crowded around us, thanking us for coming, asking questions, sharing their own personal hurts and struggles. The surprising warmth of their response heartened me.

We had much the same positive experience when we showed the video and spoke to a church youth camp. I didn't know what we could say to kids. But after seeing and hearing our story they flocked around to talk to us about personal problems, family difficulties, attempted suicides, and spiritual questions they had. Yet even after those first two positive experiences, we never imagined all the public exposure about to come our way.

The response to the national airing of "One More Season" on PBS later that year nearly overwhelmed us. Again we received letters and phone calls from all over the United States. Many people simply wanted to encourage us, quite a few wanted to help us by sending money, and a sizable number wanted help or advice on how to deal with their own hardship.

Of all the memorable responses we had to the documentary, one will always stand out. The letter carried a Canadian postmark. The author of the letter said he was a British Columbian businessman who owned a financially troubled company. When he'd lost his company, his wife had left him. He said those two crises had so depressed him that he had traveled to Seattle and checked into a downtown hotel with the intention of committing suicide. But when he had walked into his hotel room, he'd turned the television on to a PBS station showing "One More Season." By the time the show concluded he said our story had made him think of all the things he had to be grateful for—his children, his health, his friends. He wanted us to know that hearing our story turned his life around and showed him how much he had to live for.

Reading that man's letter gave me goose bumps. I remembered the reluctance we'd felt years earlier about taping the original program and why we had decided to go forward. "If it could help just one person, we ought to do it."

Our decision had been affirmed. Yet realizing our story

could have such a powerful impact on people we'd never met created a new sense of responsibility as we scrutinized our growing list of speaking invitations.

There was another big opportunity for telling our story, but one which I no longer seriously considered. In the wake of that 1985 championship game, two dozen different people approached us about movie rights to our story.

I still didn't trust Hollywood. So we'd talked to some of the producers to try to judge their interest, their sensitivity, and their commitment to accurately portraying our experiences. If we were to consider a movie, we didn't want our story sensationalized. We wanted the medical details—the ALS symptoms, my physical struggles, our hospital experiences—to be accurate.

We eventually found an experienced producer of made-for-television movies who agreed to all our stated goals. He even sent out a screenwriter to spend a few days with us and begin doing a screenplay. But the project got shelved for more than a year, the writer got busy finishing up his hit movie *Rainman*, and everyone, including us, seemed to lose enthusiasm for the project.

Then one night many months later we watched a made-for-television movie called "Right to Die," starring Raquel Welch as a wife and mother suffering from ALS. The longer I sat and watched the movie the more upset I became. The focus of the entire plot, based on a true-life story, was this woman's tragic suffering and her "courageous" fight against medical and legal establishments reluctant to recognize her "right to die." The whole movie was lopsidedly biased, propagandistic, and sympathetic to the main character's desire for death. It completely ignored or discounted any reasons she might have had for living.

The movie was so negative, so totally lacking in hope. When it ended I looked at Lucy and said, "Maybe we need to do a movie that tells another side of the story."

We contacted the producer who'd been interested in our story, and before we knew it, the project was "on" again. We insisted on doing a movie that would educate viewers and speak to those touched by Lou Gehrig's disease. Plus we wanted our movie to be positive and uplifting, not depressing like "Right to Die" which never even presented the option of living on a respirator.

The movie company assured us we could serve as technical advisors on the set to insure accuracy. And they even promised to shoot the movie on location in Los Gatos and Hawaii. That seemed an important consideration to us because it would mean our town could be a part of the movie and reap a little financial benefit from local production expenses. After all the people of Los Gatos had done for us over the years, this seemed like one small way we could give something back to the community.

This last promise was the first broken when the producer called to tell us the shooting would be done in South Carolina. He said he'd checked out Los Gatos, but the added cost of hiring technicians and other union labor in California would increase production costs by nearly half a million dollars. He said the Charleston, South Carolina area would make a great location. He could shoot the football scenes at Stratford High School in suburban Goose Creek and they could shoot all the necessary "Hawaii" scenes on the Atlantic coast in nearby Foley Beach. Though we weren't happy with this abrupt change in plans, we felt we had no choice but to accept it. We didn't want to be unreasonable.

But we kicked up a real protest when we learned the Los Gatos Wildcat team colors would be changed in the script because the South Carolina high school had red and white uniforms that could be used in the movie. "You can't do that!" Lucy told the producer. "Those are the colors of Saratoga High School—our biggest traditional rival."

"It makes no difference to the story. Who's gonna know?"

"The people of Los Gatos will know!" Lucy countered. "You just can't do that."

The producers eventually found a school with red and black uniforms they could borrow. Figuring that was as close to orange and black as we were going to get, we conceded at that point. But it wasn't the last of our differences.

Having been told we would serve as technical advisors on location Lucy began working out the details for us to go to South Carolina. Travel arrangements for us and the nurses we'd need to take were just part of the challenge; she had to make long-distance arrangements for a hospital bed, a handicap-access van, medical backup, and a zillion other details essential to an extended stay away from home.

Then just days before we were scheduled to leave, the producers told us they thought we should postpone our trip and not fly east until the third week of shooting. They gave a long list of reasons: conditions on location could be tough, the rigorous schedule and long hours could be exhausting, projects like this always begin slowly, the crew would be so preoccupied with technical things to begin with that we'd be bored, and so on.

It suddenly sounded as if the producers didn't want us around the movie set. *Were they planning other changes they weren't telling us about?* No way did I want anyone making a movie portraying the details of my life while I was stuck three thousand miles away. So we boarded our scheduled flight and flew to Charleston.

LUCY

Before we arrived in South Carolina, we'd met Michael Nouri, veteran television actor and star of the movie *Flashdance* who was slated to play Charlie in the movie. A few weeks earlier Michael had spent some time with us in Los Gatos, sharing the experience of our daily lives, and getting a feel for his character. He and Charlie hit it off immediately, in large part because they both had a mischievous streak and a similar sense of humor.

We didn't meet Pam Dawber of "Mork and Mindy" fame who was cast in my role until our first day on the set in South Carolina. But even as introductions were being made, my incorrigible husband took one look at this beautiful actress, bounced his bushy eyebrows up and down in his best "hubba-hubba" expression, and mouthed a message I interpreted. "You can be going home now, Michael," Charlie said. "I just decided I'd like to play myself."

We knew from that very first day that we'd made the right decision in coming to South Carolina. The associate producer and the director, as well as Michael and Pam, frequently asked for and took our suggestions for making the action more accurate and realistic. And despite our earlier apprehensions, everyone on the movie set made us feel welcome and respected.

Some of the first scenes shot for the movie portrayed Charlie's early coaching days. The script included a practice-field incident in which he made one of his players run laps for swearing. The sound engineer in charge of audio for the movie had rigged Charlie up with a set of headphones so he could hear not only the actor's lines, but all the technical chatter and instructions being passed between the director, the cameramen, the lighting technicians, and the sound crew. The complexity of the process fascinated Charlie. For even the simplest and shortest of scenes involving only one or two actors could take hours of set-up time and keep an army of people scurrying around behind scenes the entire time. Like a successfully executed football play, everything had to be perfectly timed and coordinated.

Right in the middle of one of the football practice scenes, an audio tape broke and the sound technician erupted with a blistering stream of profanity that suddenly ended in midsentence when she remembered who was listening over the headset. She turned and sheepishly looked over at Charlie who gave her his sternest look.

"I know, I know," she said. "Take a lap, right, Coach?" Then to my amazement, she shut down the sound equipment, removed her headphones, and took off at a trot for a quarter-mile lap around the track circling the football field while everyone else on the entire set waited and watched. By the third time she had to stop and run a lap, the rest of that movie crew had cleaned up their language. No one else wanted to run the rest of the time we were in South Carolina.

It's a strange sensation observing someone else trying to reenact your life. Michael Nouri worked particularly hard at capturing Charlie's mannerisms and regularly consulted with Charlie to get little details of movement or expression exactly right. He'd look to Charlie for an approving wink at the end of every scene. If Charlie grimaced in disapproval, Michael would hurry over and ask what the problem was.

Michael's portrayal of Charlie was so accurate that in one dramatic scene where he was fighting desperately for breath, I found myself fighting back tears and couldn't watch. It all seemed so real that I flashed back to that old familiar sense of fear and helplessness I'd lived with before Charlie had his trache.

Although we were able to give input on the movie, we had a number of frustrations with the process. The writer and producer pretty much glossed over our spiritual experience, simplified the story line by creating some imaginary "composite" characters, and omitted many people who had played important parts in our lives.

They left out important incidents that really happened because they considered them "unbelievable" or "too emotional." Yet they totally fabricated other scenes or dialog and even created fictional family conflicts between Carri and us to enhance the dramatic effect of the story.

The highlight of the experience for us was the number of wonderful relationships we developed, including warm friendships with Michael and Pam and with the local high school football coaches who were forever diagramming plays and discussing offensive strategies with Charlie. By the time we headed back home, we felt fortunate to have preserved the basic story line. But because there was so much we couldn't change about the movie, we tried to ease our frustration by telling ourselves, "It's only *loosely based* on our story. It's Pam's and Michael's movie."

Yet we felt basically satisfied that it was an encouraging, positive portrayal of life on a respirator. And the finished product, "Quiet Victory," evidently made an impact when it aired on CBS during the last week of December in 1988. Another flood of response poured in from all over the country.

CHARLIE

The loss of my head coaching job had been perhaps the greatest disappointment of my life—the bitter end of the road for me professionally. Then came the PBS documentary and soon after that the CBS movie. And those speaking invitations kept multiplying.

After we'd shared our story one night at a church men's group, a gentleman stood up and encouraged me, "Charlie, you may not be head coach at Los Gatos High School anymore. But you're still coaching—on a higher level, with more players. And you're coaching them in the most important game of all, the game of life."

And this new game was just beginning.

chapter twenty-four

A WHOLE NEW CHALLENGE

In a day and a culture where our society wrestles with right-to-life and right-to-die issues, where thoughtful people struggle to define and understand the social, economic, ethical and spiritual implications of such new and complex concepts as "quality of life" versus "quantity of life," Charlie and Lucy Wedemeyer's case demands notice because it shatters so many stereotypes.

By most contemporary standards, Charlie wouldn't rate very high on the "quality of life" scale. He remains barely alive. He can only move a few facial muscles. He can't speak. He can't eat except through a tube. He can't even breathe for himself. He spends his entire existence, twenty-four hours a day, at the end of a four-foot plastic hose attached to his life-support machinery. He can never be left alone. Just getting him out of bed requires the assistance of at least two experienced people.

And yet, despite all the limitations, sixteen years after his doctors gave him maybe a year to live, Charlie manages to lead an incredibly rich, full, rewarding, and hectic life.

CHARLIE

I'm coaching again. The year after Kale graduated from Los Gatos, I accepted the offer to be an assistant coach with the school's freshman-sophomore football team. Kale's best friend, Craig Williams, arranges time in his own schedule as a part-time college student, to help get me to practice every day and serve as my personal on-field assistant. Craig's been an integral part of our family so long that he's fluent in lip-reading and can readily serve as a back-up nurse whenever we need him. He played football for Los Gatos with Kale so knows the offense as well as my way of doing things. We've come to think of Craig as a second son: like Kale he has a way of always making me laugh. Only the dedicated help of this sensitive and fun-loving young friend makes it possible for me to handle my assistant coaching role.

That job, which I've held for five years now, has provided me the joyful opportunity to continue teaching young men while also giving me the chance to mend some interpersonal fences and restore relationships with the Los Gatos coaching staff and administration. Yet my part-time responsibilities leave me enough time, energy, and flexibility of schedule to pursue a busy speaking itinerary.

Over the course of a year, I now invest a lot more of my time in speaking than in coaching football. This must say something about God's sense of humor that he would take someone who can't even talk and have him travel all over the country on speaking engagements.

Of course, whenever possible I try to combine or at least coordinate my speaking itinerary with my continued interest in football. While Kale played two years of football for the California Golden Bears and then transferred to the University of Pacific to major in physical therapy, and complete his college football career, we attended every one of his home games. We even saw many of his away games.

Traveling on life support continues to present regular challenges. That plus our speaking schedule often make for grueling trips. (We spoke twenty-four times in one recent eighteen-day trip to Hawaii.) Yet we consider the opportunities we have to share our message of encouragement and hope to be worth the unexpected travel adventures we frequently have to endure.

Especially memorable was the time the people of Hawaii raised the money to fly us home to honor me with the Sportsman of the Year Award at the Aloha Bowl. We arrived at San Francisco International just minutes before our flight to Hawaii was scheduled to take off. Never in my life have I ever been so glad to hear a ticket agent say, "That flight's been delayed." If only we could get to the gate before they closed the door.

Minutes later, after setting an unofficial land speed record for a wheelchair, our own nine-member mini-mob reached the gate, which was already overflowing with angry, frustrated travelers still waiting impatiently to board. Linda wasn't able to go on this trip, so with Lucy and me were Carri and Kale, a regular nurse named Lisa and a couple of inexperienced nurse's aides we'd recruited at the last minute. I'd hesitated to even make the trip with so little experienced nursing help. But what changed my mind were the last-minute additions to our traveling party—Kale's buddy Craig, and Craig's cousin Mark Coulter, who'd become another honorary member of the Wedemeyer clan. I knew the three stooges—Kale, Craig, and Mark—could all fill in as capable nurses. And if serious problems developed their zany humor could keep me so thoroughly entertained I probably wouldn't worry about it.

Unfortunately, the trip was not off to an auspicious start when Lucy hurried to the counter with our tickets to check in. Due to some mix-up, the agent told her, the seats we'd reserved were already taken.

"We need to have at least three bulkhead seats together," Lucy explained. "My husband is on a respirator. Our nurse has to be on one side of him with me on the other."

"I'm sorry," said the obviously frazzled agent, "we only have one bulkhead seat left."

"Okay," Lucy smiled patiently. "I guess we'll just have to teach the passengers on either side of him how to suction his trache and monitor his respirator."

The agent never even batted an eye. She evidently didn't realize Lucy was being facetious. Or maybe ours was simply one problem more than she was able to contend with at that moment.

But no sooner had Lucy walked back to report on our predicament than a small warning buzzer sounded, indicating the battery powering my respirator was about to go dead. Although we travel with a backup battery, we had no idea how long a delay we'd have before our scheduled five-hour flight. Since we couldn't risk losing power at thirty-five thousand feet over the Pacific, Lucy walked back to the beleaguered ticket agent to ask about the prospect of the airline providing a spare battery charger that we could use to renew my power supply. When the poor woman looked at her as if she were crazy, Lucy returned to suggest to our group, "I think it's time to pray."

That's what we did. Right there in the middle of that airport hubbub the group gathered around my wheelchair and prayed that God would somehow work out the necessary details for a safe and enjoyable trip.

Within minutes of our amens the ticket agent bustled over with a handful of boarding passes. "Would nine tickets in first class do?" she asked rather huffily.

"Yes, I believe that will do just fine," Lucy deadpanned. "Thank you." The rest of us looked at each other with knowing grins. Our prayer had been answered in record time.

Moments later we spotted a big burly guy coming down the corridor toward us wheeling a battery charger roughly the size of a major appliance. Because the gate area was already so crowded, our entire party was escorted to a nearby operations office where we waited for the battery to recharge. While we sat in that office an operations supervisor walked over to talk. When he found out I had ALS, he told us his girlfriend's brother had just been diagnosed and the family was having a difficult time dealing with the news. At his urging, Lucy placed a call to the fellow's girlfriend, and while the rest of us waited for our flight, she talked for over an hour, answering questions, giving advice, and trying to offer encouragement to a family we'd never met.

Was this unexpected experience merely a coincidence? Only if you can accept the definition I heard recently from our pastor, who said, "A coincidence is a small miracle where God prefers to remain anonymous."

So after a nine-hour delay, we finally boarded our flight with fully charged batteries. And while we sat back and relaxed in first-class comfort, I thought about the important lesson illustrated by this "coincidental" experience. As a lifelong perfectionist, I need occasional reminders to show me that when things seem most discouraging, when I can do nothing to solve the problems confronting me, I can turn to God and know that he's in ultimate control. And I've seen enough such "coincidences" to convince me of that.

So whether or not I understand it or even see it from where I am, he's got a better game plan for my life than I could ever come up with on my own.

LUCY

God's plan for our lives these past few years has brought so many highlights it's impossible to recount them all. For someone who can't move, Charlie gets around. In addition to his busy coaching and speaking routines, he's been honored with such special opportunities as throwing out the ceremonial first pitch for a San Francisco Giants game—on several different occasions. The first time we'd wheeled Charlie out to the mound before the game, Charlie looked at Will Clark, the Giant's star first baseman who'd come out to take the pitch, and then looked back to me and said, "You throw it for me."

"Oh no!" I told him. "It's your job." I placed the ball

under the palm of his right hand and wrapped his fingers around it. As I prepared to help Charlie make a sidearm delivery I prayed that I wouldn't embarrass him, I looked at Will. "Ready?"

He nodded. And I looked at Charlie. "Ready?"

Just as I picked up his hand, Charlie's lips began to move. "Wait a minute!" he said.

"What's wrong?"

"Give me two fingers."

For a few seconds I couldn't understand what Charlie meant. Then it hit me. "Hold on," I told Will. I let go of Charlie's hand and put two fingers to his lips so Charlie could stick out his tongue and lick them. Charlie wanted to throw a spitter. Will Clark caught our sidearm delivery and went back to the dugout, shaking his head and laughing.

The next year the Giants invited Charlie back to do the first-pitch honors. When catcher Terry Kennedy walked out to the mound to take the "throw" he laughingly said, "No spitballs this time, Charlie. All right?"

"Okay!" Charlie grinned. But this time he was ready with a huge metal file he'd had Linda dig out of a toolbox and hide on his lap so he could scuff the ball and "throw" another illegal pitch.

Then there was the time Charlie was asked to take part in the official coin toss before a football game between Kale's University of Pacific team and the University of Hawaii in Honolulu's Aloha Stadium. Knowing he couldn't actually flip the coin, Charlie experimented with alternatives.

First he asked his nurses to carefully place a quarter on the top of his nose. Then he practiced scrunching up his face and wiggling his nose until the coin fell to the floor. Not content with such an undignified procedure, Charlie settled on Plan C. He'd have someone hold his arm out and place a coin on the back of his hand. When a second person would slap his hand from the bottom the coin flipped up as pretty as you please. After all that rehearsal time however, Charlie was a bit disappointed when we wheeled him out to the 50-yard line before the game and the referee explained that his role was merely ceremonial: collegiate rules require the referee to make the actual coin toss.

It seems many of Charlie's special opportunities continue to revolve around sports. Each fall for several years now, Charlie has been asked to coach in an annual powder-puff charity football game between the San Francisco '49ers' wives and the wives of the Oakland Athletics. After assessing his team during the initial practice the first year, Charlie immediately announced, "This is the best looking football team I've ever had the privilege to coach!" So I quickly learned I had to keep an eye on my husband. I also learned that Joe Montana wasn't the only member of his family who could throw a football.

One of Charlie's more unusual opportunities has been the chance to serve as one of the judges in a big pasta cooking contest held annually in Los Gatos to benefit the Muscular Dystrophy Association. We ladle in a spoonful of each dish, Charlie chews a bit and rolls it around on his tongue for taste. Then, since he can't swallow, Linda quickly suctions the food from his mouth and Charlie gives his rating for the dish. It's a role Charlie savors every year.

A couple years ago, Charlie made front page news when he accepted an invitation to take a complimentary hot-air balloon ride. Because he couldn't exactly go up by himself, he wanted Linda and me to join him, his wheelchair, all his medical gear, and our pilot in what promised to be a very cramped gondola for a memorable flight over the scenic landscape of northern California's wine country. I wasn't too crazy about the idea. But Charlie kept badgering me until I gave in and told him, "I'll go up in a balloon with you this one time. But only if you promise me you'll never suggest we take up bungee jumping."

He's kept that bargain—so far.

But one of Charlie's biggest honors came when he was selected to receive the California Governor's Trophy for the 1991 Disabled Employee of the Year. After that he was nominated for and won the 1992 President's Award for Disabled American of the Year.

We flew to Washington, D.C. to receive Charlie's award right during the middle of primary season when the president himself was off jetting around the country on a campaign trip. During a special ceremony before 4,000 people in the ballroom of the Washington Hilton Hotel, Charlie made a brief acceptance speech at the conclusion of which he brought down the house when he asked me to tell our distinguished audience: "Charlie says thank you again, but he has to confess being very disappointed President Bush couldn't be here today. He says he wanted to tell the president to *'Read my lips.'*"

Life with Charlie is never dull.

chapter twenty-five
OFFERING HOPE

LUCY

It's enormously rewarding to be able to share the lessons we've learned with other ALS victims and their families. But we've been amazed to find that our experience speaks to a much wider audience. More than half of our speaking engagements are sponsored by churches. But we often give inspirational talks for civic organizations and motivational speeches for business groups. Occasionally we speak at conventions or give after-dinner talks at banquets.

Elementary school kids are always fascinated with Charlie's medical paraphernalia. To set them at ease, before we begin our school talks, we often select one child from the audience and teach him how to suction Charlie's mouth. But students still invariably gasp in alarm when we tell them, "Charlie hasn't had a swallow of food in almost eight years." Then we show them his stomach tube and explain how we feed Charlie.

How does Charlie actually speak to groups when he can't talk? Over the years we've devised a pretty efficient three-person system. Usually our primary nurse, Linda, accompanies us so that when we get Charlie on the platform she sits on one side and I sit on the other. Because it would take too long to read Charlie's lips for an entire speech, we get together ahead of time to pray and determine what we will say. Then, on stage we'll alternate: While I'm talking Linda suctions Charlie and reads his lips; when she's talking I take over the nurse-interpreter role. For no matter how carefully we've prepared a talk, Charlie loves to interrupt and to ad lib his own one-liners, tell a few stories, and make for himself a few of the points he feels are especially important.

Just describing our system makes it sound awkward. But it works. And we continue to marvel at the kind of responses we get wherever Charlie speaks and the variety of people who seem to relate to our struggles.

Not long ago we spoke at an inner-city high school in Seattle. At the close of the assembly we did what we often do and opened the floor for questions. One of the first kids to stand in that audience was a great big linebacker on the varsity football team. "Charlie, I just wanted to know . . . ," he began, ". . . would it be all right for me to come down and give you a hug?"

"Sure," Charlie grinned.

And right there in front of the entire student body, this tough, macho football player walked from the back of the auditorium, up onto the stage, and gave Charlie a hug. It was all I could do to not cry.

I'm often moved to tears by the responses we get when we speak. There are just so many hurting people in the world who need encouragement and help.

I remember the teenage girl who wrote to tell us her story. She'd been born as the result of her mother's rape. Her stepfather molested her. And she'd attempted suicide more than once. She said that listening to Charlie talk about God's love was the first time in her life she ever felt she might be a special person with a reason to be alive.

Then there was Andre, a sad little nine-year-old boy we met when Charlie was asked to speak at a Catholic boys' home. Andre's father had beaten Andre and his little brother all their lives. But they weren't made wards of the state until after their father had slit their mother's throat right in front of the boys.

We selected Andre out of the crowd to be our special helper, teaching him to suction Charlie's mouth and letting him trail along on our guided tour of the facility. When we went out to the parking lot at the end of our visit, he jumped into our van the moment we opened the door. "Please let me go home with you, Charlie!"

Charlie grinned at him. "You'd have to mow my lawn and do lots and lots of chores."

"That's okay," Andre responded. "I can do lots of things. You'll see." It nearly broke my heart to leave him behind.

We went back to that boys' home a second time several months later. Andre was still there. The moment Charlie spotted him I called him out of the crowd of children waiting for us, "Hey, Andre. Charlie says he wants to talk to you."

The little guy got this surprised look on his face and then swaggered out to greet us. "You remembered my name, Charlie! I can't believe it. You actually remembered my name!"

It's heartbreaking to realize how hungry some children are for a little bit of personal attention, for the world of hope they can find in the smallest sliver of human kindnesses. We'll never forget Andre.

Neither will I ever forget the first time Charlie was invited to speak in a prison—Hawaii's Halawa State Prison. We had no idea what to expect or what to say to a truly captive audience. Charlie laughingly wondered if he'd see some of his old friends from the tough Kalihi Valley neighborhood he'd lived in as a boy.

The room where we spoke could only hold a fraction of the prison's total population. So only selected prisoners who'd earned the privilege came to hear us.

These seemingly disinterested, stone-faced men sat stiffly in front of us as we began. Some of them remembered

Charlie from his high school and college playing days but what really seemed to connect with them was when Charlie told them, "I used to feel like a prisoner given a life sentence in my own body. . . ." And as we began to simply share our story an amazing change took place in that room. These "tough" prisoners were soon responding much like any other audience, laughing at Charlie's jokes, listening intently with interest and compassion. I saw tears running down several faces as we talked about our struggles and Charlie told them how his relationship with God had set him free and given him peace.

Afterward the men swarmed around Charlie to thank him for coming and ask questions that indicated they could relate to us in ways I'd not foreseen. I remember one man in particular who wanted to know how Charlie could discipline our children. "All I can do," he said, "is talk to my kids on the phone."

But the most memorable reaction of that day came a few minutes later. To leave the prison, we had to walk out through a long courtyard lined on either side by tall, stark buildings with double tiers of cells. As Kale pushed Charlie down that courtyard, some of the prisoners in those cellblocks, most of whom had been locked in their cells and had had to watch our presentation on the prison's closed-circuit television, began to call out: "Hey, Charlie!" Then more and more added their voices. "Charlie! Over here Charlie!" By the time we reached the prison gate the chant resounded through the whole prison, "Charlie—Charlie—Charlie," in what may have been the most spine-tingling tribute we've ever had when we've spoken anywhere.

So many people struggle with the same basic human issues of life. Even people we seldom stop and think about.

CHARLIE

We've been in prisons several times now—but only for short-term speaking engagements. Twice we've been invited to San Quentin.

After we spoke to a group from the general prison population the first time, officials asked if we'd be willing to return and speak to some of the more "volatile prisoners." Lucy gulped and said, "Yes."

We soon realized we were in for an experience because we received very detailed instructions regarding this visit. Whenever possible we like to show a shortened twenty-seven-minute version of the *One More Season* documentary video so that our audience will know our basic story and struggles. But because the violent offenders included pedophiles and men convicted of sex crimes, officials asked that we provide them with a video that didn't include the two- to three-second flash of home movie footage showing Carri and Kale as preschoolers playing in a bathtub. So we dubbed a special version with that scene taken out.

We were also instructed that it was very important for us to arrive at the prison at least a half-hour before we were scheduled to speak so that we could be escorted in and be safely positioned when the prisoners arrived. There would be guards in the room at all times to make sure none of the men crossed a line painted on the floor between the marked off area in the front of the room where we would be and the rest of the room where the prisoners would be sitting. We were told that all these important precautions were "for your protection."

On top of all this, our friend Brent Jones told us about the speaking experience he and some of the other San Francisco '49er football players had had at San Quentin. He said prison officials had warned these NFL players "If some prisoner grabs you and holds you hostage, you're on your own."

With all that incentive, we made sure we left home in plenty of time to reach San Quentin early. At least that's what we told ourselves sitting in a San Francisco traffic jam waiting to get on the Golden Gate Bridge. An hour later, when we finally reached the bridge, we weren't so sure.

By the time we pulled up at the San Quentin guard gate,

it was not only past our required arrival time, it was long past the time we'd been scheduled to begin speaking.

The chaplain and a guard waited for us right inside the first security checkpoint. "I'm afraid the men are already waiting for you in the room," the chaplain told us. "We'll need to hurry."

When we slipped into the very back of the meeting room the prisoners were watching an uncut, sixty-minute tape of *One More Season*, which someone had dug up. They wildly cheered the football segments, jeering and booing the referees in that first St. Francis game we lost. Minutes later, when the room practically exploded with applause and cheers after the championship game ended the video, I wondered whether Lucy, Linda, Carri, and I would make it through this raucous crowd of hardened criminals to the front of the room where we were supposed to speak.

I'd spotted an inmate we'd met on our first visit to the prison. So I had Lucy ask Frank to push me to the front. I figured his presence would make it easier to navigate the crowd. I needn't have worried. As we began to inch our way forward and the inmates recognized us from the video, that entire roomful of prisoners stood and applauded until we reached the front of the room.

When we finished speaking they gave us yet another standing ovation. And then, as the guards began herding the crowd out of the room and back to their cells, more than half a dozen of the men slipped behind the guards. Quickly surrounding us, they began hugging me and thanking us for coming even as the guards waded in and began moving them away.

Frank pushed my wheelchair out toward the gate when it was time to head home only to stop when we reached a wide white stripe painted on the walkway, "This is as far as I can go, Charlie," he said, glancing up at an armed guard standing and watching us intently from a catwalk high above our heads. Lucy waved a friendly greeting up at the guard, who never smiled or made any reaction at all.

The next thing I knew, Frank had bent down close to me

and was whispering: "You know, Charlie, last night I was making plans to commit suicide. I just didn't think I could stand it in here any longer. But I wanted to tell you that after hearing you speak, I believe there must be some reason God wants me to keep living too. So thanks."

With that he was gone. And the chaplain pushed me the rest of the way out to the prison gates.

chapter twenty-six

FINDING
NEW STRENGTH

LUCY

What I've found most exciting these past few years isn't the recognition or honors Charlie has received. It's not the memorable opportunities we've had, the places we've traveled, or the things we've been privileged to do. What has meant the most to me has been watching my husband not merely manage to survive and live an active life but seeing him continue to learn and grow as a person.

Today it seems hard to believe Charlie was once so self-conscious he almost refused to go to that first fund raiser the community held in his honor back in 1983 because he wasn't comfortable with public attention. Put Charlie in front of any group now, whether it's an audience of NASA scientists or in a classroom full of school children, and he practically lights up.

Sometimes, when we're up in front of some church, civic, or school group, I'll be reading his lips, watching his expressions, sensing the rapport you get from an especially responsive audience, and I'll marvel: *Look at him! He's loving this! He's having such a good time that his enjoyment is contagious!*

How did this change happen? The biggest difference has been a spiritual one.

Having a meaningful personal relationship with the Lord, knowing he's loved and accepted by the Creator of the universe who is willing to forgive human mistakes and imperfections, has made Charlie more comfortable with himself. And in this process of becoming less self-conscious, I see how Charlie has become more others-conscious. And just as his Christian faith has helped him focus on other people's needs, it's given him added concern for others and a greater desire to reach out and try to meet those needs.

On a stage isn't the only place I've seen this transformation. Our home life has also changed dramatically over the past few years.

I only vaguely remember those days when Charlie felt so uncomfortable and self-conscious that he never wanted company in his bedroom and would refuse to see visitors until he was shaved, had his hair combed, and had all the wrinkles ironed out of his shirt. Today our family room doubles as Charlie's bedroom because he doesn't want to miss out on any of the action. And this past year, during months of remodeling when friends from a local church volunteered to enlarge our family room so that Charlie could entertain more visitors at a time, he commandeered the breakfast area of our kitchen. He considered that the perfect location because he could not only oversee all the construction from there, but he could better instruct and supervise his nurses and me in the preparation of his favorite recipes he insisted we feed the steady stream of carpenters, plumbers, electricians, and roofers traipsing through the house at all hours of the day and night.

Charlie always enjoyed planning creative theme parties that usually featured some hilarious games designed to make participants look and feel silly. Whether it was teaching our haole friends traditional Hawaiian hula dances or hosting a five-year-old-theme party when Kale and his best friend Craig Williams turned 16 and making all their macho football player buddies ride in tricycle races and play kiddie games, Charlie always had a knack for getting everyone, like it or not, to act silly.

He still loves to do that. But as Charlie has become less self-conscious in recent years I've seen another significant change: he takes himself less seriously today. He worries much less about what others think about him. This same guy, who never wanted to go out to eat for fear strangers might stare at him, now loves few things more than a big restaurant meal with a big group of friends, watching them enjoy good food, sharing in boisterous laughter, and hopefully recruiting a waiter or another diner to help pull some practical joke on an unsuspecting member of our dinner party.

The same guy who got so upset when I accidentally mashed his precious Los Gatos baseball cap in a car door now thinks it's funny when a friend pushing him through the crowded International Market in Honolulu stops in a women's shop and tries the most outlandish hats on Charlie for size. This same guy who quit shopping because he was too self-conscious to fumble for change in his pocket thought it was a riot the time my friend Suzanne and I parked his wheelchair amidst a huge stuffed animal jungle in the toy section of an exclusive downtown department store. We plopped a giant orangutan on his lap, wrapped its arms around Charlie's neck and then snuck away to hide where we could watch the surprised reactions of other shoppers when they suddenly noticed the man in the wheelchair with the Kong-sized monkey on his lap was real and not part of some bizarre, avant-garde marketing display.

I think we've both grown and learned a number of important lessons the past few years that have enriched our marriage and family. Because seven out of ten people diagnosed with a terminal illness eventually face the added tragedy of a divorce, we realize this is another area where our faith has made a very real difference.

Not only can we depend on God to provide us with emotional, spiritual, and physical resources to go on when the last of our human strength deserts us, but as we strive to be more Christ-like Christians, we've found that God gives us sensitivity and insight we never had before. When we're truly honest with God, we have to be more honest with ourselves and with each other.

With our new perspective on life, we realize the picky little things that can slowly eat away at a marriage from the inside, the petty irritations and conflicts that destroy so many relationships don't really matter at all. Because we realize communication is a common problem in most marriages, we've learned to make it a priority in ours. In spite of or perhaps because of the added challenges we face in this area, I think we're communicating better now than we ever have.

It's easy for many husbands and wives to casually listen to each other's words without stopping and really hearing everything being said or understanding the feelings behind the words. But if I intend to have any kind of meaningful conversation at all with Charlie, we have to stop and get face to face. Even then we can't rely just on vocabulary. We have to watch for every clue we can find—in subtle facial expressions and in each other's eyes—to make certain we understand.

All these lessons have helped as much in our parenting as they have in our marriage. Kale had always been an easy child to raise; through the influence of Charlie's nephew Blane, he'd actually made his own personal commitment to Christ a couple years before Charlie and I did, when he was only twelve years old.

But we went through a period with Carri that tested and tried every parenting skill we ever thought we had. We worried because her dreams of establishing a singing career in the rock music scene seemed to draw her farther and farther away from our family and the values we believed in. Only because we had begun to understand God's model and see the important distinction he makes between approval of someone's actions and loving acceptance of them as a person were we able to keep the communication lines open with our daughter.

I have to admit, our attempts to demonstrate acceptance and love for Carri expanded our musical horizons. There were some memorable if not exactly wonderful evenings spent sitting in the back corner shadows of a seedy rock club and biker bar, trying not to inhale too much smoke, waiting until Carri came on to sing. (Only then would we remove the protective cotton balls from our ears.)

We worried and prayed a lot about Carri, her friends, and her future. And those prayers were answered after she went to a Christian crusade with Kale and experienced her own spiritual rebirth. Today she's attending Bible college in San Jose, writing and recording her first album, and regularly traveling with us to minister and to sing where we've been asked to speak. But I sometimes wonder where she'd be if Charlie and I hadn't learned our lessons about the importance of maintaining clear communication lines in any relationship.

And then there's laughter—our sense of humor is one of the most important emotional and spiritual survival tools we've found. If we hadn't learned to laugh, and continued to laugh through everything we've been through, I doubt either Charlie or I would be alive today.

Laughter has been our therapy. It's the simplest stress management strategy we've ever seen. And much cheaper than a psychiatrist.

For example, Charlie coached a recent football practice from a familiar perch, his wheelchair sitting eighteen inches above ground level on the mechanical lift platform extending from the side of our van. A tired football player, leaning against the van accidentally bumped one of the outside control switches and the lift platform supporting Charlie and his wheelchair automatically began to fold up. Before anyone could stop it, the electric lift had tipped Charlie, his wheelchair, and all his life-support equipment tumbling over backward into the van.

By the time Linda could reach Charlie he was lying with his head pressed against the van floor, his wheelchair on top of him, the respirator hose still hooked at his trache, and he was laughing hysterically. What could have been a heart-stopping trauma was instantly transformed into a hilarious story Charlie couldn't wait to tell the next time we spoke. And Charlie's laughter enabled me to reassure the mortified player that everything was really okay, although I wondered if I shouldn't bring a sign to practice the next day to post on the van, saying, "Please do not fold, spindle, or mutilate the coach."

Our children have always seemed to understand the importance of laughter, dressing up in silly costumes to make their dad laugh, mimicking friends, and reenacting humorous experiences from school. Kale in particular always had a knack for sensing tension and diffusing it with humor. I remember one time with the family in the van heading to a television interview in San Francisco. We'd had a long tiring day, were running late as usual, and we all were feeling a little uptight about the interview.

Carri particularly was not thrilled about this excursion. "What are they going to ask us?" she mumbled. "I don't know what to say."

"Okay," Kale suggested. "Let's rehearse a little so we'll feel better prepared."

"I don't think so."

"Come on. It can't hurt."

"Okay, okay," Carri agreed. "What's a good starting question?"

Kale put on his deep, full announcer's voice. *"We're here this evening talking to Carri and Kale Wedemeyer. Can either of you tell our audience how you have been affected by your father's illness?"*

"What illness?"

"Dad's sick? Why didn't anyone tell us?"

"You . . . uh . . . didn't know your father has ALS?"

"Really? ALS? You know . . . that would explain the wheelchair."

"Wheelchair? Oh, wow . . . I *thought* Dad seemed a lot shorter than he used to be."

"It explains a lot of things. Like why he doesn't talk to us anymore."

"You too? Well that sure makes me feel better. I figured he was just really mad at me. But I've spent years now trying to remember what I could have done."

The two of them went on and on. By the time we reached the television station, they were contemplating trying out their comedy routine on the air. I was thankful they weren't asked the right questions because Charlie was all for the plan.

He's more of a prankster than ever, and the poor victims who fall for his gags get teased unmercifully forever and ever. Fortunately he will only go so far with me before I remind him that I can pull his plug. Sometimes that threat is all I have to keep my husband in line.

Not only does humor ease the tension and make life more manageable for us, but it sets other people at ease. Laughter helps them forget about wheelchairs and respirators and illness and death and allows us to have normal conversations and relationships.

Charlie's family is a good example. They felt so uncomfortable in those first years after the diagnosis. They didn't know how to act around us, whether to talk about the ALS or pretend it didn't exist. But after I told Georgie-boy he needed to tell jokes and tease Charlie like he always had, everything changed. Today Charlie's family feels completely free to discuss ALS, ask any question they have about Charlie's condition, even joke about it.

One of the last times we visited Charlie's brother Kenneth in San Diego, he proudly showed us his new pet birds—one of which was chattering away. Thinking he'd give Kenneth a hard time Charlie observed, "One of them isn't talking at all. What's wrong with him?"

"Oh, Charlie," Kenneth replied, eyeing his brother. "That bird has ALS."

Charlie shot right back. "I guess that explains why he has such skinny legs."

chapter twenty-seven
TOMORROW

CHARLIE

Having had a terminal illness for more than sixteen years has forced me to think a lot about the basic issues of life and death. While I hope a few valuable lessons have begun to sink in, I have to confess there are still many questions for which I have no answers.

I could spend a dozen lifetimes asking why questions? "Why must life include so much struggle and pain? Why has my family had to go through all this? Why hasn't God answered prayer by miraculously healing me? (Wouldn't that be a terrific story?) Out of billions of people in the world, why did I get ALS? Why me?"

I know I can't answer any of those questions, which is one reason I don't even ask them. Instead I've come to believe it's not our responsibility to know why, but to trust that God has a reason and a purpose for everything he allows to happen to us. And he can salvage good out of any circumstance. In my case I believe he has chosen me as one of his ambassadors to bring his message of hope and encouragement to others wherever I can.

So instead of worrying and wondering "why?" about the negatives, I find it helps to focus on the positive.

I've been so fortunate. I've lived so much longer than anyone ever expected. I've enjoyed so many experiences and made so many memories. I still have my mind. I can communicate with the people around me.

I've been truly blessed to live in the supportive, caring community of Los Gatos, to claim so many supportive friends, to belong to a loving extended family, and to have so many dedicated nurses to care for me. God gave me two wonderful children who continue to bring me such joy and happiness. And on top of all these blessings, I have Lucy.

Many happy, loving husbands can honestly say "I don't know what I'd do without my wife; I couldn't live without her." But for me those words have extra meaning. Every morning I wake up, every single day I continue to live, is a testimony to God's grace and Lucy's devotion.

Her sacrificial efforts to keep me alive however have exacted a toll on her health. All those years of heavy, awkward lifting have left her with two degenerative discs in her back that make it prohibitively painful to do such simple tasks as carrying a purse when she shops or writing personal thank-you notes to our many generous friends and benefactors. The rotator cuff in her right shoulder is also shot; so she can't throw a football like she used to. But I have to tease her and remind her about the pretty, young reporter from *People* magazine who had the temerity to ask her, "Except for your crow's feet, how do you stay looking so young?"

Even when my loving wife isn't threatening to pull my plug, staying alive continues to be a difficult physical and financial challenge. Lucy loves her full-time career as a real-estate broker, which not only provides our primary family income but also allows her the flexibility needed to travel with me and cope with the often-crazy schedule of our complicated daily lives.

Coordinating my nursing care with all of our activities can make for a bigger logistical nightmare than ever. There's still too little time for sleep. And our medical expenses, even since our insurance finally agreed to pay part of our home nursing bill, total nearly $50,000 a year. If it weren't for regular donations to the medical trust fund our friends established, plus Lucy's real estate and financial planning expertise that have enabled her to often sell equity shares in our own home to generate needed cash from time to time, we'd have a hard time staying solvent.

While my physical condition has remained fairly stable for the past six or seven years now, that could change tomorrow with a progressive disease like ALS. In recent months I've detected a slight weakening in the muscles of my leg, which I can voluntarily stiffen to help make it easier to be maneuvered out of bed and into a wheelchair. As happens to many ALS victims, I may eventually lose all remaining muscle control, even in my face, and be left with no means of communicating except blinking. It could happen—I just don't know when.

However I do know this: whatever tomorrow holds, God will give me the resources I need to deal with it. And Lucy will be by my side, looking out for me, loving me always.

I realize the end will eventually come. But God has taken away my old fear of death. I'm spiritually ready to go, and I'm looking forward to one of those new bodies the Bible promises we'll all get in heaven.

But I'd rather not go right away, because I'm still having a lot of fun here on earth. I've places to go, people to meet, things to do.

Next weekend I'm again coaching the San Francisco '49er wives in a charity flag-football game. (And they're still the best looking team I've ever coached.) I just received an invitation to speak at Folsom Prison. (I may be in and out of prisons the rest of my life.) Our frosh-soph football team scored an impressive victory last Friday night and looks to be even better next season. Someday I hope to see Carri and Kale stand at the altar and pledge their love to someone who will make them as happy as Lucy has made me. Eventually I even hope to have grandchildren I can spoil.

You never know. Because "When?" is another one of those life-and-death questions no one but God can answer.

I thought my time would come long ago. Instead I've outlived so many people who were special to me. Both my dear parents are gone now. Georgie-boy, my nephew who was more like a little brother to me, who made me laugh during some of my darkest days, died almost a decade ago.

Then there was Mark Coulter, Kale's and Carri's friend, who provided much needed medical and comedy relief on our Aloha Bowl trip. Mark spent hours in our home every week, willing to tackle any necessary construction and repair jobs, or simply entertain me. His youthful vitality and outrageous humor made him a welcome addition to any Wedemeyer activity and a friend to each of us. His accidental drowning death shocked and devastated our entire family just months before we began working on this book.

A little over a year ago, a friend whose boys played football for me at Los Gatos, was diagnosed with cancer and given six months to live. Our family spent much of this past New Year's Day with Jim Farwell and his wife Sue and his sons in his hospital room. For months we'd been sharing with Jim how he could experience God's presence and peace in the midst of his pain and suffering. He had come to a new understanding of God's love and about the wonderful future that awaits us all in heaven. Jim's fear of death diminished, and on New Year's Day, when we prayed, both he and Sue invited Christ into their hearts. A few weeks later, he accepted death like a valiant soldier, with family and friends by his side.

So if there's one thing Lucy and I have learned through our experience and through the loss of so many friends and loved ones, if there's one thing we try to get across every time we're asked to speak somewhere—it's this: Tomorrow is not promised to anyone. We're all terminal.

Every day is a gift. It's up to us to make the most of it.

TO THOSE FACING
TERMINAL ILLNESS

With their life experiences, with all the spiritual, relational and character lessons they have learned over the years, the public recognition they've received, plus the media's widespread exposure of their story, Charlie and Lucy often find themselves uniquely positioned to help a wide variety of people. Yet they always have a special interest in helping those in similar situations, not just ALS victims, but those battling other terminal illnesses.

For several years now Charlie has served as honorary chairman of San Francisco's ALS Research Foundation, and he's just been asked to serve as national spokesperson for the ALS Association. Lucy plays an active role in Bay Area ALS support groups and has a real burden for helping the families of ALS victims. They spend hours on the phone most weeks giving encouragement and advice to spouses and families of ALS victims around the country who have called for help.

LUCY

In addition to what we've already shared, we have several points we try to make with families facing a terminal illness. "Be honest enough to let other people know your needs and then don't be too proud to accept their help." This lesson took a while to sink in for us. Yet so many individuals and groups in our town of Los Gatos have been so generous, staging fund raising events, volunteering to do things for us, or providing resources we couldn't afford on our own.

Television star Michael Landon, who has since died of cancer himself, read about Charlie in a Honolulu newspaper during one of our Hawaiian visits a few years ago. Though he was in the islands on a family vacation, this busy celebrity took the time to track us down at our hotel and wrote us a generous check to help with ongoing medical expenses.

But for every celebrity who has wanted to help in a big financial way, there have been dozens of neighborhood friends who volunteer to do needed yard work, children who send nickels and dimes along with their precious notes, and little old ladies who send checks for five dollars and promise their much appreciated prayers.

While we used to feel reluctant to accept any kind of help, we now tell other ALS families they need to remember, "People want to do something. And when you can graciously accept their help it not only benefits you, but you're enabling them to experience the joy and satisfaction that comes from generosity and service to others."

Whenever we can, we share our faith with others suffering from terminal disease and explain what a valuable resource that has been in our lives. And we encourage other families to get involved in a caring, supportive church.

For a couple years after that first dramatic experience with God back in January of 1985, Charlie didn't want to attend regular church services for fear the sound of his respirator and suction machine would be a distraction during worship. But after we began accepting speaking engagements and sharing about our faith, a local minister came to us and said, "If you're going to go around speaking about your faith, you really need to be a part of a local church. Not only so you can be spiritually accountable to the body of Christ, but to provide you with a spiritual base, a family of faith that can nourish you and help you grow spiritually."

We knew we needed that. But we still didn't want to be a disruption. "You won't be," one of my friends insisted. "Just come to church with me next Sunday." We did. And by the time we visited the second Sunday, one of the church members had built a special ramp for Charlie's wheelchair near the back of the sanctuary so he could sit without tipping forward on the church's sloping floor.

We've been attending church there at Calvary ever since. Charlie is now officially considered part of the staff with the title Minister at Large and receives an annual salary of $1.00 for his work. And our church family has become a critically important part of our lives.

We never tell families facing terminal illness that it's going to be easy. It's not. Some days you'll be ready to give up. Caring for a person with a terminal illness is a lot like caring for an elderly parent or grandparent. It can and will wear you down—physically and emotionally. That's why you need to find support.

We warn people about an important lesson we've learned. When life's frustrations become too much to bear, it's easy to lash out at the closest target. Usually that's a loved one. And if you happen to be the target, it's important to remember that when anger explodes it may have little or nothing to do with you or the incident that triggered it. It's more likely the result of suppressed fear, frustration, or pain. And sometimes stopping to realize that will keep you from absorbing the blast and taking it on yourself.

If you're battling a terminal illness, it's important to try to dwell on the positive and to find things to focus on outside of yourself. Get out with people. Look for ways to reach out to others; we regularly cruise spinal-cord-injury wards to try to encourage patients struggling to face the reality of life in a wheelchair.

Try to develop some new interests or hobbies. Charlie has learned Spanish and become quite the gourmet chef in recent years. With the help of his nurse Lynette—who spreads ingredients, bowls, and utensils on stools and chairs and every other available surface around his bed— Charlie creates an amazing array of wonderful dishes.

We can't emphasize enough how important it is to keep the lines of communication open with friends and family. Sometimes it's hard.

A friend who played on the basketball team with Charlie during our days at Punahou flew from Seattle to spend a day with us after he was diagnosed with terminal cancer. "How do you cope?" he wanted to know. "I feel so alone. So isolated from friends and family. No one knows what to say to me, so they avoid me. They'll ask my family how I'm doing, but no one ever talks directly to me about my condition."

We saw the same thing happening last year when our friend Jim Farwell contracted cancer. Mutual friends would ask us all the time, "How's Jim doing?" Other friends would say "I saw Jim downtown the other day, but I didn't know what to say to him, so I ducked around the corner before he saw me."

So to break the ice, we threw a party for Jim and invited lots of friends. Jim proudly showed off the new IV pump he wore to administer his intravenous chemotherapy, talked candidly about the treatments he'd gone through, and put everyone at ease. Our friends' attitude toward Jim turned around 180 degrees.

We can't be afraid to communicate.

CHARLIE

Wherever we speak, to whatever audience, I always try to warn people. Sometime in our lives we'll all be faced with some circumstance that will seem too difficult to cope with. When that time comes, we have to make a choice because God gives each one of us the power of choice. We can choose to be miserable, feel sorry for ourselves, throw our own private pity party, and cause everyone around us to be miserable, too.

Or we can choose to face our trials with God's help, knowing that we'll come out the other side as stronger people for the experience. We all have that choice.

In summary I'd like to borrow a quote from my friend, author Tim Hansel, who suffers from his own chronic pain and observes in his book, *You Gotta Keep Dancing*, what is true in each of our lives: "Pain and suffering is inevitable, but misery is optional."

We must make the choice.

appendix two

THE WEDEMEYER STORY TIMELINE

1964   Lucy and Charlie become sweethearts
       Charlie named to *Parade*'s High School
           All-American team

1965   Charlie graduates from Honolulu's Punahou
           Academy
       Enters Michigan State University on football
           scholarship

1966   Charlie goes to the Rose Bowl as an
           MSU Spartan
       Lucy and Charlie get married
       Charlie plays back-up QB on MSU national
           championship team

1967   Daughter Carri born

1968   Charlie named Back of the Year for the
           MSU Spartans
       Selected to play in East-West College
           All-Star Game
       Also plays in the Hula Bowl

1969   Charlie graduates from MSU

Teaches/coaches junior high school in
Flint, Michigan

1970   Charlie granted grad fellowship at
Central Michigan University
Named Hawaii's "Prep Athlete of Decade" for
the 1960s
Son Kale born

1971   Charlie receives a Master's in Community
Education
Wedemeyers move to San Jose, California
Charlie named Director of Community Education
in local school district

1972   Charlie resigns administrative job to return
to classroom
Becomes math teacher/assistant football coach
at Los Gatos High

1976   Charlie begins noticing weakness in his hands

1977   Lucy learns about Charlie's symptoms
Charlie named head coach of
Los Gatos Wildcats
First team goes 8–2 and wins league
championship
Initial medical tests are "inconclusive"

1978   Charlie told he has ALS, Lou Gehrig's
disease
Inform families
Lucy earns real estate license
League Champs, Wildcats go 8–3, lose
first round playoff game
Wedemeyers begin search for cures

1979   Mobility becomes a challenge
Charlie begins falling
The Los Gatos Wildcats have a 7–3 season

1980   Charlie gives up driving
Speech becomes more slurred

The 7–3 Wildcats are league champs third time
  in four years
Charlie named West Valley Coach of the Year

1981   Honolulu paper goes public with the
          Wedemeyer's story
        Wedemeyers given notice that Charlie can
          no longer teach
        Charlie featured on local TV show
          "Extraordinary People"
        Los Gatos Wildcats go 7–3

1982   Lucy earns real estate broker's license
        "Extraordinary People" segment wins
          an Emmy
        Charlie begins using wheelchair
        Rides in golf cart on the football field
        The Wildcats win the league with 9–2 season
        But lose in first round of playoffs again
        Charlie named Coach of the Year again

1983   ALS affects Charlie's throat—ability to breathe
          and eat
        Charlie loses weight and strength
        Lucy joins Charlie on sidelines as cart
          driver/interpreter
        Wildcats go 9–1, take league championship
          again
        Lose first round playoff game once again
        Los Gatos community sponsors "We Love
          Charlie" fund raiser

1984   Wedemeyers take assistant coaches on
          Hawaiian thank-you trip
        Hire part-time nurses to help care for Charlie
        Charlie often has a battle to breathe
        The Wildcats go undefeated in regular season
        Charlie earns Coach of the Year honors for
          third time
        Loses CCS to St. Francis in
          heartbreaker

1985   Losing his battle to live, Charlie weighs less
          than one hundred pounds
        The Wedemeyers find spiritual peace and
          strength
        The NFL Alumni sponsor fund raiser dinner
          honoring Charlie
        Charlie quits breathing
        Emergency tracheotomy, goes on life support
        The "last" trip home to Hawaii
        Wildcats drop opener before going 8–1 in
          regular season
        Rematch with St. Francis in playoff finals
        Los Gatos wins CCS championship

1986   Charlie fired as head coach of
          Los Gatos Wildcats

1987   First speaking engagements
        National broadcast of PBS documentary
          One More Season

1988   Charlie begins assistant coaching job with Los
          Gatos's freshman-sophomore football team
        Lucy receives Rockwell Distinguished Service
          Award from the California Coaches Associa-
          tion
        Wedemeyers' story told in CBS movie
          "Quiet Victory"

1989   Charlie named Sportsman of the Year at
          Aloha Bowl

1990   Charlie takes first hot air balloon ride

1991   Charlie receives California Governor's Trophy
          for Disabled Employee of the Year

1992   Charlie awarded President's Trophy for
          Disabled American of the Year

1993   Lucy and Charlie publish their book
        Charlie's Victory
        New documentary released: "A Message of
        Love and Hope"

Special Thanks

If this could be a book filled entirely with "thank-you's" we would still miss a multitude of incredible people who have touched our lives and our hearts. They've supported us not only emotionally and financially but with their blessed prayers, for which we are forever grateful and wish to express our thanks.

We're greatly indebted to our treasured friends Dave and Jan Dravecky, whose story of tragedy and triumph continues to inspire us. Although we'd been encouraged to write a book by caring friends like Zig Ziglar and Tim Hansel, we didn't anticipate the curve ball that Dave would throw at us. He was so adamant that we needed to write this book that he actually sent his own literary agent to our door. There was no backing out!

Sealy Yates quickly became far more than our agent. He and his wife, Susan, are wonderful advisors and wise Christian friends who have helped us keep our sense of humor through the book-writing challenge and the publishing maze (not to mention all the brownies). We had no idea of the demands that lay ahead.

Our thanks also to all those who worked on the book itself: Jim Buick and our other friends at Zondervan Publishing House; publisher Scott Bolinder, for his unflagging belief that our story could inspire and help others; and our editor,

John Sloan, for his dedication, hard work, and all (or at least most) of those phone calls. We appreciate our writer, Gregg Lewis, for all the late-night interviews and for helping us squeeze more than twenty-four hours into our chaotic days, for enduring our silly sense of humor, and for helping us excavate a lifetime of buried memories and forgotten emotions.

It's not enough to thank these people who've played such a big role in making this book a reality, without acknowledging several other groups that have contributed so much to our lives.

The first people we must thank are all our wonderful nurses who keep us both going. They not only provide medical care, they (and their families) have become part of our extended family. The biggest debt of gratitude goes to Linda Peevyhouse, her husband, Wayne, and their three sons, for the sacrifice they have made so that Linda could serve as our primary nurse for almost seven years now. Linda's not only an outstanding and tireless medical professional but a committed Christian friend.

The second group we want to extend our appreciation to are those gentlemen involved with Los Gatos High football for the past twenty years. First, there were Charlie's assistant coaches, whose commitment of time and energy allowed him to continue as head coach through 1985: Butch Cattolico, Larry Matthews, Eric Van Patten, Steve Bauer, and Stan Perry. Today there's a special coaching assistant, interpreter, chauffeur, sometimes nurse, second son, and Kale's best friend Craig Williams, who makes it physically and logistically possible for Charlie to continue as an assistant coach on Los Gatos's frosh-soph team. Craig's contagious enthusiasm, selfless spirit, his positive attitude, his sense of humor, and his willingness to help at all hours are all often beyond belief. We love him dearly!

Every Los Gatos football team Charlie has coached has been special. The respect his players show for him and their easy acceptance of Charlie's ALS have helped keep the fun in coaching. We truly appreciate the extra effort all the frosh-soph coaches make to keep Charlie coaching. The continuing contact with so many players and fellow coaches over the years has enriched our lives.

When Charlie was first diagnosed with ALS, we never imagined that our needs would become so great. But then we never dreamed there'd be such an outpouring of love, concern, and support from so many individuals and groups from in and around our wonderful little town of Los Gatos. The magnitude of our community's kindness is truly miraculous in today's seemingly cold world. So many people stretched out their compassionate arms to offer us warmth against the chill of uncertainties we have faced.

Mahalo nui loa to Los Gatos High School—administration, faculty, staff, students, parents, and alumni have all reached out to us with help. The myriad of Lions Club members astound us with their constant assistance. Johnny Smart and the Los Gatos Athletic Association supervise the trust fund for Charlie's medical expenses. Ed Burk of the Los Gatos Athletic Club and many local businesses and restaurants have all contributed to our family. Renson's Automotive keeps our poor van running; and when they can't, they come and rescue us. Even students from crosstown rival, Saratoga High, at the direction of the vice-principal and dear friend Karen Hyde, have staged fundraisers and done yard work.

We've been blessed by the prayerful support of Calvary Church and our pastors Fred Wilson and Bill Allison. Our friends at Calvary and at Los Gatos Christian Church have not only prayed but have raised funds to help offset Charlie's medical expenses. We want to thank Paul Tokar for enabling Charlie to be part of Men's Bible Study Fellowship, which has greatly helped Charlie grow spiritually.

We're especially grateful to Larry Petulla and his staff for providing intense physical therapy for our family as we struggled to keep Charlie mobile. Appreciation also to the chiropractors who gave of their time and skills to keep Lucy's neck and back from sidelining her. We owe so much to Jacqueline Schindler for her selfless compassion as she helped and prayed Lucy through myotherapy and deep muscle massage. When all else failed, our close friend Suzanne Meinhardt would clear the dinner dishes and use her kitchen table to practice her new expertise in myo-therapy—using Lucy as guinea pig. What are friends for?

Only the understanding and the caring assistance shown by Lucy's associates in real estate—from her broker, Al Gibson, her manager, Dan Wilson, wonderful secretaries Kathy and Vicki, title officer and friend Joyce Vasters, many fellow agents, and even her clients—has made it possible for her to maintain a real estate career while simultaneously caring for Charlie and keeping him active both in coaching and in public speaking.

So many wonderful, giving people have shared their skills and creativity to help us. Local contractor Jim Valenta commandeered a battalion of volunteer contractors, crafts-men, and carpenters, along with special friends Brian Derby, our beloved Mark Coulter, and Lucy's brothers when they could come from Hawaii, to remodel our home to meet Charlie's needs. It is mind-boggling to think of all those who have donated their time and their expertise—especially families of former players, such as the Niemiecs. We are tremendously blessed by their help and their cherished friendships.

So many financial benefactors have helped us over the years—from little children who've written and sent dimes and nickels to the generosity of Wayne Catlett, who has given us the use of his cellular phone in case of emergency when we're on the road. Some generous friends we've never met in person—like Bette Perot and her caring and giving brother Ross.

We've been blessed with amazing support and precious friendships from the NFL Alumni Association; the San Francisco '49ers—from the coaches and staff to the players and former players and their wives—especially Roger Craig, Brent Jones, Pete Kugler, Ronnie Lott, Joe Montana, Jerry

Rice, and a great giver from the heart, conditioning coach Ben Parks.

We will always appreciate the generosity and the calls and letters from former teammates and friends from our Michigan State days. Especially Tony Conti, who calls often to delight Charlie with a new supply of corny jokes, and Francie (Mrs. Duffy) Daugherty, for her encouragement and support over the years.

Dr. Norris and his wife, Dee, at the ALS Research Foundation in San Francisco are friends who have always offered encouragement and advice whenever we've needed it. And we're beholden to the San Francisco Giants and the Golden State Warriors for their help in raising funds for research.

Another friend at the national ALS Association, Lynn Klein, serves as an expert informational resource and referral service when people call us with questions about Lou Gehrig's disease. We're grateful, too, for MDA and their fight against ALS. We're especially thankful for their equipment provisions when we travel.

We are still overwhelmed at the incredible response to the films about our lives. We're truly grateful to Crystal Bullet Productions. Deb and Ken thought they were filming the final days of a dying man when they started the ball rolling with their award-winning 1981 documentary. The people at the Landsburg Co., who produced the CBS movie, are to be applauded for not only believing in the project but for all the loving and caring people involved in making the film. We thank them for allowing us to be a part of their "movie family" and for keeping in touch—especially Michael "Potato" Nouri.

A new, soon-to-be-released documentary, "A Message of Love and Hope: The Charlie Wedemeyer Story," is the work of a producer from Hawaii, Don Mapes, and the Video Film Group. It's a project empowered by prayer and uncommon faith. Bless you, Don.

We're privileged to call Hawaii home, even though we reside in California. The islands have showered us with amazing love and incredible aloha spirit. Our Hawaiian friends deserve so much more than a simple *mahalo*. Island people have given to us from the depths of their hearts. We thank classmates and all of the Punahou Ohana, including Puna Chillingsworth, Wanda Williams, Tom Gentry, and Butch Cook. We've been overwhelmed at the gracious generosity extended to us by Dr. Kelley, Chuck Comeau, and Ron Lee of the Outrigger Hotel. Charlie loves "playing tourist," and the Outrigger staff treat him like a king. And we appreciate all the airlines, who work so hard to make traveling a positive experience for us.

Tears of gratitude have filled our eyes while reading letters written by former rivals from Charlie's playing days who wanted to help. And from retired "oldies" who recall stories of watching Charlie run and share many precious memories.

We thank God for our strong prayer warriors: Morris Takushi of Fellowship Ministries for his humble spirit and tireless efforts; and Suzanne Maurer, our head cheerleader, booking agent, travel secretary, prayer partner, dear friend, and one-woman personal PR agency.

Our family has been blessed over the years with so many whole-family friendships. Because we've lived so far from our Hawaiian home, these families have become like extended family to us and our children. We have so many special people in our lives it's impossible to name them all, but we want to thank a few close friends, people we can count on day or night, who've laughed and cried with us and prayed that we'd hang on: the Andersons, the Bohns, the Boulwares, the Bowmans, the Coulters, the Eaffs, the Farwells, the Handleys, the Harrises, the Lees, the Meinhardts, the Niemiecs, the Petullas, the Oulds, the Pecklers, the Siewerts, the Ursinys, and the Williamses. Plus other special friends Joan Matthews, Cathy Brock, Diane Carlson, Sheri Cusimano, Helen Petrianos, Anna Steiner, and hundreds more. We love you all.

And finally we'd like to acknowledge the eternal and insurmountable debt of gratitude we owe to our own families—the Dangler and the Wedemeyer ohanas. From Charlie's loving (and now deceased) parents, his siblings: brother Herman and wife, Carol; brother Kenneth and wife, Tiny; brother Earl and wife, Barbara; sister Ruth and husband, Tom; sister Jewel and husband, Bob; sister Winona and husband, George; sister Bridget and husband, Whitney; sister Penny and husband, Take; plus all their keikis, the nieces and nephews, aunties and uncles. Also Lucy's family, from her caring, deceased father to her precious mother, Marcia, brother Tim and wife, Dian, sister Antoinette, brother Breck, the nieces, and Uncle Bud and Uncle Dave.

You have provided comfort and concern most families never know. You've given when you had nothing to give. *Mahalo nui loa* for your unconditional love.

Expressing thanks remains surprisingly difficult and emotionally agonizing for us. Each act of kindness, each need for a note of gratitude tugs at our hearts and floods us with reminders of all the traumatic reasons that people are so generous. We have to push aside embarrassment and pride to focus on the blessings. We really just want to reach out and hug you all so close and share our joyful tears of love and heartfelt thanksgiving. We thank God for each of you.

To so many we owe so much. We've expressed but a token of our gratitude. May this book be a small tribute to all who have contributed to our story and our lives. Without the Lord Jesus Christ there would be no story, no victory.

Mahalo nui loa me ke aloha pumehana. Aloha ke Akua ia oe. God bless you one and all.

Charlie and Lucy Wedemeyer

Lucy and Charlie Wedemeyer still reside in Los Gatos, California. Those interested in arranging speaking engagements may contact them through Sealy Yates, 505 S. Main Street, Suite 1000, Orange, California 92668.

Those interested in helping to financially support the ministry of the Wedemeyers in reaching out to those who are hurting in a world that offers little hope or encouragement can send tax-deductible donations to The Wedemeyer Family Foundation, c/o Sealy Yates, 505 S. Main Street, Suite 1000, Orange, California 92668.

For further information or answers to questions about ALS, you may call the National ALS Association's toll-free hotline: 1-800-782-4747.